Popular Culture and Philosophy®

iPod and Philosophy

iCon of an ePoch

Edited by

D.E. WITTKOWER

OPEN COURT
Chicago and La Salle, Illinois

Popular Culture and Philosophy®
Series Editor: George A. Reisch

iPod

AND PHILOSOPHY
iCon of an ePoch

MENU

EDITED BY D. E. WITTKOWER

Volume 34 in the series, Popular Culture and Philosophy®, edited by George A. Reisch

To order books from Open Court, call 1-800-815-2280, or visit our website at www.opencourtbooks.com.

Open Court Publishing Company is a division of Carus Publishing Company.

Printed and bound in the United States of America..

Library of Congress Cataloging-in-Publication Data

iPod and philosophy : iCon of an ePoch / edited by D.E. Wittkower.
    p. cm.—(Popular culture and philosophy ; v. 34)
    Summary: "Essays examine philosophical aspects of the iPod portable audio player, focusing on its status as a cultural icon and object with many meanings"— Provided by publisher.
    Includes bibliographical references and index.
    ISBN 978-0-8126-9651-6 (trade paper : alk. paper)
    1. iPod (Digital music player)—Social aspects. 2. Digital music players—Social aspects. 3. Music—Social aspects. I. Wittkower, D. E., 1977-
    ML3916.I76 2008
    006.5—dc22

                           2008034306

To The Decemberists, Erin McKeown, Jonathan Coulton,
The Go! Team, Iron and Wine, Andrew Bird,
The Magnetic Fields, Rilo Kiley, The Weakerthans,
Neutral Milk Hotel, The Postal Service, The Mountain Goats,
and everybody else who helped me put this book together

Menu

What Do We Hear when We Listen to Our iPods?

D.E. WITTKOWER

Every night, as I go to sleep, my cat—the distinguished gentleman from Tennessee, Wallace Beauford Neely—gazes intently out the window. Sometimes he sees something. He perks up, his ears forward, intent. I stare out the window, uncomprehending, seeing nothing but trees under the streetlight. He sniffs at my face, also uncomprehending.

What is it that Wallace is seeing? What interests him so? I haven't the faintest idea. I might imagine it's a bird, or another cat—*the enemy!*—but that's not based on anything I've seen, only on my imagining of what he might care about.

On the other hand, when I get ready to go on campus in the morning, NPR is blasting out of my clock radio, so that I can hear Renée Montagne and Steve Inskeep from down the hall in the kitchen, and Wallace curls up next to the radio! His senses are clearly sharper than mine—except his common sense, as attested to by his attempts to jump on things just a bit too far away, and his obvious hatred for writing implements of any form. (String and wires are also suspect.) Yet, he seems perfectly willing to sleep quite close to the radio.

Now, I'm sure that you'd be glad to hear much more about my wonderful cat, but I suppose I ought to get to some kind of point anyway. The point is this: hearing is a far more particular and selective thing than we generally recognize. Consider these sounds: A whistling of the wind through leafless branches. A distant owl call. A rustling of a bush, behind you.

The rustling has a different character than the rest; and the rest only have a meaningful quality to them since we expect that they lead up to that rustling. The rustling is the appearance of a face: it is the sudden appearance of an other. When we realize that another is there, with us, the world is sucked away from us; reoriented towards this foreign and unknown viewer. What has he seen? What were we doing? Where is he now?

This is, at least, the view put forth by Jean-Paul Sartre in *Being and Nothingness*. He claims that the other is a 'void within being'. He gives the example of the voyeur, peeking through a keyhole. The voyeur is fully engaged in the scene unfolding in the room beyond, until he hears something—*a footstep?*—from behind. The scene, in his perception, reorients itself. He is no longer an observer, but becomes aware of his reality as a thing to be observed—terrifyingly aware!

The question for us, here, is this: When do we hear the face of the other? When and how, as we listen to the various sounds of our lives, do we discover that we are already-along-with another thinking being, who may be a threat, an ally, or perhaps even our victim?

Hearing as a Social Act

Imagine what it would be like if you could actually *hear* everything that you heard. What do I mean by that? Think of your experience of that particular shade of yellow as you stand, awestruck, before a painting. Or your experience of that note—that note of false resolution of a chord, or the seventh note, suspended at the moment of highest tension at the center of a symphonic movement or a saxophone solo, and held for long enough to make you itch for it to move forward. Think of that moment when the beauty and power of a composition overwhelms you and pulls you along with it. What would it be like to experience every color and every sound that way?

It would be unbearable. Incomprehensible. And so, like Wallace, we filter out sensory input into various categories. Renée Montagne's voice just doesn't count as sound of a relevant kind for him. The distant movement of a bird at night does. And things work out the other way round for me.

The selectivity of the senses is partly biologically conditioned. Everybody's ears perk up at a baby's cry in the distance. Everybody jumps a little at the snake's hiss. But our senses are not just biologically conditioned, but socially conditioned as well. Can you just "tune out" a TV? I used to be able to, but ever since I got rid of my TV at home, whenever I'm out in a bar or restaurant, I need to keep TVs out of my line-of-sight, otherwise I won't be able to pay attention to the conversation. TVs are shiny, colorful, ever-changing things, filled with images designed by intelligent and highly trained people to grab your attention! Yet, many of us have learned to ignore them entirely, and can even read with the TV on, right in front of us.

In his early work, back when his work was much more clearly philosophy than economics, Karl Marx claimed that we were estranged from our own senses. To explain this claim—and to extend it into our world, today—consider what you see when you look at someone else. In what situations do we look at people, on a day-to-day basis? They include these: Does that person work here, and can he help me find the aisle the light bulbs are in? No, thank you, I would not like an apple pie with that. Where did our waiter go?

We encounter others through our relationships—especially our economic relationships. We see someone as their profession, as their class, as their race, as someone wearing sunglasses that are *so* last year; we see the other as a collection of objects, functions, prices, and conspicuous consumption; and we tend to think of ourselves in the same way! This is why *Fight Club* needed to remind us that we are not our khakis.

It only stands to reason that the iPod® mobile digital device[1] will be another way that our encounters are *conditioned*, that is, another way which *both limits* how we find each other, and which, at the same time, *allows* us to find each other.

Hearing and the iPod

So what, then, is it that we hear when we listen to our iPods?

- **Do we hear the face of the artist, speaking through us through the distance of electronics and the distorting medium of the music industry?**

- **Do we hear the art or the artistry speaking to us directly?**

---

[1] You may notice and perhaps (after you see it crop up over and over again) be bothered by the phrase "mobile digital device." This is the generic term specified by Apple Inc. for the iPod, and always accompanies the first mention of the iPod in each chapter. This helps satisfy guidelines for acceptable use of trademarked terms set down by Apple Inc.

- **Do we hear our own adopted social identity—metal-head, goth, punk, emo kid, indie-rocker—reflected back to us?**

- **Do we hear a mere affirmation that we are listening to what is—and, by association, that we ourselves *are*—popular, hip, funky, cool, badass, obscure, or refined?**

- **Or do we hear nothing at all? Maybe when we listen to our iPods, we do so in order to close ourselves off from a world that we find threatening, strange, annoying, exhausting, or simply dull.**

Clearly, at different times, we hear all of these things when we listen to our iPods. When we place ourselves into our audio cocoon, we isolate ourselves; and yet, we isolate ourselves within a world of culture, expression, and individual and social meanings. And, when we attempt to encounter the other through her music, we can't help but hear our own identity reflected back: *I* am the kind of person who listens to Amy Winehouse, we hear; *I* am the kind of person who listens to Ella Fitzgerald, we hear; *I* am the kind of person who listens to The Dresden Dolls, we hear; *I* am the kind of person who listens to Sarah Brightman, we hear; *I* am the kind of person who listens to Kylie Minogue, we hear.[2] When we are alone, we seek (and find) community; when we are in among the crowd, we seek (and find) private meanings.

Consider this image: Odysseus by the *sirenum scopuli*—the rocky islands that were home to the Sirens in Homer's *Odyssey*.[3] The Sirens sang a beautiful song that caused any man hearing it to steer his boat towards them . . . and into the rocks, which would

---

[2] I have been informed by Andrew Hickey, one of the Australian contributors to this volume, that this is a poor example. Apparently, the kind of person who listens to Kylie Minogue is also the kind of person who does not admit to being the kind of person who would listen to Kylie Minogue. Her success, he reports, is something of a national mystery, saying "I don't know of anyone who wantonly admits to being a fan of dear Kylie."

[3] Apologies to Theodor Adorno and Max Horkheimer, who use this myth in a different but very closely related way in their brilliant but difficult *Dialectic of Enlightenment*. Apologies also to Robert Bittlestone, whose book titled *Odysseus Unbound* is more-or-less totally unrelated to this whole discussion.

be his demise. Odysseus, wishing to hear the song without losing his life, stopped the ears of all his oarsmen with wax, leaving only his own free. Then he ordered himself to be tied to the mast, so he would be immobile and unable to act.

Which are we? Are we Odysseus, who hears the voice of the other, distant, disconnected from action, unable to go meet them, but aware of the compulsion to do so? Or do we silence the other, in order that we are able to move forward, to act, and to participate in our day-to-day re-creation of our society through our mere consumption?

How can we bridge the gap? How can we become Odysseus unbound?

Listening to Technology

Most fields of learning don't take seriously theories put forth two thousand years ago. In philosophy, though, things are different from in most fields: we deal with those thoughts and questions that are of constant and continuing relevance to human life. So while it would be unusual in other disciplines, it makes sense that philosophy takes seriously what was said by Socrates, even two thousand years after he said it.

A side-effect, however, is that philosophy, in taking the big view, tends to find itself a little distant from the hustle and bustle of daily life, and often doesn't look at what's happening just now or at how things are changing right now. Arthur Schopenhauer expressed this in his advice: "Mind not the times, but the eternities."

Some of us are a little closer to the ground than others, though. Most of us writing here are scholars concerned in various ways with social and political philosophy, and the philosophy of technology. This means that, aside from these thematic connections, there are also certain names that you'll see cropping up frequently. This is because there are relatively few philosophers who have really taken technology seriously. You'll hear a lot about many different people, but most often, you'll hear about these three main lines of thought: that of Martin Heidegger, that of John Dewey, and that of Karl Marx and those who extended his work into the twentieth and twenty-first Century (including Georg Lukács, Theodor Adorno, and Jürgen Habermas). Donna Haraway and Neil Postman, contemporary American theorists, also crop up here and there, as do French theorists Michel DeCerteau and Michel Foucault.

I should make a final note about Karl Marx in particular. Marx is one of the first philosophers (some would argue, *the* first) who took technology seriously, and his philosophical work has given rise to a great amount of exciting social and political philosophy, including some of the very first important philosophy that took popular culture seriously. For this reason, you'll notice that he comes up pretty frequently in this book. I thought it might be worth saying, first, that this does not mean that we, the authors, are a bunch of raging communists, and second, that you, dear reader, actually *already* take Marx's ideas seriously – even if you are a dyed-in-the-wool right wing free-market fundamentalist.

Marx is too often and too easily identified with those who call themselves "Marxists." Marx gets a bad rap, and it's for a very good reason: many, many people have been killed in his name. Marx has the poor fortune of being one of those great thinkers who had disciples who – it seems often almost willfully – failed to understand him, and used his words to justify mass-murder. He at least has the consolation of being in good company in this respect; he has this misfortune in common with Mohammed, Jesus of Nazareth, and Friedrich Nietzsche.

Anyhow, Marx saw how the free market led to human rights abuses, and thought that things would change. They did, but not the way he thought they would. And things got better, at least in the Western world. We limit the work-week now. We outlawed child labor. We now have public education systems. But many of the more abstract things he worried are still with us – a feeling of disconnection from one another. Our experience of our work-lives as meaningless drudgery. Our seeming inability to just go out there and create something that really makes a difference. Furthermore, the human rights abuses that Marx saw in Industrial England haven't disappeared – they've just been outsourced.

The point of all this is pretty simple: Marx was concerned with the same kinds of things that we worry about today, and taking Marx's ideas seriously does not necessarily mean that you want to overthrow the government and take down the whole capitalist system (although in some cases, it may mean that). What taking Marx's ideas seriously today means, instead, is something more like this:

> *The self is created socially; I discover and define myself within the particular society I am born into. The ways that we end up thinking about each other, in our society today, creates divisions between us. And we*

should work towards finding a way of living together where we are not divided by class, race, or gender; and where we are able to be creative, self-determining beings.

And with that, we turn to the iPod, both as a product of our society and as a location where we can find thought, dialog, education, identity, community, and meaning—or fail to find all of these things . . . depending.

OBJECT

1
Wittgenstein's iPod, or, The Familiar among Us

ALF REHN

The white earbuds give us all away. Some of us, the ones who like to have it all hang out, have gone for the lanyard earphones for the Nano, displaying the iPod mobile digital device on our chest like a less-than-ironic cross. Others tuck theirs into a pocket, with only the white cables signaling their devotion. Some carry the clip-on, colorized Shuffle as a badge of honor. All of us are, however, recognizable.

Even dangerously so. At one point, police chiefs in the United States asked kids not to wear the Jobs-sanctioned headphones, as recognition led to redistribution—as in having your iPod jacked and redistributed to someone less fortunate but more "entrepreneurial." So being familiarly adorned with the accouterments of the iPod can lead to many things, not all of them good. However, the iPod itself will always already be a *familiar* sign, an easily deciphered part of the wearer. It is, for want of a better notion, part of the family of modern man.

The notion of *being familiar* is not altogether simple. It is one of those words and ideas that we all instantly recognize—it is familiar to us, after all—but it is far less clear exactly how it works. What exactly is it that we recognize in the iPod? The shape? The color? The coolness factor? And how come we can recognize the funky clip of the iPod Shuffle as being related to the decidedly different iPod Touch? Is there an "iPodness" that we can recognize, and what does this consist of? How come we so immediately become accustomed to the darned things?

Regardless of what it is, we cannot escape the fact that the iPod creates a familiarity. Much like we could earlier seek comfort in the

3

fact that no matter where in the world you went, you could see the golden arches of McDonald's and be re-assured that there was something you would know, something familiar, we can now travel to the far reaches of the earth and say "It has to be somewhat civilized, that guy with the machete is listening to his iPod." When I walk the streets of my own city, listening to Bill Hicks on my black, lanyarded Nano, I can see others in the iPod-family pass by and smile knowingly. Some have old, beat-up 2Gs, others the "little fatty." I can feel slightly superior to the former and envious of the latter, but still feel we all belong to the family of Steve's Greatest Gift, all connected and recognizable. Maybe it's because, through it, we all become part of the Family of Mac (as in "Cult of," not as in "related to" cool but weird Uncle Steve). And this is what fascinates me. Hold on, I'll try to explain why.

"Hey, You Got an iPod!"

Much has been made of the iPod's exterior. The white box, the wheel, and the aforementioned earbuds have become both icons and the butt of numerous jokes. However, lest we forget, the iPod doesn't even exist anymore, at least not as something you can buy from Apple. Sure, some may have the old, original iPod in a drawer somewhere, but the iPod is a rapidly changing beast. At the moment of writing, the closest thing to the original, "real" thing would be the "iPod classic," a sleek music machine that comes in black or light gray, with an integrated Click Wheel controller and a new interface (Cover Flow).

If we compare this to the original iPod, several things stand out. The original (not the "Classic") had a small black-and-white screen, a physical wheel that collected grime, bulky buttons around this wheel, and the iconic white surface. If we compare this to the iPod Classic, the direct similarities are not that clear. Yes, there is the positioning of the elements – the screen above, the wheel below, both occupying about 50% of the front (with the screen getting somewhat less). The wheel is still round, and the proportions are about the same. We can somehow discern that the design is in fact the same, even though the elements that create it have noticeable differences.

This feeling of comfortable recognition does not stop at the little white box (now no longer white) itself. We can use the idea of the iPod to talk about a lot of things. Companies refer to themselves as wanting to be the "iPod of," for example, software or machinery. Particularly beautiful products are referred to as "the iPod of," for example, toilets [*sic*]. There seems to be an "iPodness" that other companies covet, a kind of guaranteed quality and style that can be borrowed from the music-box of St. Jobs. But when someone refers to a particularly elegant faucet as "the iPod of taps," he or she obviously don't mean that the faucet has a small screen and a click-wheel (at least not yet). Instead there seems to be some more abstract quality that connects all things elegant and covetable into a universe of iPod-like things—an iPodness hovering over the world.

There seems to be at least two different familiarities operating here. On the one hand the physical qualities of the iPod, creating a sense of shared design and inherited style. On the other hand, the more abstract quality of being like an iPod in coolness factor, (desired) rate of adoption, and overall ease-of-use. The family seems to accommodate both those that look alike and those who just seem to fit in. Things can obviously be familiar in many different ways, but the way in which this is created differs. To make a tortured analogy, some men date women who look like their mothers, others date women who behave like their mothers. We all have issues.

Why Has Jonathan Such a Big Nose?

It can be really difficult to explain what a person looks like, but it is even more difficult to explain what a family looks like. Still, we are very good at discerning such similarities. In the same way, it is really difficult to explain what is meant by a sport, as, for example, water polo has very few things in common with boxing, yet they both are sports (unlike curling, for which there is simply no explanation). We rarely have difficulty identifying something as a sport, even when we really cannot explain why we think it is. For instance, there seem to be sport-like qualities to cricket, yet I cannot for the life of me figure out what they might be. Maybe it's in the clothes. This problem, which is a problem of definitions, has occupied many thinkers but maybe none so much as Ludwig Wittgenstein.

For how do you define an iPod? It comes in many forms and kinds, and is becoming almost a template with which one can discuss a number of things. Not all iPods have screens, and with the iPhone and the iPod touch, not all have click-wheels either. With the iPhone, the capacity to play music is starting to blend into the background as yet one more function, and with a Shuffle, you might not even know what music is on there. And "thing I own that among other things plays some of the songs I've downloaded" sounds like a somewhat awkward definition. Even if we were to discount the abstract, almost-likes, it is clear that creating a perfect definition is very difficult, possibly impossible. Wittgenstein battled with the same issue, but also presented a rather ingenious solution to it all. Rather than hunt for the perfect definition, he says, we should observe how similar things can be grouped together by their "family resemblances."

In a family, not everyone looks alike. Still, there tends to be a set of similar features, distributed across the family. Some might have dad's eyes but not his mouth, others mom's hair but not her build. Two people from the same family might look very little like each other, but still obviously be from the same family—for instance so that a sister might have Dad's eyes and Mom's mouth, whereas a brother might have Dad's mouth and Mom's eyes. They are unlike each other, but share in the greater set of family resemblance. There is, in families and in the world in general, a situation so that "if you look at them you will not see something that is common to *all*, but similarities, relationships, and a whole series of them at that,"[1] and our work should focus on tracing this rather than looking for absolute general certainties. We need to look for connections and overlaps, tendencies and similarities, not some essential, eternal thing. Your father's nose may be a prominent thing, majestic in size and tagged on both Flickr and Google Earth, but that does not mean that your family is defined by that nose, or that this is what makes the people in your family look like each other. At least according to Wittgenstein.

What does this mean for looking at the iPod? Well, obviously there are quite a few resemblances within even its more limited family. A Shuffle has a click-wheel, but no screen. A "Touch" has only a screen. A "Classic" has both, and the new Nano ("little fatty") is a small version of a Classic. It would perhaps be easiest to say that the Classic is the fundamental, essential form, and all the others versions of it. The Touch has evolved into one direction, the

---

[1] Ludwig Wittgenstein, *Philosophical Investigations* (Oxford: Blackwell, 1958), §66, p. 31.

Shuffle into another, and they both share in the general familiarity of the gold standard of the "real" one. In one way this isn't so strange, as the word "classic" does connote a standard of some sort. But how does something get to be a standard? And how does this work in practice?

Meet the Fockers

The difficult thing in assessing the iPodness of the iPod is the realization that there might be no such thing, at least not in any essential sense. Instead, there are a number of things that we look for, a number of vaguely defined things that we relate to each other into a kind of lattice we can attach our understandings to. Trying to philosophically come to grips with the problem of recognition thus means that we are not only talking about the iPod, we are talking about ourselves as well.

Many iPod aficionados have commented on the fact that the first time one comes across the beloved box, one feels almost instantly drawn to it. The surface, the user interface, the experience itself—amplified if one is standing in an Apple Store—all seem to communicate friendliness and that there is no barrier between the user and the music. The iPod is not only easy to use, it is in a sense familiar before the fact. Much has been made of this, and although there are a few minor issues which seem less than logical—having to press Play and keep it down in order to shut the iPod off seems somewhat counter-intuitive—the logic and orderly set-up makes the user feel familiar-with-use in a very short period of time. Like a friend you haven't had contact with since college, but who you can "sync" with immediately, Steve's Gift to Us All seems almost insidious in the way it can infiltrate our cynical barriers.

Apple has very consciously worked at keeping this so. If we take the newest interface, Cover Flow, this becomes even more apparent. Rather than flicking through a series of folders, presented in a list, we can flick through album covers in a lovely approximation of the real thing. It is as if you were there! It's just like going through the stacks at the old record-store, except you can't flirt with the girl in the other aisle! It's like going through a friend's rack of LPs! (Note that the Cover Flow experience is specifically geared towards the memories of those old enough to remember LPs . . . You know, Steve's generation.) Only it's not. Not by a long shot. No one has ever gone through albums in the manner of Cover

Flow, as most albums do not float weightlessly in space, moving fluidly as you guide your fingers across the great mass of them. The experience of Cover Flow is in fact completely alien, physically impossible in the real world and in a sense never-before-seen. Yet it seems an *instantly familiar* experience, completely understandable and logical. How can this be? How can we recognize something that is not only strange, but literally impossible, as familiar?

It would seem that familiarity does not require recognition. Rather, familiarity requires for us to be able to find enough little hints and similarities in order for us to create a conceptual family of likenesses—so that Cover Flow and the more traditional box of albums get to share in the familiar act of flicking through. Familiarity would then be not a thing pre-existing in the world, but something that humans form in their making sense of the world. It would be a human creation, not an innate thing.

On the Go in Boise

One of the things that make the iPod such a friendly companion might be that it makes it very easy to create familiarities. In fact, one of the built-in games on the newer models even automates this. The "Music Quiz" game plays you a song, and your task is to recognize it as quickly as you can. Well, not really recognize, but rather guess as well as you can from an offered list of possibilities while the clock is ticking down. The game assumes you are already familiar with your music, and uses this to turn your own collection of music into a game. If you are good at the game you are awarded with points, but also with a feeling of order, as you clearly are able to recognize that which should already be familiar to you—a familiarity made new and fed back to you. Within the box, the familiar can be endlessly recreated.

Playlists are of course one of the most important ways to do this. Rather than trusting the chaos of all your songs, or the shuffle-function (which is an entirely different thing), you set up your playlists in iTunes, and the trusty synchronization feature makes it possible to transfer this familiar way of ordering your music onto your iPod. You can then either trust these ready-mades, or take a walk on the wild side and create a new (but reassuringly familiar) playlist from the already present material.

Sync(hronization) itself is a technology of familiarity. Even though your Mac (or, Steve forbid, your PC) is very unlike your iPod, syncing the two makes them familiar to each other. Your contacts come along, identical on the two machines, as do your images (of your family, no doubt) and so on. Sync, of any kind, creates familiarity between two devices, and the touted seamlessness of the iPod's syncing points towards an age when all devices might be "familiar." This obviously raises the specter of another way to use the word, as a familiar can also denote a spirit (often inhabiting the form of an animal) who serves a witch. Maybe our technological age has gone beyond the use of animals in this respect . . . (What is that you say, Nano of mine? I can't tell them about you? But I don't want to ki . . . Sssch, I'm writing this now, okay?)

This then makes it possible to make the entire world familiar to you. Regardless of whether you're having a huckleberry pie in Boise or eating bibimbap in Korea, you can rest easy knowing that as long as you have your iPod, you always have a familiar soundscape to metaphorically lean on. In a manner not unlike the comfort of knowing that a Big Mac is the same everywhere in the world, the iPod can make any place seem less strange, less different. The co-branded system of Nike+iPod has a more extreme version of this, allowing the user to set a "PowerSong"—a song you can call up when you need an extra boost in motivation. Rather than serving up a list of songs, this enables the user to have an instantly recognizable (and completely unsurprising) song come up at the touch of a button. Again, whether you're jogging in Central Park, or biking in Stockholm, the iPod can make the environment familiar.

To See the World in a Clickwheel

This potential for universalizing our experiences has been one of the things people criticize in the iPod. If you are going to shield yourself from the differences in the world just by putting on the white buds and sticking to your predefined playlists, why even go to foreign places? The banality of shutting yourself within the iPod's aural familiarity would seem to be something like an *evil* side of familiarity. Where the act of making familiar seems to be a good thing when we are fundamentally lost—not understanding what is going on and looking for clues to make sense of things—ready-made familiarity seems to make the world more distant and unimportant.

What, in effect, is it that we do when we turn up our "Foreign Lands" playlist in a place unknown to us? In the simplest sense, we replace foreign and alien sounds with familiar ones. We choose not to completely give in to the experience of being somewhere foreign, and instead combine the new sensations we get through sight and touch (and smell, particularly so if we're in Paris) with the reassuringly familiar sounds emanating from our chosen mechanism of distancing ourselves.

If we're lucky, we might even come across something as familiar as an Apple Store, and be able to stand in a foreign city, listening to music we chose back home, looking at a new iPod in the shop window, instantly familiar to us. Here, though, we see two slightly different kinds of familiarity. The music, our lived experience with the iPod, is familiar because the iPod is a machine that creates these kinds of familiarities. The iPod in the window is familiar because we have created ways of looking at the world within which the iPod stands as a symbol through which we can understand things. Many things.

I Know You'll Like This

To state that the iPod is universally familiar might be a bit of an exaggeration, but not a huge one. The little white box that is no longer white is sold all over the globe, and used by American farmers as well as Russian middle managers. If you walk through an electronics market in China, you will be inundated with offers to buy copies and clones of it. You can find it being sold in every airport, sometimes even in vending machines, and it turns up as a prize in lotteries around the world. But the global iPod is not the whole story.

To engage with an iPod also means that you become part of a universalized experience. Not only do you become part of the general family of the iPod, recognizable in the street, but also entangled in a set of understandings that tries to make you familiar to both your iPod and to the system behind it. While we are used to thinking that information-gathering and the manufacture of systemic meaning are human endeavors, the fact is that the iPod also tries to make you familiar to it. For instance, the iPod tracks the number of times you've played a specific song and encourages you to rate the songs you have on it. This information is then used to make better guesses about what to play back to you, for instance so that higher rated songs, and songs you like to play, are more likely to turn up when you shuffle songs.

Although it might seem aphilosophical to ascribe agency to a music player, this kind of thinking has been quite popular in, for example, the Actor-Network Theory of people like Bruno Latour and John Law.

Here, in ANT, the radical claim was that agency was not only something that humans had, but that machines or technology also exhibited the same. Rather than just study the world as expressions of human wants and desires, ANT argued for taking the technological network and the things themselves into account, on their own terms. This infuriated some people, who accused this line of thinking of being willfully obscurantist and little more than a cobbled set of superficial frippery placed to cover up a shambolic core (a little like Microsoft Vista, in this regard), but it did manage to bring the technological object back into the analytic spotlight.

Even though we might shy away from saying that the iPod could choose to act in certain ways (and not in others), it isn't so far-fetched to say that objects act, and that they limit or enable our actions in specific ways—with the iPod certain things become possible that otherwise would not, and the iPod also sets behavioral limits for how we act. Just like an ATM can handle only one person or transaction at a time and therefore makes us stand in line to take out money, the iPod increasingly makes choices for you. Granted, you can disable this, but who among us hasn't trusted the shuffle function from time to time? Part of the way in which an object such as the iPod becomes familiar and universalized is that the technological rules and limits of the object "trains" us into specific behaviors, so that we know how to flick our fingers or turn the click-wheel in the correct way, and thus integrate ourselves into the iPod's life-world. But then again, this is true of all technology, and even though looking towards how specific interactions with the object become familiar to us can teach us something, it is only part of the bigger picture.

We could perhaps say that the iPod is hardwired to become friendly with you, and programmed to make itself familiar to you. But this is not all. If we look at the extensions of the iPod, such as the iTunes-software and the related iTunes Store, the attempt to tie the user of the iPod into a web of familiarity is greatly enhanced. Attempting to buy, for example, a song by Sly and the Family Stone will instantly lead to being suggested "Top Songs" and push you towards "Listeners Also Bought." In further extension, the logic is that the more you buy, the better the system will know you (you will become familiar to the universal iPod system) and the better it will be able to serve you.

So maybe it is not you becoming familiar with the iPod, but the iPod becoming familiar with you?

The Familiar Familiar

So who is really familiar to whom? And what is being familiar or made familiar? Maybe, in the tradition of a "normal" family (whatever that is), familiarity involves a complex negotiation of relationships and a fluid line between who is family and who isn't. In fact, just as there really isn't anything like a "normal family" in the world, just different kinds of actual families, there is no "iPod" either, not any longer (once there was, but now we have a family that somehow shares a familiar iPodness). This would in fact correspond well to Wittgenstein's general theory of knowledge, as he tended to be wary of well-defined concepts. Paraphrasing him, we could say that it seems a little insane to claim that just because it is difficult to draw the line exactly where family ends and a more general kinship begins, families aren't real. Actually, he said "Many words . . . don't have a strict meaning. But this is not a defect. To think it is would be like saying that the light of my reading lamp is no real light at all because it has no sharp boundary,"[2] but still.

We could thus say that, in the iPod, we have quite a few different familiarities. On the one hand, the iPod has become a familiar symbol to us, so familiar in fact that we use it to talk about other things, which then in their turn could be seen as parts of the greater iPod family. Or at least hang-around members, for lest we forget, in the contemporary economy there are few things more desirable than being similar to the iPod. On the other, the iPod can be used to create familiarity where there is none, such as when running in an unfamiliar terrain or when traveling in foreign lands. By being portable and by making it possible to customize experiences, the iPod is something akin to a digital security blanket.

On the third hand (for many, the quality of philosophy can only properly be measured by the amount of hands involved—and philosophy doesn't care if you've only got two), the iPod tries very hard

---

[2] Ludwig Wittgenstein, *The Blue and Brown Books* (New York: Harper and Row, 1965), p. 27.

to make itself familiar to you. It imports things from your computer, it tries to learn from you, and it is positioned as an unintrusive and wholly intuitive little buddy. That technology can show this kind of agency sometimes feels quite eerie, but we should pay heed to it, as it questions exactly who is getting familiar with whom. Clearly, the iPod is also a way for Apple to be more familiar with you, but we'll leave the issues of integrity for another chapter.

So not only are there many ways to be familiar, there are many familiars as well. Sound familiar?

On the Heresy of the Zune

But what about things that seem familiar, but shouldn't be? With a product as successful as the little white box (which still isn't quite as white any longer), there will be copies and attempts to mimic the form, function and fabulousness of the thing we know and love. How should we understand these?

The anti-iPod, as it were, must be the Microsoft Zune. Any Mac-fan worth his or her salt will instantly react to the mention of this monstrosity with derision and scorn. Although it looked somewhat similar, it was clearly an alien, evil intrusion. It was bigger, it was differently colored, and most importantly, created in the forges of Hell. It was both familiar and clearly wrong, a both-and. We might even compare it to a zombie[3]—recognizably both human and horribly non-human.

True, the Zune might eat your soul instead of your flesh (unlike that shambling, flesh-eating monster Steven Ballmer, who'll eat both), but it was still clearly an evil presence—an abomination unto the One True Steve. The truly evil thing about it was not that the Evil Empire created it, but that it so clearly tried to look like the iPod. It took a lovely familiar thing, and created a perverse replica of it, something like a deranged Elvis-impersonator with extensive plastic surgery and a welded-on automatically rotating artificial pelvis (but not as cool). It was familiar, but clearly had no right to be. Just as Windows Vista looks like what would happen if OS X got drunk and started projectile vomiting, the Zune looks like an iPod in particularly ill-advised drag, making this specific case of familiarity threatening and abject.

---

[3] See Richard Greene and K. Silem Muhammad, eds., *The Undead and Philosophy* (Chicago: Open Court, 2006).

In fact, this twisted familiarity did create an admirable play on recognition and the iPod-Zune dichotomy. Owing to the similarity in use and difference in size, a way to create Zune replicas out of regular paper printed with the image of this hellspawn was quickly distributed on the net, with the following ostensible use: By making a replica Zune, and hiding one's iPod within it, one could achieve a one-two familiarity punch. By making the iPod look less familiar through masquerading it as another familiar thing, the Zune, one could (arguably) make it less desirable to thieves. This play with familiarities again shows that recognition is not an entirely neutral thing . . . We might even here see a politics of familiarity. Luckily, there is no time to delve into this (as we would then be too close to comfort for a bevy of Derrida's hairier discussions). Let it just be said that familiarity is not easy, even when it works.

What Was on Wittgenstein's iPod?

There's a fun game you can play with your friends or your iPod (whichever is dearest to you) in which one tries to imagine what songs would be on the most-played playlist of famous people. Imagining the potential playlists of people like Andrew Jackson or the Pope[4] makes it possible for us to make these people seem a little less abstract. Or at least show off how familiar we are with them. So what would be on Wittgenstein's iPod?

My guess is that it would have quite a lot of modern classical on it, from which you could infer that he liked atonal music. But I also think he'd have a bunch of simple beerhall tunes on there, and possibly a few British music hall pieces (like "I'm 'Enery the Eighth, I Am"), things that made him feel good and which could balance the odd soundscapes that form such great backgrounds to his philosophy. He'd sit there, listening to Schoenberg and being one with

---

[4] *Editor's note.* Pope Benedict XVI apparently actually does have an iPod—a 2GB white Nano. At one time at least, it contained Beethoven, Mozart, Chopin, Tchaikovsky, and Stravinsky, as well as a few podcasts, including a radio drama about St. Thomas Becket and a feature on Pope Pius XI's creation of Vatican Radio. See Carol Glatz, "Vatican Radio Employees Present Pope with Specially Loaded iPod Nano," *Catholic News Service*, March 3rd, 2006, http://www.catholicnews .com/data/stories/cns/0601282.htm (accessed March 12th, 2008). It's anybody's guess what's on the old PopePod these days. He seems like a classy guy to me, so I'd guess Hank Sr. For the record, Alf guessed he'd be listening to David Hasselhoff. He is, after all, German.

his philosophy, and then switch to a rousing "Krakauer Polka" and feel a little more at home.

It just goes to show that familiarity is not one singular thing. Rather, when we talk about familiarity we in fact talk about several different things, phenomena that share some family likenesses but which are not easily reducible to one single thing. Familiarity can be about recognition, but it can also be about substituting recognition. It can be about similar things, or just about seeing similarities where there really are none—familiarity as parsimony in sense-making. Put an iPod Mini (the colorful and chubby version that preceded the Nano) next to an iPod Touch, and very few things seem to unite them. Still, as humans, we are very good at connecting the few family resemblances they do show in such a way to make them seem similar.

Compare the familiarity of listening to the Beach Boys' classic "Wouldn't It Be Nice" while in Kabul to the sensation of seeing a new iPod for the first time in your favorite store. There is almost nothing that unites these two things, yet both share in some sensation of familiarity. What the iPod does, and what is fantastic about it, is that it creates not one but a bunch of potential familiarities. The impossibility of clearly defining these, and the obviousness of them still being somehow connected, is as good an illustration as any of how Wittgenstein tried to move philosophy away from being too enthralled with exact definitions, and how he instead argued that we need to celebrate natural language and the multitude of (language) games we play. The iPod can be used in many ways, just like language can. Personally, I like to think that Wittgenstein would have loved an iPod. And I think he would have gone for the same look I prefer—black Nano, lanyard headphones. Showing off, yet utterly practical. Like philosophy, really.

2

The Moment of the Blobject Has Passed

FRANCIS RAVEN

The history of design can be viewed as a swinging pendulum between the poles of what I term beauty and truth, or more safely, between frivolity and functionality. The swinging between these poles echoes the feelings of society, as we move between idealism and realism. The rise of the blobject—objects characterized by curved, flowing shapes—in the late 1990s is the moment when the design pole of beauty merged with technology. The introduction of the iPod mobile digital device in the fall of 2001 marks the decline of the blobject and the full collision of these two extremes of beauty and function. If the blobject began as an attempt at unifying beauty and truth, the iPod represents the culmination of this merging. This culmination followed broader trends in society as we tried, in the post-9/11 world, to find a middle place between beauty and truth. Indeed, as newer generations of the iPods move further from the blobject, they track broader changes in design. That is, you can read what role we feel design should play in our lives, and more, the philosophical zeitgeist of our culture, right off the face of the latest iPod.

Waves of Beauty and Truth

We live in a designed world. Everything you see, touch, feel, and taste has been designed. This includes the chair you're sitting in, the pants you're wearing, and the car you drive. Further, this world is not randomly designed, but is put together according to the philosophical commitments of the day. This wasn't always the case. Sure, pants were designed: they were designed to keep you warm;

cars were designed to drive. Some things, of course, were always designed for more aesthetic pleasures. But it's only recently that everything we touch, see, or feel has been designed for those pleasures. As Virginia Postrel writes in her 2004 book, *The Substance of Style*,

> Aesthetics is no longer the luxury that it once was, and that has allowed people to pick and choose styles that appeal to them as individuals. Advances in technology and product design combined with the mixing of cultures have all allowed for a greater range of aesthetic choices. This has also meant a huge growth in industries that focus on personal aesthetics.

Today almost every industry wants its products to have style, including functional items—like music players. Style, though, is something that changes over time. As Rob Horning writes, style is

> often described paradoxically enough as an indescribable quality, as something timeless, which is precisely what makes it so useful to the fashion industry. Style can be deployed to mystify the perpetual scheduled changes in fashion that the industry requires, allowing the contradiction of timeless trends to seem altogether natural.[1]

In other words, it's only recently that everything, every single thing you see, would have taken part in the tidal cycle of design history.

One way to view these ebbs and flows of design is as an undulation between two extremes, which we can call Beauty Waves and Truth Waves. When we're in the midst of a Beauty Wave we believe that beauty is all. Movements such as these are what one would call decorative. In the extreme case the function of objects produced by these movements does not matter. Objects are deemed worthy if they improve the aesthetic value of the designed object at hand (whether it be a bed, a car, or a computer) and this aesthetic value is assessed without reference to the object's function.

When we're in the midst of a Truth Wave, on the other hand, we believe that function and truth are all. These movements are what one would call functionalist. During them, design decisions

---

[1] Rob Horning, "Too Many Mirrors," *Pop Matters*, (August 17th, 2007), www.popmatters.com/pm/columns/article/46866/too-many-mirrors/ (accessed March 10th, 2008).

are made with reference only to the function of a particular design object (whether it be a building, a desk, or a bicycle). In the extreme case, it wouldn't matter what the design object looked like, only that it performed its function well. When such functional objects are seen as beautiful in a Truth Wave, they are "beautiful of a kind." That is, when we consider the beauty of something we consider it with reference to the kind of thing that it is; if it does not perform its function well then we don't think it could ever be beautiful. Our aesthetic expectations of such a work are shaped by its non-aesthetic features. Hence, in the case of designed objects, our aesthetic expectations are shaped by whether they fulfill their functions.

Art Nouveau is the prime example of a Beauty Wave in design. Art Nouveau is a design style that was immensely popular between 1890 and 1914 and which was characterized by its use of "sinuous, elongated, curvy lines" and "stylized flowers, leaves, roots, buds and seedpods."[2] According to the promotional brochure from the National Gallery's recent exhibit *Art Nouveau, 1890–1914*, "Art Nouveau was a concerted attempt to create an international style based on decoration." It was

> characterized by writhing plant forms and an opposition to the historicism which had plagued the nineteenth century. There was a tension implicit throughout the movement between the decorative and the modern, which can be seen in the work of individual designers as well as in the chronology of the whole.[3]

Thus, Art Nouveau was awash in decorative flourishes unattached to the function of the objects they adorned.

But then World War I began and the beauty (or frivolity, depending on who you ask) of Art Nouveau was laid aside for the basic industrial functionalism of Art Deco (in both its Art Moderne and its International Style aspects). Art Deco emphasized straight clean lines and geometrical forms, in a word, functionality. The functionalism of the era was especially visible in what was known at the International Style of architecture (itself a wing of the Art Deco movement). The Swiss architect Le Corbusier, considered the

---

[2] BBC—Homes, *Period Style: Art Nouveau*, BBC Online, www.bbc.co.uk/homes/design/period_artnouveau.shtml (accessed March 11th, 2008).

[3] Shearer West, *The Bulfinch Guide to Art History* (New York: Bulfinch, 1996).

father of this architectural movement, in an exemplary statement, wrote that a modern house should be a "machine for living."[4] Of course, functionalism in design is often itself only another decorative style, but it is a style that shows society's desire for efficiency, its desire for truth.

Now consider a more recent shift in design. Design in the late 1960s and 1970s was characterized by excess and exuberance (along with shag carpets and floral psychedelia). These are the same qualities that Art Nouveau's Beauty Wave trafficked in. As a popular Interior Design website puts it, "The late 1960s and the early '70s also saw an Art Nouveau revival, which fused with psychedelia. As a result, by the middle of the decade, there seemed to be swirls everywhere: on ceilings, on wallpaper, on floors."[5] This particular Beauty Wave and its excesses weren't reigned in very quickly as the Reagan Era's "Me Generation" brought ostentation to an entirely new level. The Beauty Wave began to be replaced by another Truth Wave with the introduction of the Internet. By the 1990s, the computer was the focus of our lives and thus, of much of design. It's hard to think of it this way now, but there isn't much that's more purely functional than a computer. It also altered design, as computer-aided design is now the norm. I will return to this point when I discuss the genesis of the blobject. For now, we can see that the undulations of design and fashion pulse a wave of beauty and then a wave of truth.

Blobject

Now consider the Blobject. The term is a portmanteau of the words 'blobby' and 'object'. So, a blobject is a blobby object. The two prime examples of blobjects are the iMac and Volkswagen's new Beetle (which will forever be called 'new'). Both of these products emerged onto the market in 1998, the year of the blobject. In order to understand constantly changing contemporary terminology it's often helpful to look at Wikipedia, since users from a variety of vantage points can alter Wikipedia entries. Wikipedia's entry on blobjects reads, in part, "A Blobject is most often a colorful, mass-produced, plastic-based, emotionally engaging con-

---

[4] Le Corbusier, *Towards a New Architecture* (Mineola: Dover, 1985).

[5] Behr Process Corporation, "The '70s are Back? Outta Sight!," Behr Website, www.behr.com/behrx/inspiration/artistic_7.jsp (accessed March 11th, 2008).

sumer product with a curvilinear, flowing shape. This fluid and curvaceous form is the blobject's most distinctive feature." Again, blobjects are blobby.

Science-fiction writer Bruce Sterling has identified many prime examples of the blobject. The include, of course, the iMac and the New Beetle, but many more blobjects were also put in front of consumers in the late 1990s, such as the Gillette MACH3 Razor with its curvilinear grip, an Oral-B toothbrush, Marc Newson's Orgone Chair, the Swatch Twinphone with its curved handle and its rounded cradle, the Philips USB Desktop video camera, pens with "bulbous silicone-grips," and the "laser-guided Microsoft Explorer mouse, gliding under one's sweaty palm with a slick red glare like a molten hockey puck."[6] Rounded objects, mostly of molded plastic, could be found in all areas of society. Furniture, office supplies, and technological gadgets became blobby.

Furthermore, blobjects all fit loosely together to form a lifestyle. It's no accident that the new Volkswagon Beetle is often paired with the iPod, which I will finally arrive at in a moment; it was part of a well-developed advertising campaign. According to a 2003 Volkswagen press release,

> Adhering to the philosophy that one good thing deserves another, two icons of American popular culture—Volkswagen and Apple Computers—are joining forces to provide 2003 New Beetle sedan buyers with a complimentary Apple iPod, the world's top-selling digital music player. Volkswagen of America, Inc. and Apple Computers have dubbed the new initiative: 'Pods Unite'.

The unity of the lifestyle implied by blobjects completely enveloped the consumer world. But how do blobjects fit into the ocean controlled by the Beauty and Truth Waves I previously outlined? That is, was the lifestyle's unity one of beauty or of truth?

The blobject first appears to be a new Beauty Wave of design sweeping over our consumer world. Blobjects are swoopy and curvaceous, suggesting decoration and an aesthetic divorced from function. They are also sleek and streamlined in the words of Steven Skov Holt, the originator of the term 'blobject.' He writes:

---

[6] Bruce Sterling, "Blobjects and Biodesign," *Artbyte: The Magazine of Digital Culture*, March–April, 2000.

The blobject appears to be our generation's parallel to streamlining. It can be applied, or integrated, anywhere and everywhere, and although it is not the fastest form on the block (streamlining and true low-drag coefficient forms win that title), the blobject is the smoothest, sleekest, and swoopiest of all our forms.[7]

This integration of curvaceous design and streamlining represents the two waves of Beauty and Truth beginning to merge. The blobject foreshadows the iPod, which completely merges the two waves.

That beauty and efficiency were able to begin to merge in design was in no small part due to the fact that computers are capable of molding new materials to alter the way we live. The computer made it possible for blobbiness to be efficient and possess a functional aesthetic. So while blobjects are part of the Beauty Wave of design they have elements of the Truth Wave; they are a synergy of decoration and function. The blobject as we know it today would not be possible without computer-aided drafting software. This is perhaps the biggest difference between the blobjects and their Art Nouveau counterparts.

As Bruce Sterling puts it, "Computer-aided design lends itself to playful interaction. The severe linear dictations of paper, T-square, and mechanical pencil are as dead as the slide rule, as is the fear that precious design drawings will be defaced by a careless ink smear or a drop of sweat."[8] Computers did change the design world by *showing* the possible regardless of the mind doing the designing. That is, while a piece of paper shows what is possible within a single designer's mind, a computer program has the capability of showing what the materials at hand are capable of (what is possible for them) without reference to the designer's mind. While this allows more variation and fluidity in design, it equally cuts down on the contribution of the individual designer. It denigrates the designer and downplays her contribution to the final product. This is part of the tradeoff that's been made in contemporary design: personality has been traded for the furthest reaches of the possible.

---

[7] Steven Skov Holt, "Fluid Blobs in Motion" in *Blobjects and Beyond* (San Francisco: Chronicle Books, 2005), pp. 85–99.

[8] Bruce Sterling, "The Kandy-Kolored Blobject" in *Blobjects and Beyond*, pp. 71–84.

This dependence on computers makes blobjects an indication of how deeply technology has penetrated our lives. They are design's response to how rapidly technology transformed individuals and society in the period following the release of the personal computer. This infiltration of technology was discussed by Martin Heidegger. As Michael Heim nicely explains:

> What Heidegger called 'the essence of technology' infiltrates human existence more intimately than anything humans could create. The danger of technology lies in the transformation of the human being, by which human actions and aspirations are fundamentally distorted. Not that machines can run amok, or even that we might misunderstand ourselves through a faulty comparison with machines. Instead, technology enters the inmost recesses of human existence, transforming the way we know and think and will. Technology is, in essence, a mode of human existence, and we could not appreciate its mental infiltrations until the computer became a major cultural phenomenon.[9]

Blobjects arose in part because of and in part as a response to technology entering the innermost recesses of human existence. By the time of the iPod, the infiltration of technology into our lives had gone further than ever before. The blobject can be seen as a response to this infiltration. It is the search for more organic, human forms in the midst of machines. The blobject's mushrooming curves cushion us within its soft edges. It is thus no coincidence that the year of the blobject was 1998. What was happening that year? The techboom of the late mid-90s was burning out, even if it didn't look like it. The implication: the bubble—of the blobject and the economy—could save us from the uncertainties of the post-modern world (or, at least, keep us in the warm rays of Silicon Valley).

Behind the Beauty and Truth Waves

The design phases of Beauty and Truth echo deeper currents in society. The philosophical poles of idealism and realism can be said to be the hidden forces behind the tides of Beauty and Truth. The realist takes what is given and thus corresponds to design's

---

[9] Michael Heim, *The Metaphysics of Virtual Reality* (New York: Oxford University Press, 1993).

cold hard facts whereas the idealist believes that ideas matter more. Hence, realism corresponds to the Truth Wave while idealism corresponds to the Beauty Wave.

Realism as a philosophical doctrine—metaphysical realism—is "the view that there is a world of objects and properties that is independent of our thought and discourse (including our schemes of concepts) about such a world."[10] It is the view that, regardless of our philosophical, scientific, and linguistic frameworks, the world is what it is, and what we believe does not change that world. In effect, it's the philosophical belief that we don't have that much control over what is real and what is not. It is perhaps not surprising then that Truth waves in design often follow periods of rapid social change or upheaval. A strong belief in realism would lead to very functional, efficient designs such as are prevalent during the wash of a Truth Wave.

Idealism is the philosophical belief that our ideas, not things, are what's real. As George Berkeley famously wrote "esse est percipi" (*to be is to be perceived*), that is, physical things exist only to the extent to which they are perceived. This would mean that a world of physical objects containing no ideas would not, in any ordinary understanding of the word, be real. Only what we think can be considered real. With idealism, our ideas, unattached to the functions of objects, have a free space to roam. Thus, rises in idealism can be associated with the more decorative, imaginative designs found in the curl of a Beauty Wave.

However, in some sense, we keep wanting to make the case that beauty is truth—that this dichotomy between idealism and realism, between decoration and function, between beauty and truth, might be a false one. Enter the iPod.

iPod

The iPod was finally introduced to the world on October 23rd, 2001, just five weeks after 9/11. Jobs proclaimed it "a major, major breakthrough." To say that an entertainment product is a major breakthrough just weeks after the largest tragedy America had seen in decades smacks of a new level of hubris, but it turned out to be

---

[10] Terry Horgan and Mark Timmons, "Conceptual Relativity and Metaphysical Realism," *Philosophical Issues* 12 (2002), pp. 74–96.

true: the iPod was a major breakthrough for contemporary life. One hundred million iPods have been sold—an iPod for every seventy people worldwide. Now *that's* technology infiltrating our lives. Before the iPod was introduced Leander Kahney reported in an article for *Wired*, "Digital music players were either big and clunky or small and useless." Before the iPod, personal digital music players had not come into their own either on a design or a technological level. The iPod did both. But you know about the importance of the iPod, and if you're unsure of it, other chapters in this volume will loudly proclaim that importance.

Is the iPod a blobject? This question turns on which model you are looking at. One of the Apple team's response is quite telling. Vinnie Chieco, one of those assigned the task of making the iPod user friendly, said "As soon as I saw the white iPod, I thought *2001* . . . Open the pod bay door, Hal!" This reference to Stanley Kubrick's 1968 movie (incidentally, the way the iPod's name was arrived at) is significant in that the late 1960s and early 1970s were the last resurgence of Art Nouveau until the blobject's entrance in the late '90s. To put it succinctly, the iPod is a *minimalist* blobject. Or, at least, the first generation was. It was all smooth curved edges, but nothing screamed that it was, in fact, a blob, such as being pure blob. Its dedication to functionalism entailed that it did not shout such things. The iPod is the bloject that did not blob. The iPod is the exact moment when the blobjectification of the world ended.

Perhaps a new term is needed. *Christian Science Monitor* staff writer Gregory M. Lamb reported that "the 'squircle' or square circle, as seen in the rounded rectangle of an iPod music player or many digital cameras, represents a hybrid approach, but not a 'full on' blobject." So, technically, the iPod should be seen as a squircle, which is something of a minimalist blobject. Perhaps its popularity has something to do with the fact that it is a minimalist interpretation of the trendiest design movement around. Often what makes its way into popular culture isn't the most cutting-edge thing, but a slightly more digestible (or acceptable) version of that cutting-edge paradigm. Popular culture is essentially conservative. We often critically admire the most radical and cutting-edge arts while purchasing a milder version of these works. This is most obviously the case at Target where the principle of good-design-for-the-masses has been successfully brought to market. We can have our design and eat it too.

The squircle is where the Beauty and Truth Waves fully meet. It's the middle ground between the pleasure principle and the reality principle. The pleasure principle is Freud's term for the desire for immediate gratification—this is opposed to the reality principle, which entails the deferral of that gratification. Quite simply, the pleasure principle drives one to seek pleasure and to avoid pain. However, as one matures, one learns the need to sometimes endure pain and defer gratification because of the exigencies and obstacles of reality: "An ego thus educated has become reasonable; it no longer lets itself be governed by the pleasure principle, but obeys the reality principle, which also at bottom seeks to obtain pleasure, but pleasure which is assured through taking account of reality, even though it is pleasure postponed and diminished."[11] The blobject, and the Beauty Wave of design in general, is a perfect expression of the pleasure principle. The Truth Wave is exemplary of the reality principle and the iPod, in all its generations, is wedged between the pleasure and the reality principles.

The iPod got wedged so firmly because it was born at a historical moment. The iPod signaled that the moment of the blobject had passed, that the Truth Wave and the Beauty Wave had merged—we were in a post-9/11 world. 9/11 is the societal background that precipitated the decline of the blobject. After 9/11, excess was reigned in under the rubric of security, a supreme sort of functionality that is supposed to outweigh all others. Or that's what we thought. We thought that 9/11 woke us up, but really we were still caught up in our pleasure bubble, caught up in our blobjecture. The blobjects still multiplied after 9/11. We were less sure after 9/11, but we kept up the belief that the bubble could save us (and added the belief that it could save us from international terrorism). We were shyer with the minimal blobjectification of the iPod, but we were determined to say that we would determine the course of our own lives. We wanted truth *and* beauty.

However, what really changed things, and caused the merging of the Beauty and Truth Waves, is what is wearing us down: the war in Iraq. In the same way that the Vietnam War arguably created a generation of politically aware individuals the Iraq War is

---

[11] Sigmund Freud, *Introductory Lectures* (New York: Norton, 1989).

creating a generation of people who are aware that sometimes reality must be faced head on. The first moment of that realization was 9/11, but it took the Iraq War to solidify. It took the thousands wounded and dead, the idealism of Iraqi democracy shattered, and an administration mired in flabbergasting lies to solidify the reality principle, but now that principle can be seen from the rhetoric of our politics to the design of our humble consumer products, such as the iPod. After years of war in Iraq, we finally succumbed; we knew that we did not control our destinies; the world was cold; we finally let go of our beneficent belief in the bubble.

There was no final funeral for the blobject, but our iPods now have edges. Our lives have edges. We want things that work, honest things. We know now that things can look cool and that those things can fool us.

Navigating this merger is difficult. As Rob Seward writes,

The iPod is designed to look simple and easy to use. There appears to be an initiative to make the interface look as simple as possible. Putting a volume wheel on the side of the iPod might make the operation a little easier, since I often end up scanning back and forth within a track when I want to just change the volume. Here, however, the perception of ease of use is more important than actual ease of use.[12]

But can function and beauty really be merged? It's not that design after the moment of the blobject is necessarily more functional, but that it *feels* more functional, more in touch with reality. We can organize our songs by artist or title or playlist and have a squircle object that fits so well in the palm of our hands. We can have the white headphones that are nothing if not stylish. We feel safer in their presence. We feel more in touch with reality with the more straightforward lines and designs that followed the moment of the blobject.

We're constantly navigating the distance between truth and beauty. Part of what it means to be a twenty-first-century, technologically literate consumer is to believe that, with the help of computers, beauty isn't necessarily in conflict with efficiency and truth. The iPod exemplifies our faith in this principle.

---

[12] Rob Seward, "iPod Design Analysis," Personal Website, January 30th, 2006 http://stage.itp.nyu.edu/~rus200/blog/archives/2006/01/ipod_design_ana.html

That's not to say that the iPod will resolve all our problems: there will always be items (and design movements) that are judged to be more beautiful, just as there will always be items judged to be more efficacious. What I have tried to show in this chapter is that belief in the design of the iPod is belief in the fact that we don't have to compromise between truth and beauty.

3

Don't Delete These Memories: The iPod and Materiality

ANDREW WELLS GARNAR

I've been a collector most of my life—toys, comics, games (video and otherwise), books, more recently DVDs, and music. More than anything, the music is what matters most to me. I started off my music collection with a few LPs, but they're prone to scratches and aren't too portable. Rather quickly, I moved over to tapes, which given the world of the late 1980s was a practical choice. At that time, CD players were still rather expensive, as were the CDs themselves. I did collect tapes, both ones that I purchased as well as those I dubbed from friends. But for as much as tapes were more portable than LPs, they had the habit of getting caught in the player, especially after too much listening, and were a pain to organize. Those boxes made for holding tapes were always a serious hassle.

Things changed Christmas of 1991, when the family got its first CD player and the possibility of owning CDs was made much more reasonable. I got one CD as a present and quickly bought up a few more, days later. From then on I would get CDs whenever I had enough money. With the exception of my first term at college, when I had no CD player of my own, there was never any looking back. With the exception of mix tapes—a whole other issue—I don't think I have gotten in any way, shape or form a tape since the end of 1992. Fine by me.

CDs are important for several reasons. First, CDs sound better than tapes and the ease with which I can skip tracks still delights me. (How many CDs by groups with two or more singer-songwriters are made listenable by this function? Uncle Tupelo; Hüsker Dü: I'm looking at you.) Second, in a very important way, CDs, as opposed to tapes, are worth collecting (I'm not touching LPs here. Contemporary LP-collectors scare me and I will not offend). Outside of sound quality and the typically limited or tiny or somewhat fragile cover art and liner notes, there wasn't much reason to prefer a store-bought original over a dubbed tape. Given the dimensions of CDs, except the very rare mini-CD singles, the CD case allowed for much better packaging. Not only could the cover art be reproduced larger, but if lyrics or notes were included, they could be read without the aid of a magnifying glass. Furthermore, there was the CD package itself.

While many packages were just the standard jewel case, with either the solid bottom or clear (latter being preferable since there is more possibilities for the packaging), some artists managed to have produced rather elegant packaging for their CDs. Take the Rachels' *Music for Egon Schiele* (Quarterstick Records [Qs35cd]) as an example. Assuming one can palate their music, this is a CD worth buying and owning, simply because the envelopes (not even a proper jewel case), the liner notes, the disc's physical design, and the music make a complete package. This could have never been with a tape, and harkens back to the heyday of LP manufacturing (I am thinking here of the first pressing of the Rolling Stones' *Sticky Fingers* or Led Zeppelin's *In Through the Out Door*). The whole shebang made an object of, dare I say, art.

Lastly, CDs can be organized (also part of my collecting fetish) in ways that are at least much easier than tapes and probably LPs as well. CDs, especially when put on a rack or flat surface, can be lined up very neatly. Tapes were always very clunky in this respect. LPs fare better, except that they are much larger and heavier. Not only is owning the original CD important for collecting, so is the physical location of it with respect to the rest of the collection.

I keep my CDs meticulously organized, broadly divided by genre (classical, jazz, not-[classical or jazz], those that fit nowhere else) and then sorted alphabetically and so on. Outside of making it simpler to find the CDs, this is also a two-fold statement. On the one hand, it makes clear how I think they should be ordered. This is important for when people, usually other collectors, come by and browse, or when I do the same in someone else's collection. If nothing else, it's a good topic for conversation. On the other hand, it's a way to say to whoever is looking: "I have a lot of CDs." (I gave up counting somewhere around 1,200 or so. Estimates now range from 1,500 to 2,000.) Boasting, but important for my ego.

The sheer number of CDs serves to make clear I take my music seriously.

Certain discs are passing fancies; the whole ensemble marks my passion for collecting, which, for whatever reasons, has become a symbol of who I am.

The Everyday World of Bodies

What's important to note about all this madness is that it is a *material practice*. While the music encoded on the discs is simply ones and zeros, and anything with speakers that can read this sort of binary code is able to play the music, this is not my whole story. Along with the pleasures of listening to music, there's a peculiar pleasure of owning the artifact and the duties that come with it. This pleasure is always essentially bodily, spatial. It only emerges through my body's relation with the objects themselves, in particular as I arrange them on their shelves. I can read through the liner notes at my leisure, study the package's art, and determine if a particular disc is out of order. Every part of the practice goes beyond the simple binary code burned into the disc and involves a material relationship between myself, the CD, and ultimately the entire collection altogether. It involves a physical doing on my part, holding and sorting the CDs, soaking up the room filled with them, searching through the collection to find what I will take into the office and so forth. Particular elements of collecting might be abstractable from the artifact itself, like putting songs from my collection onto my iPod mobile digital device, but the whole practice requires me to be materially engaged with the practice.

Furthermore, each disc, in principle and quite often in practice as well, has a story, a memory, attached to it. Following David Hume's writings on the operations of the human mind, there's a constant association between a particular CD and memories: a gift, a bad day, marking a trip, a good day, new release Tuesday, and what the CD meant in this context.[1] When laid out on the CD racks, and given enough time, I could reconstruct the better part of the last sixteen years of my life through the CDs themselves. (A different manner of organization?)

---

[1] See David Hume A *Treatise of Human Nature: Second Edition* (Oxford: Clarendon, 1888), especially Book I, Part III and Book II, Part II.

Again, the songs on the discs are vital for the story, but also incomplete. What makes the story work is the artifact. Sometimes a song might conjure a memory, but so too can a CD. Pulling out my copy of New Order's *Lowlife* brings back my trip to go buy blue hair dye (a significant memory since my hair is long gone. Probably expedited by blue hair dye and the requisite bleaching), since it was purchased on that occasion. Someone else's copy need not have the same effect, and usually doesn't. This is because I was there and the events are tightly bound together.

A New Amusement

My concerns about the materiality of the CD come into clearer focus when we turn to the iPod. I got my iPod in August of 2006. My long-serving and long-suffering portable CD player was obviously about to die. Always needing music near by, and looking ahead to a trip to Europe and knowing that there was at least one album I *had* to have with me, the question arose: Do I buy a new portable CD player or an iPod? After comparisons, I went with the iPod. It was the right choice, both for the trip and in general. I don't deny the appeal of the iPod: the design, the size, the interface, the fact I can keep many songs on it, and the possibilities for moving between songs. It is a rather elegant device.

But there's a noticeable change in the relationship to my music. There's a shift away from thinking in terms of albums towards thinking in terms of songs. While I have my iPod organized around "artists" and then "albums," this is simply done to expedite finding songs. Unlike listening to an album on CD, where even if I skip tracks I usually listen to the bulk of the album from start to finish, the iPod allows for a very "non-linear" relationship with songs.

When I went out walking with my CD player, there was a gentle art to making sure that I could get through as much as I could of a given album in the amount of time I would be out walking, without repeating the album. The iPod makes such neurotic concerns irrelevant. I might start off listening to one album on the iPod, but a song will trigger a desire to move on to something else (either another album by the artist, a different performance of the song, memories of other songs dating from the era of the first, or those days when I go through and listen to every song on my iPod with the title "Disappointed" or "Drive"). This is quite fun. It is aided by the large amount of storage space on the iPod I purchased, so I can shift genres or styles very quickly. Such movement would basically be impossible with conventional CD players and is a definite draw of the iPod.

This sea-change in the experience of music, from albums to songs, has been aided by the rise of on-line music sharing and sites like iTunes, which I will refer to collectively as "iMedia." The iTunes Store is of particular note since it makes the purchasing of individual songs possible. The basic idea here is: "Don't like the rest of the album? Just get the song you want!" Sites like Napster in its heyday and the iTunes Store today make this practice perfectly acceptable—and in a way qualitatively different from that of the mix. If a song was included on a mix, at least among my friends it was there to entice you to get the rest of the album. Again, a gentle art: finding a particular track that is both exemplary and representative, but that makes purchasing the album itself still worthwhile. Or the song was extraordinarily hard to find, usually a b-side from an obscure single. In which case the song's inclusion was a boastful gift of sorts ("I have this, but will give to you . . .").

It's with the rise of iMedia that the collector in me balks. The concern is two-fold. First, although the iTunes Store does allow for the downloading of the album art, liner notes and so on, it's not the same as owning the artifact itself. With the downloaded album, everything is mediated through the iPod or the computer. With the artifact, I can take it with me, touch, hold it, shelve it in whatever way, read the liner notes anywhere without worrying about the interface. If I do this with iMedia on my iPod, I have to worry over the amount of charge on the battery, making the size readable and the like. In essence, iMedia cannot replicate these various material relations totally, especially given the rather extravagant packaging in albums like the Rachels', mentioned above.

[handwritten marginalia: "everything mediated by computer"]

The other concern here I will call "the sanctity of the album." Two points. One, some albums were released to be just that: albums. A fully conceived work from start to end, where *Sgt. Peppers*, XTC's *Skylarking*, and Elvis Costello's *North* are shimmering examples (Many works of "classical" music where you have several movements serve as excellent examples as well. And yes, I detest the move towards "classical samplers" for the same reason). While some cuts might be stronger than others, an irreducibly important part of the experience is the entire experience from the first note until the last moment. With these classic albums (and *many* others), as well as classical music CDs, to purchase tracks in piecemeal fashion is a moral crime.

Furthermore, I mentioned earlier my appreciation for the "skip button" on CD players. Yet, for as much as I can be a chronic track-skipper with certain albums, I never regret that I have those tracks to skip over. Hüsker Dü is a case a good example. My apologies to Grant Hart, but I've always been more of a Bob Mould guy. But that said, sometimes I am just in the mood, generally a good mood, for listening to Grant's songs alongside Bob's. This was not always true. And if I had simply acquired Bob's Hüsker Dü-era work from whichever iMedia vendor, I would never have learned this. Such an oversight is nothing less than a mistake.

Deeper into iPhenomena

Now we have moved into strange and somewhat dangerous place. We must tread carefully. Three themes emerge from the discussion thus far:

1. The stark differences between the material practice of collecting CDs and the iPod phenomenon (iPhenomenon?) of individual song acquisition;

2. The constraints of listening to CDs and the freedom the iPod allows the listener; and

3. That I cannot be simply for or against one medium or the other.

Given my love for collecting and love for my iPod, navigating these oppositions is necessary. Perhaps why I see this as important is nothing more than pompously dressed-up self-interest, in that it provides a bulwark to argue for why artists, presumably via record companies and bricks-'n'-mortar record stores, must continue to feed my desire for artifacts and not simply move over entirely to what I've referred to as iMedia. Yet I hope that something more can be said to justify the importance of CDs.

To make this more general, and hopefully significant, case, I will argue two points. First, that the iPod in conjunction with iMedia represents a dangerous way of thinking of ourselves. Second, that a wholesale move away from the materiality of the CD would mark an irreparable, genuine loss.

The entire iPhenomenon discussed here illustrates a particular aspect of contemporary life in the United States, and probably elsewhere too. Fliply put, this involves the tendency to place the lowercase letter "i" in front of a word to indicate a move away from "the real world" to something virtual, electronic, digital, based in information or how-ever-else-you-want-to-describe-it. There is much to reject in this language, but it is still significant.

First, the real-virtual distinction is metaphysically untenable because much of what gets called "the real world" involves the virtual, and, conversely, the world of information ("virtual reality") produces some very concrete material effects (the songs on my iPod, routed through speakers, produce noise, and Chinese citizens using the Web in certain unorthodox ways get detained). Coming out of our earlier discussion, a more reasonable way of parsing the differences here would be the to talk about different ways in which reality "works." Both "real reality" and "virtual reality" are real, but in different ways that hinge on the sorts of practices through which we engage with these worlds. And fundamentally, all of this will be connected to material practices (the hard drive or iPod on which the songs are stored, the power plant that supplies electricity, the cables through which I connect to the Web). Echoing William James, the important question is "How is the *practice* real?"[2] In which case, speaking in terms of "real" versus "virtual," without qualification, obscures much.

That said, this language of "real" and "virtual" remains significant *because* it obscures matters. The iPhenomenon reveals a peculiar desire to move beyond the material world, at least among those who can afford to do so. The hyperbolic formulation is: "the body is no longer really necessary!" The general drift of this iPhenomenon moves towards the gradual erasure of materiality. On the one hand, the body is taken as unimportant on a cultural level. On the other, even those living in the over-industrialized United States still require a body to move through the world. Likewise, the music becomes disengaged from physical artifacts, LPs, CDs, or (heaven help us) tapes. Songs are loaded onto iTunes from whatever source and then transferred to the iPod. While material things clearly play roles in such a story, the songs themselves need not have ever been permanently stored on a material artifact, in contrast with the older media.

---

[2] This follows James's *Pragmatism* and *A Pluralistic Universe*, both in William James, *Writings, 1902–1910* (Library of America, 1987).

The freedom that the iPod allows relies on just this erasure of materiality. My ability to jump from song to song to song on a whim requires a disengagement from the artifact. And this is fine, so far as it goes. So too with acquiring of songs versus collecting CDs. I am free to circumvent the artist's (and sometimes the record label's) intentions by only acquiring those songs that, on a particular day, I want. What is at work here is a corollary to the bourgeoisie's "single, unconscionable freedom—Free Trade:"[3] we have the freedom to consume!

We're All Light? Really?

This freedom that the iPhenomenon provides reflects a trend within hyper-industrialized nations to emphasize the liberty of "the virtual world." Along with this new-found liberty comes a certain denigration of the material world. The body, once the center around which the storm of experience was anchored, becomes a fashion accessory—plastic, in several senses (Public Enemy's "Plastic Nation" off of their collaboration with Paris, *Rebirth of a Nation*, is instructive on this point). The other curious thing about this freedom is that it occurs wholly through commodities. The iTunes Store allows for what might be termed "micro-consumption" in that individual songs can be purchased. The music increasingly moves towards simply being another thing to be consumed like food or fashion.

This last comment should raise eyebrows. "What makes consumption of CDs *any different* from acquiring songs via iMedia? Both CDs and songs are artifacts of sorts. And both are meant to be bought and sold. So, on what grounds can you assert that one is better than another?" No doubt a serious objection.

What we must be careful about is delineating sorts of freedom. Freedom, by and large, is about possible actions one might take. This always requires a context in which the possibilities arise. The CD and the iPod establish different sorts of possible actions and, hence, different patterns of freedom. But this is not to say that these are ethically or politically equivalent. To the claim that "One regime of consumption is the same as another!" we must reply "Not in the least." Instead, what collectors, and consumers generally, must do is determine what is gained and lost with respect to each pattern.

---

[3] Karl Marx and Friedrich Engels *The Communist Manifesto* (New York: International Publishers, 1948), p. 11.

Before lurching towards a conclusion, I think it is fair to say that there is a general tendency to see "iFreedom" as naturally superior. While, tentatively, this might be the case, such a conclusion is usually arrived at for the wrong reason. The seamless move from admitting that this whatever-you're-talking-about is "our latest technology" to the conclusion that it must be "our best technology so far" involves a set of, philosophically speaking, non sequiturs. Ideologically, though, such a move is the only permissible one because without the basic assumption that newer is better, our hyper-industrial economy, society, and culture would collapse.

To bring this point home, return to my earlier claim that something of genuine significance is lost in moving to iMedia and away from the materiality of collecting. Why? For as much as the CD carries similar information, basically the same audible ones and zeros as the MP3s on my iPod, CDs serve as reminder of my material existence. In these topsy-turvy postmodern days, this remains important. Two questions then: (1) how does CD collecting do this? and (2) why care about bodies and materiality?

There are two main answers to the first question. Part of the appeal of the store-bought CD is that I must deal with the artists (via the record company and layers of distribution) on their own terms. This ranges from the packaging of the CD, which can flow into the experience of the music (for instance, I always hear the Sundays' *Reading, Writing, and Arithmetic* as a blue album because of the blue-tinged photo on the cover), to addressing the contents and ordering of the tracks (why that song? why that order?). While this does exemplify a certain sort of commodity fetishism, here there is a distinct difference from acquiring iMedia.

With the CD, I encounter artists and deal with their intentions. I might skip over tracks, but this is a constant decision, which I make over and over again. In downloading songs from iTunes and the like, it's what suits me. Solipsism for the information age! Bumping up against the CD—both its music and its packaging— forces me to encounter the artist; a "confrontation" at the boundary between my experience and the artist's (albeit highly mediated) production is forged. While I consume the music, both in a capitalist *and* a nigh-gustatory sense, the CD, understood as an album from start to finish, determines part of the incorporation.

This peculiar artifact can force me to wrestle with not simply what I want, but what the artist wanted as well. I learn from the CD. My relationship to the work is, at least in principle, always capable of growing. A case in point is my experience with John Coltrane's album *My Favorite Things*. Only four tracks, the first three, each in its own way, were revelations to me about what could be done with a quartet (still true). For several years, I kept stumbling over the final track, "But Not for Me," which struck me as an excellent performance of a goofy song, something Trane could have done in his sleep. Then one afternoon I was listening to the disc for the umpteenth time and it dawned on me: the album had to end with that performance of that song. To put something else as path-breaking as the others after them, especially after their performance of "Summertime," would have been too much, would have been too hard on the listener. It suddenly felt like, for as much fun as the rest of the CD is, Trane was telling me "now let's just play around." From then on, I found the album incomplete without going through every song. It must be heard as a process from the first note to the last.

Progress Is a Myth that Truly Makes Life Worthwhile

With iFreedom, it's all about me and an immediate sating of my desires. I acquire what I want, based on whatever moves me. But the intents of the artist, however mediated, do not necessarily faze the iMedia consumer. The music is there to be consumed, like anything else in our culture: fast food or television for example. There is little more at work here than a strange solipsistic egoism. The world of iMedia exists for my desires alone.

This is further reinforced given the sheer physicality of my CD collecting. In a way that brings together both David Hume and Gaston Bachelard, the practice ties together space, sound and memory.[4] When I am in amongst my collection, there is a relation to the objects and, in turn, the memories associated with both the object and noise encoded upon it. In a properly broad sense, the relation is a material relation in that it entails living with and through these physical objects. Again, we see this "confrontation" between self and other, where "the other" involves both the CD and the artists, and in which the two meet and negotiate how they

---

[4] Again, Hume's *Treatise* is important here, as well as Bachelard's *The Poetics of Space* (Boston: Beacon Press, 1964).

are connected. Since the CD has some sort of relative permanence, how I relate to the whole deal has limits. This is a negotiation between me and the artist-via-the-CD because I bring a set of associations, feelings and memories to the interaction that must navigate the contents of the CD if it is to be a meaningful experience.

While there are encounters between me and the contents of my iPod, these are not analogous. My songs on the iPod can draw up memories, the associations and power of those memories is different and, in significant ways, weaker. The lack of a physical object attached to the experience, however arbitrarily, leads to a certain fluidity in the feelings evoked. Any song on my iPod can be deleted and put back on at my whim. The richness of how my music and my memories are entwined is largely reinforced only through the material practice of collecting. To lose this is to lose part of myself and my history.

Outside of the rather personal question of this loss—a matter of memory and identity—there is a larger issue with regards to the significance of materiality here. As Michel Foucault, Friedrich Nietzsche and, before them, Marx illustrate, the body has always been a central site for exploitation, oppression, domination, though how this is done varies from case-to-case.[5] As Foucault makes clear in *The History of Sexuality*, modern industry was made possible only through the cultivation of particular sorts of bodies. Yet the necessity of going to the gym to maintain a healthy body (where one might listen to an iPod?) is rather different from the squalid, out-sourced working conditions that Dylan Wittkower notes in the Introduction to this book, and which are discussed in more depth by Peter Schaeffer in the next chapter.

To remake ourselves such that "the body is not so important anymore" does not liberate us from such dangers. Instead, such domination continues on but is less of an "issue" because "the body is not so important anymore." The supposed freedom that the iPod, iMedia, and iLiving allows for does nothing to challenge such domination, and is sometimes reliant on these practices. With the former, iLiving provides no ground on which to challenge the

---

[5] See Michel Foucault's *Discipline and Punish: The Birth of the Prison* (New York: Vintage, 1976) and *The History of Sexuality: An Introduction, Volume 1* (New York: Vintage, 1978) as well as Friedrich Nietzsche's *Genealogy of Morals* in *The Basic Writings of Nietzsche* (New York: Modern Library, 1966). Anything by Marx will do, but *The Communist Manifesto* is a good place to start.

continuing disciplining of human bodies in potentially destructive ways. One specific example of this is the continued prevalence of eating disorders among girls and young women.[6] As to the latter, that iLiving relies on domination of bodies, one can point to the sometimes exploitive labor used to produce the artifacts (monitors, iPods, printers) that make iLiving possible, as well as the environmental hazards that result from such production (both in the process of production and the "e-waste" once discarded). For these reasons, despite ideological claims to the contrary, the body and materiality remain very important.

This "iFreedom" is little more than a freedom for those within the iron cage. That is, a freedom for those for who no longer care that they are oppressed because they feel themselves to be "comfortable." On this score, the CD is perhaps marginally better if only because I must physically interact with it, those always reinforcing my corporeality and, in principle, relating me to other material persons.

Should we smash our iPods? Of course not. That would be silly. They are delightful gadgets for many reasons. Instead we must be cautious of not being like the man-child with a new tool, trying to do everything with it, regardless of how inept such attempts prove. The world of iMedia has definite virtues, but preserving a place for the relatively clunky world of CDs, LPs, CD players and bodies remains important. This entails a balancing act: not one or the other but a plurality of media.

---

[6] See Susan Bordo's *Unbearable Weight: Feminism, Western Culture, and the Body*, (Berkeley: University of California Press, 1993), especially pp. 139–164, for a succinct introduction to these concerns.

4

Alive and Clicking

PETER D. SCHAEFER

It's merely inert matter composed of plastic and circuits. Yet when I touch the click wheel, it comes to life. I can feel the iPod mobile digital device buzz with excitement as I scroll through my options. It whirs and clicks, demanding my attention, and I'm more than willing to provide it. My iPod keeps me company like a little traveling companion who obeys my every wish. I know that the device is only as alive as I make it out to be, yet I can't seem to shake the feeling that my iPod is somehow special. Yet, as special as it seems to be, I know that the iPod is a commodity—mass produced and electronically identical to millions of others, many of which probably even have the same albums and videos as mine loaded on their hard drive.

It's quite common to develop a personal relationship with inanimate objects. Especially in the modern world, we look to products to make meaning for ourselves and for the world around us. The industrial revolution and mass production altered our relationships to people and things. During the era of artisan craftsmanship, we could know the person who manufactured the things we buy. Now, we are separated more than ever from the conditions of production and the people who create the commodities we purchase and live our lives along with.

The Apple of My Eye

iPod users are no longer satisfied with the institutional white case and earbuds. As a fashion accessory, portable media players give us a means to build identity by adapting and adding to the device.

People buy different covers or "skins" that indicate consumer allegiance to various cultural trends. Some even crack open the pristine iPod case to alter the machine's circuitry, change screen colors, or install a different operating system. There are a wide range of ways to personalize an iPod, and there's a fine line between personalization and personification, at which point the machine ceases to be merely an electronic device and starts to seem like a member of the family.

Personification may be the best explanation for the iPod's popularity. They come as an empty vessel, free of content, allowing us to fill the device with our personal files. Still, they are charming little vessels, even when empty. Apple works hard to design products that foster a personal connection. Their machines look capable of life, thanks in part to their shape.

Since the first iMac in 1998, Apple has created products with flowing shapes and organic lines. The beige-box aesthetic of the 1984 Macintosh gave way to colors and rounded corners. The iMac G4 looked more like a bulbous alien life form than a desktop computer. The name "iPod" itself suggests a living creature. It arrives as a pod, yet it is up to the consumer to fill the pod with seeds that grow into something like a second-self.

If you're like me, you have almost as much fun putting content on the iPod as you do listening and watching. When I bought my first iPod, I spent countless hours tailoring my player. I carefully formatted file names through iTunes, created playlists, and downloaded content. One way in which I define myself is through my favorite music, movies, and television shows. So choosing content for my iPod was a process of self-definition. I filled my iPod, and my identity became more and more clearly established with respect to the vast landscape of popular culture in our networked world. Who am I? I'm an R.E.M. (entire discography), John Coltrane, and *The Office*-kind of guy.

But my iPod contains more than just cultural products. It has my most personal memories, such as a photo of me and my fiancée in the Netherlands after we got engaged. It also holds backups of my writing and other important documents. I feel that if I were ever to lose my iPod, the person who found it would have immediate access to my innermost thoughts by listening to my music, watching my videos, viewing my photos, and reading the files—there would be no need to talk to the real me. My iPod has a life all its own and reflects my innermost feelings. It lives in its little black velvet sleeve and quietly waits to come to life until it is needed.

Apple is well aware of the connection consumers establish with their iPods, and the company offers to engrave inscriptions on the back cover. This makes it possible to have a unique iPod (if you choose a unique inscription), but it's not the same as *personifying* iPods. Apple's marketing nudges us to think of iPods as being persons, like the "I'm a Mac" character played by actor Justin Long in the famous Apple commercials. The commercials represent PCs as stodgy bean counters, while Macs are casual, hip, and versatile. The marketing for iPods suggests that iPods are alive, boldly visible against a high contrast field of color. The only definable feature of the ads is the signature white iPod and earbuds, which stand out against the black figure. The person holding the iPod appears as blank as a new iPod actually is, as if only the iPod brings these.featureless figures to life. It makes them cool, attractive, and intriguing, and in the video version it makes them dance to the vivacious rhythms emanating from the device.

While Apple does its best to create ways to make the iPod into a living entity, other companies have helped foster the personal connection. The number of iPod accessories available continues to grow as many companies capitalize on its popularity. BMW, for example, was the first automobile company to offer an embedded interface for iPods. Now Levi's makes 'iPod-compatible' jeans that feature a pocket designed for the player. Even *haute couture* companies such as Prada and Marc Jacobs produce iPod accessories, such as cases with suede lining and calf leather covers. If one uses an iPod while jogging, Apple sells an armband to strap on a Nano. For a more cozy connection, Apple sells tiny socks to keep the cute little thing safe and warm. There's no place or activity or social class where iPods are not welcome and useful. They are, as they say, a way of life. What then has created this commodity-based lifestyle in which we feel such a personal connection to a portable media player? For an answer to this question, we can turn to nineteenth-century political philosophy.

The Conditions of iPod Production

While Karl Marx is well known as the political philosopher who gave rise to communism, his earliest writings about capitalism focused less on politics and more on theories of industrial production. Writing in the era of the first factories, Marx saw the division between the workers in a factory and the owner of a factory as a foundational source of conflict. This was before the rise of a large white-collar class, in a world in which nearly everyone worked long hours for little pay. A privileged few lived in luxury while most workers could barely afford life's basic necessities.

The social conditions that Marx criticized were represented in novels by Charles Dickens, Upton Sinclair, and others. Books like *Hard Times* and *The Jungle* are filled with vivid scenes of back-breaking labor. Workers' sweat seems to pour from the page. These novels give a sense of the pain and injustice felt by the working class that can speak to the motivations for Marxist philosophy. Karl Marx believed that people would never be equal until the tensions were reconciled between those who labor to produce commodities and the capitalists who own the means of production. In contemporary terms, Marx wanted Steve Jobs to have the same access to resources as you or I, or as a person who assembles iPods in a factory. This doesn't mean that we should all travel in private jets and run Fortune 500 companies. Instead, a hardliner Marxist would argue for somehing like an egalitarian distribution of wealth, regardless of one's social position.

The way that workers and capitalists are set in opposition to each other forms the basis of society viewed from a Marxist perspective. The antagonism at the heart of manufacturing is channeled by the commodities produced, leading workers to have a peculiar relationship to the things they create. As Marx wrote in his famous treatise *Capital*:

> Even if we consider just the *formal* relation, the *general* form of capitalist production, which is common to both its more and its less advanced forms, we see that the *means of production,* the *material conditions of labour,* are not subject to the worker, but he to them. Capital *employs* labour. This in itself exhibits the relationship in its simple form and entails the personification of things and the reification of persons.[1]

For Marx, workers become *alienated* from the product of their labor—that is, since their work is subject to the conditions created

---

[1] Karl Marx, *Capital Volume 1* (London: Penguin, 1976), p. 1054, italics in original.

by their employers, the laborers do not actually own what they produce. They do not feel the kind of attachment to these products that the traditional artisan once did. Labor is a process that is hidden away in the commodities. Think of all the work it takes to make an iPod. While some of its production is done by machines, not all of it is. Someone had to assemble the various parts, but, as consumers, that is not visible to us.

My iPod came in a package that was so utterly simple and inviting that it seemed to unwrap itself. The box was elegant. The instructions didn't ask me to do anything more than install iTunes and plug in my iPod. I barely lifted a finger before I had music on my iPod and could dance around like one of the shadowy hipsters in the commercials. Everything about the iPod and its packaging is designed to make it easy to use, and the work that went into designing, manufacturing, packaging, and distributing the device to me was hidden from view.

This isn't unique to iPods, however. Modern mass-production severs producers from consumers. Take the shoes that I'm wearing. I know nothing about the life of the person who manufactured them. He could be a teenager in Bangladesh working to support a family of five. She could be a sixty-year-old grandmother in Portugal working to save up for retirement. I wear these shoes nearly every day, yet I know as much about the person who assembled them as I do about the cow whose leather was used to produce them. Still, my shoes are important to me. Besides their obvious functions, they connect me to others. They help establish my position in society, and their style tells others how I see myself. I have an intimate connection to these shoes, but someone else made them, and that someone is a complete mystery to me.

A commodity, whether it's a pair of shoes or an iPod, takes on its own life independent from the conditions of its original production. For Marx, this gulf between the producer of a commodity and the person who buys it and uses it creates problems. The worker on a factory floor doesn't get to see people walking around with their shoes and iPods. Actually, the majority of the people who manufacture iPods couldn't even afford to buy an iPod. Marx uses the term "reification" (*Verdinglichung*—literally, "thingification") to refer to the way that the market tends to make us reduce people and workers to mere labor-power, while, at the same time, we begin to see human, life-like qualities in manufactured products. Reification is the process whereby the workers who produce things become, themselves, treated more and more like things, and their humanity is transferred to the things they produce, which we treat more and more like people.

Now, you might ask, How did I get from nineteenth-century Dickensian factory conditions to contemporary consumer electronics? How could reification, a concept from more than one hundred years ago, still be relevant today? Because, for one reason, globalization has increased the geographical distance between producers and consumers. Most consumers are used to seeing "Made in China" labels, and wouldn't necessarily think twice about the conditions of production necessary for the commodities to exist. According to Marx, the system is structured so that we forget about the work that goes into a product. The principle of exchange means that every commodity can be boiled down to its monetary worth and disconnected from the human element involved in creating the product.

This is not to say that conditions of production are the same today as they were in the nineteenth century. For example, there is a range of social positions, such as the new middle class, making the distinction between owners of capital and the working class not quite as clear-cut as it once was. With all the talk of post-industrial capitalism, one might think that there are no more factories. Certainly, the increasing use of mechanical production has alleviated much of the toil involved in commodity production. But with electronics manufacturing in particular, there remain conditions that Marx would find familiar, were he to rise from the grave and examine companies outsourced by Apple to produce iPods. Particularly in developing nations such as China, there is a stark difference between the privileged few and the toiling workers.

The London-based newspaper *Mail on Sunday* published an exposé titled 'iPod City' that examined working conditions in Longhua, China, located approximately twenty miles from Hong Kong.[2] The article has been called "the first major sweatshop story about the electronics industry."[3] Apple outsourced production to a company called Foxconn that came under fire for its retrograde conditions of production. According to the article, the iPod factory,

---

[2] Claudia Joseph, "iPod City," *Mail on Sunday* (June 11th, 2006).

[3] Stephen Frost and Margaret Burnett, "Case Study: The Apple iPod in China," *Corporate Social Responsibility and Environmental Management* 14:2 (2007), p. 104.

operated by Foxconn, was built for two hundred thousand people. Residents of this 'iPod City' were allowed no visitors, labored for fifteen-hour shifts, lived in dormitories that house one hundred workers per room, and were paid about fifty U.S. dollars per month; a low wage even compared to other electronics manufacturing elsewhere in China. While some individuals, most notably representatives from Foxconn, decried the claims as sensational journalism, Apple investigated the claims and found violations to their code of conduct, mostly with regard to forced overtime.[4]

The conditions of production for iPods reveal a troubling paradox. On the one hand, the device is endlessly customizable, allowing consumers to tailor the product to become the embodiment of their personality. On the other hand, iPods come from a rationalized and standardized production process that leads to less-than-desirable conditions for some of the workers. The distance created between these people and those who enjoy the fruits of their labor falls in line with Marx's idea of reification. Products such as iPods have to take on the character of people and seem humanized in the eyes of consumers. Otherwise, the entire process would be inhuman, mechanical, and empty.

I think back to all the work I put into my iPod. It was a matter of minutes before I had the device set up, but I've spent hours upon hours turning my iPod into a thing resembling myself. Why do I work so hard to import CD cover art, create playlists, and make sure that my genre tags are exactly what I want them to be? Certainly these tasks have served their purposes, and by spending time customizing content I've enjoyed my iPod more. I'd even go so far as to say that my iPod has helped to make my life more exciting. When walking to the bus, I now have my own private soundtrack. I have playlists for when I'm writing, when I'm working out, and when I'm relaxing. Because of the time spent customizing my iPod, my everyday activities have a little more zest to them. Yet there may be another reason why I feel the need to put so much of myself into my iPod. Seen in the light of Marx's critique of reification, perhaps I'm trying to put back some of the humanity that has been stripped away by modern modes of mass production in a globalized economy.

---

[4] Apple Inc, "Report on iPod Manufacturing," *Apple.com* (August 17th, 2007), http://www.apple.com/hotnews/ipodreport (accessed March 12th, 2008).

The iPod World as a Reified World?

If reification helps explain our relationship to our iPods, that's due less to Marx himself (who mentions reification only a handful of times) and more to the Hungarian philosopher Georg Lukács, who explored and developed the concept of reification more fully. Like Marx, Lukács examined industrial production, but he also applied Marxist ideas to the growing expanse of commodities. The move from a sole focus on production to an expanded look at how capitalism and culture interact reflects a broader shift in Marxist philosophy writ large. A common interpretation of Marx's writings, particularly his later work, is that he put too much emphasis on the conditions of production. What happens beyond the factory floor? Marx was a trenchant observer of tensions between capital and labor, but to have a philosophical understanding of cultural artifacts like iPods, one needs to take a step back—as Lukács and others have—to survey consumer terrain along with the industrial landscape.

Consider my local grocery store where I live in Brooklyn. It has a health food section that features rice, oatmeal, nuts, granola, and many similar products for sale in bulk. These products aren't labeled "Uncle Ben's" rice or "Quaker" oatmeal, nor do they come in colorful packages. They aren't marketed. They exist as commodities for sale without the personality of a consumer brand. During the mid-nineteenth century when Marx was writing, these bulk foods were all that one could buy. So one might expect that Marx would pay less attention to the life of commodities outside the factory, since they were relatively straightforward, without the layers added by consumer culture. Lukács, however, was writing in the early twentieth century when commodities were becoming branded, marketed, and taking on a personality independent from their life on the factory floor. For Lukács, the essence of the creation of commodities is that a relation between people takes on the character of a thing and thus acquires a "phantom objectivity," an autonomy that seems so strictly rational and all-embracing as to conceal every trace of its fundamental nature: the relation between people.[5]

As we saw in Marx, the capitalist mode of production disguises the human process behind products. Lukács, however, is more

---

[5] Georg Lukács, *History and Class Consciousness: Studies in Marxist Dialectics* (MIT Press, 1971), p. 83.

interested in considering how commodities affect experience beyond the factory floor. Commodities, when entered into a system of markets, cease to be valued for their practical use. Instead, their value is based on principles of exchange that appear to be independent from their real purpose. Wheat, for example, has a value that is determined by a complex equation involving supply, demand, and a range of other factors impossible to comprehend entirely. All the while, the actual use for wheat as a substance with value as food, does not change, regardless of the whims of the market. "Phantom objectivity," for Lukács, refers to this appearance of value that has nothing to do with the way a consumer would use the product.

iPods can also be seen in the light of this process of abstraction and the creation of this phantom objectivity. Apple stock goes up and down, yet this fluctuation is only tangentially related to the use value given by consumers. Journalists reporting on the economy refer to the whims of the market as an independent creature, with its own capricious tendencies. For Lukács, this phantom objectivity indicates that the human processes behind commodity production have been effaced from a consumer's reality.

Lukács says reification functions both objectively and subjectively. Objectively, the market economy creates a system of valuation with its own rules that appear fixed, rational, and independent from human control. Commodities relate to one another via the principles of exchange, yet these principles are abstracted from the utility of the product. The worker responsible for the creation of the commodity, as well as the consumer who uses it, have no immediate control over the objective process that determines its worth. Subjectively, on the other hand, the experience of reification depends upon the whims of the market economy which imprints new meanings on the product that affect consumer experience.

In a modern world of mass produced commodities, we relate to one another through products over which we have little to no control. Workers, and by extension consumers, suffer as a result of having to impose personal qualities to a dispossessed object. For iPods, the objective experience of reification is the way that Apple stock and market forces determine the value of the media player. The subjective experience of reification is the way that iPodders feel the need to personalize the device. This has dire consequences according to Lukács, who sees the process of reificiation shaping not just industrial production, but the entire world.

The penetration of the market into the everyday conditions of experience for individuals happens, according to Lukács, through the commodity and its essential abstraction. So we're not just talking about products like iPods, but rather our experience with other people in general. Since we aren't living in pre-modern communities with close connection to the people who produce the products we use, and modern production processes are rife with exploitation of the working classes by the powerful elite, our social relationships are harmed. Products carry with them vestiges of human production, yet the objective determinants of the market strip the commodity of these social relations. Our interactions with each other then begin to take on the character of this abstract relation to commodities. The modern world is a reified world and we can imagine no other. "The reified world appears…as the only possible world, the only conceptually accessible, comprehensible world vouchsafed to us humans" (p. 110). Our access to the object, both in terms of its utility and its human origins, inhibits access to the richness of all life experience.

In a world where people establish their personalities in part by the products they use, the only reality we can access is the one created by commodities. Right now, I'm sitting in a coffee shop, working on this chapter while listening to my iPod. I'm completely absorbed in my own little reality, separated from the people around me in an iPod sound-bubble. I'm interacting with my iPod, I'm interacting with my laptop, but I haven't said a word to another human being close by. One could say that the startling success of portable media players such as iPods demonstrates the extent to which we depend on commodities for our "human" connections.

Lukács would view the circumstances of iPod use as evidence that we are increasingly unable to relate to each other in a reified world. For example, I look at my students waiting for class to begin and see many of them immersed in their iPod world. Instead of building connections to each other, they have developed a finely-tuned relationship to a thing. Similarly, sometimes my fiancée and I go about our tasks at home while having our own individual iPod experience. I listen to my fifth-generation Video iPod and she listens to her iPod Shuffle, and we pass each other like ships in the night, oblivious to the world of human experience beyond our reified relations.

This is a rather bleak way of looking at human-iPod relations. Yet, while reification remains an important way of understanding the success of portable media players, it doesn't explain all aspects of our efforts to relate to commodities such as iPods.

Modding Mavens and the Limits of Reification

iPod devotees are not reification casualties, incapable of human contact. Many use their personal connection to the machines to achieve progressive and humanitarian goals. There's a vast community of iPod enthusiasts who come up with new and creative uses for the machine. Those who modify iPods and their peripherals in ways not imagined by Apple call into question the severity of Lukács's reification thesis, if only because these consumers give *new* meaning to their iPods through creative engagement. Rather than being locked into the system of valuation imposed by the market, iPod users who modify, or "mod," find alternatives for what iPods are and what they can do.

Modding re-inscribes a human element lost by modern mass production. At the same time, it engages with the rest of society. For example, some iPod modders try to find ways to foster connections between the environmental movement and consumer electronic use. Rather than depending on wall sockets to recharge their iPod, some modders explore renewable energy sources. One modder created a way to power his iPod while riding his bicycle. He was inspired by a hand crank flashlight whose mechanism mirrors the pedals of a bicycle. The modder used the same principle to create an iPod that operates when away from a power grid and without fossil fuels or even wind turbines.

Several websites post step-by-step instructions on how to mod iPods and peripherals. The modder who created the bicycle charger used one of these sites to connect to other iPod users with environmental sympathies. He detailed how to fasten the charger to a bicycle, making it possible for other people to replicate his invention. The personal investment with the commodity inspired him to push beyond the boundaries of the reified product, and to find environmentally responsible ways to power his iPod.

People with visual impairments often have difficulty interfacing with iPods, and many activists have criticized Apple for not considering the needs of persons with visual impairments. The small size of iPod screens makes it difficult for them to read the text selected via the scroll wheel. Unlike web browsers that allow for text enlarging, or the Mac OS X, which allows the user to zoom in on any part of the screen, iPods have no such option. One inno-vating iPod modder rose to the challenge and reshaped the iPod interface to provide a more controlled interaction with the tech-nology.

The mod builds on a third-party accessory for the iPod: a radio frequency-based remote control. There are numerous remotes on the market for portable media players, yet these interfaces use many small buttons that are similar in size and shape, rendering it practically useless for the needs of less dexterous consumers. Instead of the usual drive towards the ever-smaller, the modder built a rectangular box approximately 6" X 8" to replace the tiny device. On the top of the adapted remote one finds five large con-tact switches that allow for volume control, play/pause, and for-ward/reverse. The modded iPod interface reproduces the austerity of the original iPod design but with inputs easier to navigate. This iPod user took his interest in the device and tried to make it usable for a previously overlooked minority population who, nevertheless, has a right to the world of possibilities opened up by iPods.

While it may be true that we are living in a reified world, per-haps it's not as cold and inhuman of a place as Lukács feared it would become. Consumer modding is a sign of hope for a reified world. By personalizing and personifying these machines, users can reach through the device and make contact with the social world at large and begin to redress the dehumanizing aspects of commodity production. Through the process of re-inscribing the humanity lost in mass production, it is possible to find ways of liv-ing that are more in harmony with digital technology.

Still, the philosophy of Marx and Lukács strikes a dissonant chord that rings true today. iPods occupy a unique position in con-temporary culture. They are intimate to their owners, yet they sym-bolize a wide-scale pop-culture trend. No iPod has exactly the same content as another, yet they come from a standardized production process. Not everyone can be a modder. But since, as much as iPods might appear alive and clicking, it is the user that has breathed life into the inert matter composing its plastic and circuits, there may be ways for iPodders generally to move beyond their private spheres of engagement and breathe some life into our reified world.[6]

---

[6] I thank Margaret Schwartz and Dylan Wittkower for their insightful contribu-tions to this chapter.

THOUGHT

5
Philosophy Audiobooks?

LIBRIVOX VOLUNTEERS

JIM MOWATT: Welcome, welcome, welcome, to the LibriVox Community Podcast, show number twenty. That was Justin Barrett, with "If You've Only Got a Moustache." You'll find that in *The Folk Ballad Collection*, which is in *Readers Wanted: Short Works* on the forums. Wonderful rendition there; I make no apologies for playing the entire track—great fun!

I suppose, really, that it should have some relevance to this week's topic. But I'm afraid it doesn't. The only song I know that is related to this week's topic is the Monty Python song, "The Philosophers Song," but it'll be some time before that's out of copyright. Did you spot what the topic is there? Yes, that's right: philosophy. And why is it that I want to feature philosophy this week on the community podcast? I can tell you why in one easy word: that easy word is "enthusiasm."

There's a group of our volunteers recording *The Critique of Pure Reason*. I looked in on the Kant thread, and there was a very in-depth debate on the translation that they were going to do. I mean, they'd already got partway through, and then the notion of another translation came up, and everybody joined in to discuss the idea.

Now, this or that translation of Kant doesn't mean very much to me, but to all the participants, it meant so much to every one of them, and that enthusiasm and that delight in their subject was quite something to witness. Now, I have a deep respect for this subject, and for people trained in philosophical thinking. It trains the mind, and helps you focus on what's really being said, and what's just useless waffle. And speaking of useless waffle, I ought to get out of the way, and let some of my guest speakers on who can talk much more knowledgably about philosophy.

I asked each of these people quite a few questions regarding their recordings of philosophy texts on LibriVox. I wanted to know about their motivations for recording philosophy texts, and about why they thought it was a good medium for philosophy texts.

So first up, here's D.E. Wittkower, talking about what enthuses him about such recordings:

D.E. Wittkower: The main reason why I've been excited about trying to record more philosophy texts is just to increase the accessibility of these texts to people who, for various reasons, prefer audio formats. So, these are in part for those who aren't able to read easily, or at all.

On that topic, I actually ran into a student of mine this morning who had expressed interest in audio-format books—*apropos* of nothing. It just came out in conversation; he didn't know I was engaged in this project. As he told me, he ends up reading the kind of dense texts that he has to read for my course out loud, to himself, to better understand the text, and having it in audio format allows him to more easily engage the material. I asked him to record something, which I'm sending along with this.

Jim Mowatt: Well, you sent it, you mentioned it, so I shall play it, and I shall play it here.

Student: I've always, all through my life, had a lot of difficulty with written material, owing to some dyslexia as a child. And often, with this kind of dense material, I have to read and reread the material, and oftentimes I end up with a headache after thirty or forty pages of this kinda thing. Whereas, when it's in audio format, I engage with it much more easily, retain it, and am able to interpret it much more easily. I'm interested in these texts in particular *because* they're so dense, and the audio format gives me more of a personal relationship with the material.

Jim Mowatt: And now back to Professor Wittkower, who will talk a little bit more about philosophy in audio format.

D.E. Wittkower: The concern with accessibility here is not just for those who are not able easily to engage the material through written format, but also for those who may already have some familiarity with the text, and who would be able to benefit from having it in a more portable format.

JIM MOWATT: Now, I ought to chip in here, and just mention that I suggested to Team Kant that this wasn't a particularly good format for philosophy texts. Philosophy texts are very content-rich. When you're reading through, every single word counts, every line counts, and often it won't count on just one level. You'll be looking at a line of text, and you'll have to dig every ounce of meaning out of that line. Now, if it's just whizzing by you in audio form, it seems like you're not going to derive a great deal of benefit from a philosophical text in audio.

However, D.E. Wittkower there has already come up with one example, the student with problems with dyslexia, and there was the other example he mentioned, which involves going back over a text you already know, just as a quick revisit. I must admit, I thought of the possibility of it being a great help to somebody with problems with dyslexia, but I hadn't considered using it as a reminder of the text. Here's Ticktockman (M.L. Cohen) with some more of the advantages of philosophy in audio:

M.L. COHEN: An advantage for me, as the *reader*, in recording philosophy texts is that, as with any text, you sorta have to slow down when you're recording it, and pay attention to each part individually—skimming doesn't really work—and so, this forces you to pace yourself, and enables focusing which might not otherwise be possible. Particularly in one's adult life, with family and work and all those sorts of distractions.

With regard to the question of whether these texts are useful to listeners, I think that the answer—although this is, of course, where we differ—is an unqualified affirmative. Yes, these are extraordinarily difficult, dense texts, but that's all the more reason to make them available for listening.

Clearly these audio books will not be able to replace reading the text, but they would be an excellent supplement, such that one could, perhaps, listen to parts and then go back and carefully read sections that were unclear during your listening. Alternatively, one could read ahead of time and use this as a review, while out stuck in a traffic jam somewhere.

Another extremely important reason, in my opinion, for making these texts available as free downloads, is that—as with orphan drugs—the market, so to speak, for such audio books is likely to be limited. If you combine the limited nature of the "market" with the difficulty in reading these texts—both from a point of view of understanding and emphasizing the salient points, and even down to simple things such as the pronunciation of very unusual and arcane words—it becomes rather obvious why commercial recordings of these works are basically non-existent.

JIM MOWATT: So, Team Kant makes a fine argument for the usefulness of recording philosophical texts.[1]

---

[1] This transcription has been edited for clarity, and represents only a small portion of the original podcast. Thanks to Jim Mowatt for doing such a fine job putting this podcast together.

6

Philosophy by iPod: Wisdom to the People

SCOTT F. PARKER

[handwritten note: 6 Excellent article on philosophy in general ★#★#]

Early in 2007 I was living in Seoul, South Korea, when I decided to run in the Seoul International Marathon. Seoul's winters are cold and its streets ill-suited for running, so, to do my training, I joined a gym and ran on a treadmill. Most of the TV channels at the gym were in Korean and reading subtitles just about made me fall off of my machine; to have something to do while I ran I started listening to my iPod mobile digital device.

The iPod is a boon to the treadmill runner. Depending on how far back in technology we want to go, the previous music options available to runners were the portable CD player, which would often skip, and required changing disks; the Walkman, which required awkwardly flipping the cassette, and again, multiple albums; and the radio, which frankly sucks—for a number of reasons. The iPod, in contrast, is sleek and can contain as much music as one could reasonably want in the short term, all easily accessible.

And what goes for music on the iPod goes for information in general: the iPod is altering the way information is accessed. Music remains the particular kind of information best suited for the iPod's function. It is, after all, what it's designed for, though this doesn't mean that it can't be used for other purposes, for which some may find it more useful—one of these alternate uses being the focus of this chapter. Historically, information distribution has undergone a series of radical transformations. Once, to receive new information a person had to travel to its source or rely on word of mouth communication. Word of mouth is effective for certain kinds of transmissions, but consider the telephone game that we play as children: messages are quickly and drastically corrupted. We

59

lacked, in the past, a mechanism for distributing replicated information over distance. As papyrus, paper, scrolls, and eventually codices became more common, it became possible to transport written information over long distances without losing accuracy.

Through writing, information, became portable, though it was still time-consuming to produce. Each book had to be written out by hand, opening the possibility of introducing errors during each and every transcription, with a tendency (again, think of the telephone game) toward texts becoming increasingly corrupted over time as errors propagate. The invention of movable type allowed numerous homogenous copies of a work to be produced. As books became more common and literacy rates improved, information became decidedly more available, though its spread still faced logistical obstacles: books take time to make; they must be physically transported from press to readers, requiring time and money; and a single book is generally read only by a single person at a time—a limiting factor on the rate of distribution.

Newer technologies addressed some of these difficulties, but encountered others. The phone, radio, television, and Internet are all technologies that allow information to be distributed quickly over long distances with little or no marginal cost. In each of these cases, once you have the tool (the phone, the radio, the television, the computer) and the service (phone service, a radio station, a television network, an Internet connection) the amount of information available is limited only by others' output and the time you give to taking it in—with cable television, and ultimately the Internet, the amount of information available at all times becomes effectively infinite. You can use any of these technologies at any time (or all simultaneously, depending on which generation you belong to) and have relative control of the content you access.

However, there are problems. With radio and television, you cannot choose when to access the information you want. Radio and television are "push" media: they stream their info, and if you miss it, you miss it. Recording is an option but requires planning ahead and precise knowledge of when the content of interest will be streamed. The Internet, by contrast, is a "pull" medium: it allows its information to be retrieved whenever is convenient for the user. Because information on the Internet is archived, you can search out your interests at your leisure. However, though this will assuredly change in the near future, the Internet is not currently portable the way books are. To use the Internet you have to go to a connected computer. Wireless Internet and laptops make it portable in limited environments but not globally the way you can take a book with you anywhere you go.

The iPod is an interesting hybrid of these different aspects of information distribution, portability, accessibility, archiveability, and content control. iPods are small and light; they fit un-cumbersomely in your pocket; you can retrieve the information you've stored on it whenever you want. Of course there are technological limitations for the iPod. For one thing, a person must go to a computer that is connected to the Internet to load it with new information. For another, it must be charged periodically. Both loading and charging require physical presence in certain places where these resources, content and energy, are available. Ideally, the content and energy could be received anywhere—things we're already seeing start to happen. Despite these minor inconveniences, a user has unprecedented information control with the iPod.

This medium has been used primarily for music so far, but what about something like philosophy? Shouldn't these same features that work so well for music work for distributing other types of information, such as the written word in general and philosophy in particular?

PhilosophiPod

As did the iPod itself, I started out with music. I arranged hip-hop playlists for when I ran, but as the hours passed on the treadmill, I grew bored and wondered what else I could be listening to while I ran. It didn't take me long to discover that there are a number of sources of philosophy available for iPods (though, in full disclosure, I probably listened to more Dylan than anything else). *Philosophy Talk, The Philosophy Podcast, Philosophy Bites, LibriVox, The Sci Phi Show, Pop Philosophy!* (from Open Court), and others offer philosophical content over the Internet that can be downloaded (usually for free) to an iPod, and listened to at your convenience.

Of interest, with regards to philosophy, is the content itself. What's on these podcasts? Mostly they are discussions and interviews with philosophers about important philosophical issues, ranging from the oldest questions of free will, God, and justice to contemporary topics like stem cell research, artificial intelligence, and technology. The informal nature of these discussions allows for what is often formidable material to be made accessible to the lay population. Additionally, entire texts from the philosophical canon are available to listen to. One could "read" Friedrich Nietzsche (1844–1900)—a philosopher as delightful to the ear as any—without ever actually reading him (as many already have; in just over a year, *Twilight of the Idols* has been downloaded more than thirty thousand times from LibriVox.org).

Someone interested in philosophy can listen to the classic works of philosophy and hear them discussed by scholars. On an iPod. For free.[1] That's great for someone interested in learning more about philosophy. But is it good for *philosophy*?

The Academy

In 387 B.C.E., Plato (427–347) established his school, the Academy, in a garden on the outskirts of Athens. To study at the Academy one did not have to pledge sycophantic allegiance to Plato's thinking; one only needed commit to doing philosophy—that is, to thinking critically. "The Academy," with a capital "A," still means Plato's historic school, but when we say "the academy" with a small "a," we mean the general category of all present-day scholarly institutions where philosophy is done.

The function of the Academy, then, was to create an environment where time and energy could be devoted to doing serious philosophy without intellectual coercion. Plato was influenced in this by his own teacher, Socrates (470–399), who taught publicly but informally in the agora of Athens through dialogue, now known simply as "the Socratic method."

Several other schools were founded in ancient Greece—the Lyceum, by Aristotle (384–322 B.C.E.), and the Garden, by Epicurus (341–270 B.C.E.), among others—which flourished, floundered, and combined. They competed against one another for the next several centuries until in 529 C.E. Emperor Justinian banned what were then called "pagan teachings."[2]

Plato's Academy, Aristotle's Lyceum, and all the others made it possible for students of philosophy to study together, thereby facil-

---

[1] Again, the content is free only after buying a computer, Internet service, and iPod. This technology—and the information it provides—still favors wealth, though this becomes increasingly less true as more and more people are able to afford these things.

[2] Nigel Guy Wilson, *Encyclopedia of Ancient Greece* (Routledge, 2006), p. 568.

itating their intellectual growth. Anyone who has tried to do philosophy in any kind of systematic way knows that it is done more easily (and better) with others. Different people offer different perspectives and new ideas, can find flaws in arguments that are hard to detect for oneself, and can promote the commitment to sticking with philosophy.

Additionally, an institution devoted to philosophy offers the opportunity to study with thinkers like Plato or Aristotle: experts in philosophy. In ancient Greece, to study Plato or Aristotle, one went and studied with them. This all changed with the proliferation of the written word. By the nineteenth century it was possible, if not common, to read Hegel (1770–1831) without traveling to Berlin, or, for that matter, to read Plato without traveling back in time. Books made the works of philosophers available to any literate person with access to a library (so, some people). Like the schools, books allowed a student to observe the workings of the most brilliant minds in philosophy, often in their most polished and structured format.

However, books could not provide that other crucial function of the academy: dialogue. Whereas at the Academy you might be able to ask Plato about his theory of forms, you cannot ask a book for clarification, nor can you challenge a book, or extrapolate from it—except for yourself. Interpretations of books can also be misguided, something that is guarded against in institutions where there is an emphasis on criticism. One prominent and disturbing example of bad interpretation in philosophy comes from the Nazis who misconstrued the great individualist philosopher Nietzsche into supporting their absolute conformity. Had the Nazis had contact with Nietzsche, or had they read him in an intellectually honest environment, they would not have been allowed this bad reading.

Clearly though, despite certain shortcomings, the book was an important technological advance for philosophy. It facilitated long-distance and time-independent communication from philosophers to students. Though incomplete—philosophy requires a two-way street of communication—it is an improvement in the distribution of philosophical thinking. For people unable to attend universities, the book made the study of philosophy possible; and better (in all but the most tragic cases) to have some access to philosophy than none.

The iPod, in its capacity to distribute philosophical content, can be seen as a type of next-generation book. Its size and memory allow a person to be able to store a number of books and discussions in one's pocket. Can this technology solve the communication problem that books have not? And if so, will, or indeed, should the academy survive?

The answer to the first question is *no*: as yet, iPods do not solve the communication problem. iPods can promote exposure to philosophy, but do not assist in responding to philosophers or discussions with other students. But this limitation is likely to be temporary as iPods become increasingly interactive—the iPhone being a start. Already, there are ways to communicate now that are more efficient uses of time and money than having to travel to certain locations at certain times to meet up with similarly interested peers and instructors. Chatrooms, message boards, conference calls all can be used for discussions of philosophy. In the near future we can expect that our iPods too will be interactive, sparing us trips to the computer to join a discussion after listening to a lecture or book on our iPods. If we imagine the extreme case of digital philosophy—you have an iPod that can deliver and allow responses to any philosophy book ever written and any discussion of that book ever had, instantly—what would be the fate of philosophy in the academy? Would it be obsolete? If yes, then you can be sure, its days are numbered. But to answer that question requires a look at what exactly philosophy is.

What Is Philosophy?

The word *philosophy* itself comes from Greek and means "love of wisdom," but this isn't what we mean when we use the word now. Love might motivate our philosophy, as in: we love wisdom, so we do philosophy in order that we might obtain (some degree of) it. But what we refer to with the word *philosophy* is the whole process: a subject, a method, and a result. The subject contains metaphysics, epistemology, ethics, aesthetics, and other subdivisions. The method is critical and logical. And the results are particular conclusions, what we call *a person's philosophy*, as in "Plato's philosophy," or "Hume's."

Going back to the roots of philosophy, in Plato's *Theaetetus,* Socrates says that "Philosophy begins in wonder." Because we wonder about our world (philosophy as subject), we do philosophy—all of us—though not always explicitly. By default we all have beliefs about how the world works (philosophy as result), which we hopefully support with evidence from our lives (philosophy as method). Edward Craig makes the point in a recent podcast:

So philosophy is something that we're in. Not necessarily philosophy as the process of thought. It's one of these words, isn't it, that can denote both the process of thinking and the result. And in the sense of the result we've all got a substantial amount of philosophy. It's not as if it were something that one can avoid or not be concerned with. Though you can, of course, avoid thinking about it. ("What Is Philosophy?" *Philosophy Bites*, July 10th, 2007)

Or, to restate this in the terms I'm using, we all have philosophical results, whether or not we've put much effort into the precision of our methods. We do so because the subject of philosophy interests us. Craig again:

I certainly think philosophy's open to everybody at some level, rather in the sense that oxygen is open to everybody at some level. Because nearly everyone's got some kind of set of values, and very many people, in addition, have what you, sort of, might call some embryonic metaphysical views.

We want to understand the world and our places in it—to move from wonder to wisdom—so we make up stories to explain reality. Philosophy as process helps us determine which stories to hang on to. "Good philosophy . . . is the sort of philosophy that is constantly asking people for reasons for what they say and examining their arguments" (Craig, "What Is Philosophy?). It is toward this goal, of maintaining the good stories and eliminating the bad ones, that studying the great philosophers is a worthwhile project. Those who have been good at philosophy can assist us in developing our own stories of meaning. (This is not to suggest that everyone has his or her own truth, but that the way we narrate meaning to ourselves is pragmatic. We cannot construct our own facts, but our understanding of those facts always takes place individually and distinctly.)

So another question: Is there a difference between doing philosophy and studying philosophy? Yes, there is a difference. When we study philosophy we are compiling facts and information (for example: Kant's moral philosophy says that I cannot act in a way that I would not endorse all others to act). When we do philosophy we think for ourselves, drawing from and criticizing others' philosophies (for example: Do I agree with Kant? Aren't there exceptions to every rule? What would happen if applied his theory to my life? Would I better off? Would the world be better off?).

One of the benefits of studying philosophy is that it increases the background we have to draw from when we do our own philosophy; reading Plato, we can understand ideas that we may never have been able to articulate to ourselves. Another is that it helps us to do our own philosophy more consciously. Instead of relying on what we think we know, studying philosophy can teach us to cast doubt on our own knowledge, making us better thinkers and more modest about what we think we know.

For me, one of the joys of doing philosophy after studying it is coming to appreciate what the great philosophers have done. Reading Nietzsche is exciting; trying to think like Nietzsche humbling. Just like going to the gym and playing basketball is when I really start to understand how good Kobe Bryant is.

What Is a Philosopher?

A problem that remains in studying philosophy is deciding whom to study. Based on this essay, it seems like I think Plato is important to read, but I haven't said anything about St. Thomas Aquinas (1225–1274). Should you read him? What about someone outside of the philosophical canon, like the present Pope? Should you read him? As a philosopher? And if so, why isn't he in the canon? These are questions of authority.

The academy, like the Academy before it, establishes authority through the use of credentials. In Plato's Academy a majority vote decided who were to be Plato's successors. In modern-day universities we have a well-established system of accreditation. Students of philosophy who meet specific requirements are awarded Master's degrees or Ph.D.s in philosophy and go on to teach the next generation of students. One success of the current system is its built-in quality control: no one receives accreditation without having demonstrated mastery of the subject to the satisfaction of already accredited philosophers. This prevents a philosophy student from having to wonder about the qualifications of the instructor—they appear on an office wall somewhere and even at the end of his or her name.

But the system is not without flaws. One is that what counts as philosophy now is to a large extent determined by what the philosophers in power think is important. To make changes in this respect, one must first prove him- or herself in the field as delineated by his or her supervisors. On the one hand, this makes sense.

The senior philosophers have been studying philosophy longer and, presumably, know it better. On the other hand, there's a tendency for this power structure to stagnate around the interests in vogue at the time, and to entrench the subject within the walls of institutions removed from the everyday lives of people who may share a love of wisdom, but lack formal training.

Another, more serious, objection to our system of accreditation is whence authority ultimately derives. To take the example at hand, I am likely to be one of the only contributors to this book whose name is not followed by the letters *Ph.D.* Does this mean you shouldn't take my arguments as seriously as the others in this book? Maybe. It depends what your standards of judgment are. You might not trust me because you think I lack authority. Or you might not care; you might judge my paper by how well you think the arguments themselves hold up as you read it. If the latter is true for you, ask yourself is it because you trust the editor or publisher of this book to only allow you to read "valid" philosophy? You'll quickly realize that this begs the question. Why do you trust D.E. Wittkower—because he does have a Ph.D.? Why do you trust Open Court—because of its reputation? Well, what if they drop the ball? Do you have the confidence in your own thinking to doubt them? What if there was clean and unbroken line of approval leading all the way back to Plato and Socrates? Would that make anything I'm saying, or Wittkower says, more valid? And if not, why not? Ultimately, for all of us, the regression ends at our own minds. Whoever we decide to trust, we must first trust ourselves to make *that* decision, which means that we are, inescapably, the arbiters of our own thoughts. And as we're all drawn to certain kinds of questions (What's going on here?), we're all philosophers. Studying the great philosophers can help, and in fact, does help us with our own philosophizing, but cannot be a substitute for our own thinking. *That* is always up to us.

Democratization of Media—Philosophy for All!

Since philosophy must be for all of us, the iPod's function as a medium through which philosophy is engaged will be crucial in coming years. For someone who's interested in studying philosophy for his own ends (as if some of us are drawn by the financial rewards), iPods—when they solve the communication problem—will become a sufficient substitute for some aspects of the academy.

Personally, for an adequate study of philosophy, I recommend reading (to really spend time with a work—if you're listening, it's too easy to gloss over), complemented with listening to podcasts of relevant discussions, or following along with the text while listening to an audiobook version on your iPod. Additionally, writing (or expressing ideas some other way, such as a blog, chatroom, or discussion board) is crucial in developing understanding. (There's a reason that professors require so much of it, and it's not because they want to read stacks of term papers.) This recurring concern with the absence of dialogue is the predominant shortcoming iPods, along with other associated technologies, face in their burgeoning undermining of the academy. But this is a problem of circumstance and will be addressed shortly as the technologies continue to mature.

As the process plays out and philosophy, both from the canon and as it's done today, is increasingly democratized (more of it available online; cheaper, better iPods), the study of philosophy stands to benefit a great deal. The consequences for philosophy as a subject, however, are less clear.

The academy has been an environment in which philosophers have been allowed to devote large amounts of time to doing philosophy. If enough students decide that it is equally good (or better) to study philosophy on their own, via their iPods, as it is to study philosophy in universities, philosophy departments could shrink, thus reducing the number of people devoting their professional lives to the subject. But this is far-fetched—at least a bit—because many students of philosophy have a strong enough interest in the subject to want to do philosophy formally as well. A techno-centric alternative that could result from a strong desire to do philosophy formally and the convenience of iPod-based philosophy is a future in which the model of the academy is maintained, but relocated in virtual space. This would have the advantage of maintaining the existing credentialing of philosophy professors.

Short of a virtual academy, one lingering problem for philosophy as it proliferates in the digital world is the problem of authority. How will we know which podcasts have valid philosophical content and which are peddling poor reasoning and sophistry? This is one of the primary dangers of user-generated content: we don't know—or in any case we might not trust—the credentials of our sources. This is when we must acknowledge our own responsibility and do our own best critical thinking to make these kinds of distinctions for ourselves, making full use of available criticisms.

Assuming that interaction through iPods improves and the other big problem—communication—is solved, we can expect to see forums of philosophical exchange advance. Commenting on philosophically-themed blogs already works toward this end, but as iPods improve and we gain constant access to these forums, and communication moves into real-time, the results will be increasingly dialogical. The worst-case scenario, from the perspective of the academic philosopher, is that iPods would draw enough students to make the academy and his expertise obsolete. Surprisingly, expertise itself may not suffer in this case. Wikis offer at least the possibility that a collective might become a viable authority capable of replacing the expertise of the scholar. Kevin Kelly, editor-at-large of *Wired* magazine, sees Wikipedia as a rapidly improving collective and wonders if in the future collaborative textbooks, music, movies, and governance might be possible.[3] And if these, why not philosophy too? Not that the collective's thought should substitute for individual thought any more than an expert's thought should, only that it too can be a valuable complement.

In a podcast I listened to on one of those treadmills in Seoul, I heard the following from Harriet Baber, a philosophy professor at the University of San Diego:

> The best thing that we do as philosophers is teach undergraduates, in their first or second philosophy courses, to awaken from their dogmatic slumbers—their slumbers concerning various sorts of cultural relativism and all of the other stuff that's in the air. Unfortunately, however, I think that most of us, professionally, are being pressed by the assessment movement to produce results that can be quantified, to come up with various instruments, as they call them, where we are to come up with pre-tests and post-tests and show that our students have learned how to do calculations that they couldn't do before. . . . And we could give them tests to see if they know how to do various kinds of calculations. But that's not what we should be doing. So for practical purposes I'm wondering how we, who know better, can convince those who fund us, and those who support us, that what we're doing in awakening students from their dogmatic slumbers to be critical reasoners and good citizens is worthwhile. ("The Future of Philosophy," *Philosophy Talk*, August 1st, 2006)

---

[3] Kevin Kelly, The Edge Annual Question, 2008, www.edge.org/q2008/ q08_6 .html#kelly (accessed March 10th, 2008).

That's right. The best thing we learn from philosophers is how to do our own philosophy—a necessary skill that we must have to critically navigate our lives. Where we develop this skill in the future will be increasingly up to us. Institutionalized philosophy, as Plato envisioned it in his Academy, will retreat under the encroachment of technology. Anyone with an iPod and the willingness to challenge him- or herself critically can study philosophy with as much of history's resources as anyone has ever had at hand. But this does not spell the end of the academy: it remains the preferred environment for people who want to not only study, but also do, philosophy. It does, however, suggest that the academy's stronghold on teaching philosophy is loosening. The interesting question—an empirical question, remaining to be answered—is whether a significant increase in the number and kinds of people studying, and also doing philosophy in their spare time, will eventually supplant the focused philosophizing of a relatively small number of specialized academics.

7

Today's Cheaters, Tomorrow's Uisionaries

DANIEL STURGIS

The Sony Walkman was a pervasive appendage of the 1980s and 1990s. The Walkman was revolutionary because it allowed people to take their recorded music with them and listen to it virtually anywhere and anytime.

The iPod mobile digital device boasts massively more storage, video capacity, better batteries, and an Internet connection (either indirectly through the computer or directly with the iTouch or iPhone). It would be a mistake to think of the iPod as a Walkman on steroids. It's not simply a bigger, better Walkman, nor is it primarily a device for entertainment. The iPod has the potential to be an important educational instrument that will change how we think about how to learn and what we should know. (When I say "iPod" I am not limiting the discussion to Apple's MP3 players. As with Sony's Walkman there clearly is a value in talking about the market leader.)

The iPod supplements traditional "distance learning" (where the teacher communicates with the student at a distance), and increases the demand and opportunities for new educational experiences. The convergence of the iPod with what is called Web 2.0—the collaborative web—could transform education.

As the pervasive and portable iPod becomes more integrated into the collaborative web, an ever-increasing stock of information will be cheaply and widely accessible and sharable. Learning facts will become less valuable, while assessing their accuracy, interpreting their significance and creating with them—all in a collaborative context—will be more so. Students who are currently condemned as cheaters for making and storing digital recordings of test information will be seen as the early adopters of a new approach to education. The iPod (of the near future) will be an important part of a more creative, collaborative and philosophical era in education.

"Traditional" Distance Learning

The notion of "traditional" distance learning seems strange, since online courses are mostly a twenty-first-century phenomenon. Yet correspondence classes have been around for hundreds of years and in many ways the Internet simply made them more efficient. Rather than mailing in assignments, students can email them; students read some material online rather than from a book.

The most pervasive criticism of distance learning is that students miss out on face-to-face interaction, not only with the teacher, but with other students as well. Distance learning might seem no better than reading a book, but a lot more expensive. One is paying a hefty premium, not for better education, but for credentials. At first glance, education by iPod might seem no better. An article in *Newsweek* noted that parents felt like they were being short-changed by classes that deliver lectures by iPod when they thought that they were paying for in person instruction.[1]

Most of the students who enroll in my online Environmental Ethics course through the University of Colorado's School of Continuing Education are, from what I can infer from their information surveys, seeking credits more than greater knowledge of environmental ethics. Often, the students are in their final semesters and have not been able to put together an on-campus schedule that enables them to graduate. Sometimes the students have already left Colorado for jobs. For this reason, however, the students appreciate that the online experience is *not* meant to duplicate their on-campus course. All of these students have had extensive on-campus education. The parents (hopefully) know they're paying for an online class.

Many online classes lack face-to-face interaction, yet still create the opportunity for virtual interaction—such as participation in Internet chat rooms. Because my online class has more assignments than my on-campus class, the online students are actually required

---

[1] Peg Tyre, "Professor in your Pocket" Newsweek.com, October 16th, 2007 (accessed January 15th, 2008).

to have more interaction with me (by way of email) than my regular students. However, my online classes are self-paced classes, which means that some students are starting the class when others are finishing. Since almost no one is engaging with the same readings at the same time it has been a challenge to facilitate student-to-student interaction. iPods, or rather the podcasts, have been helpful in this regard. The School of Continuing Education recorded my on-campus lectures, which were then edited for clarity (and dead air) and put up (for free) on iTunes. These podcasts offer students access to course material at times and in places that he or she previously didn't have it—a student could have read the written commentaries on their laptop while running on the treadmill . . . but not without threat of injury. With the podcast loaded on their iPod they can listen to the lectures virtually anywhere and anytime.

Some people learn stuff better by listening to it than they do by reading it. Having access to the readings and recordings appeals to both styles of learners as well as to those students who learn best from a combination of the two approaches.

A related benefit, and probably the reason that some people learn better from auditory presentations, is that the auditory experience humanizes the material. The podcasts of the lectures give the student a voice to put with the material that they're reading. It's not like being in an intimate interactive seminar, but at many universities very few courses are like that. It's at least more human than the traditional, all-text, online experience. After hearing several podcasts some students reported to me that they felt that they were a part of the class.

While he or she cannot contribute to the discussion of the on-campus class, the online student can hear the class questions. While no face-to-face interaction occurs, they hear more than my lectures. They get the students' perspectives as well. I could put my written commentaries in the form of a dialogue, but there's something more to the experience when the student hears other voices as well as the chalk on the chalkboard. One online student said that he found that students were sometimes asking the very questions he had on his mind. As Socratic lecturers know, this is no accident. We teach the class by asking (and encourage the asking) of particular questions. In doing so, we hope that, by the idea arising from the student, they learn it better than if we simply presented it.

In a world where video images are so pervasive and compelling it's easy to forget about how compelling auditory experiences can be. Gardner Campbell writes that podcasts—when done right— have the capacity to create a theater of the mind:

> the droning voice of a professor reading from yellowed lecture notes will not be so affecting, but a voice that creates a theater of the mind— radio's time-honored heritage—can connect with the listener on a profound level. The theater of the mind can be compelling and transformative, often far more than anything witnessed visually. A gifted teacher could be said to create just such a theater of the mind, as well as the conditions whereby students may be enticed to create such a theater for themselves. At its best, podcasting can serve as training in rich interiority and in shared reflection. (Gardner Campbell, *EDUCAUSE Review* 40:6 (November–December 2005): pp. 32–47.

I'm not sure whether I am creating such a theater of the mind for my online students, but I will say that, to the extent that the on-campus students are engaged, the online ones can partake of some of those experiences. With the help of some constructive editing they even avoid some of the more boring moments of the on campus lectures.

Not only is listening to a lecture a *different kind of experience* from reading, it is less oppressive and less demanding. For many students it's easier to listen to a podcast than to read my written commentaries. The traditionalist might gripe that this is precisely the problem with podcast education, and, indeed, most people learn better when they are forced to concentrate and block out other intrusions rather than multi-task. However, the relevant question is whether the student gets anything more from the podcasts then from the written commentaries alone.

The convenience of the podcasts counts heavily in favor of the view that the student gets some benefit from them. Most students already own and regularly use an iPod. Even those without iPods can stream the lectures while they do something else. The student can easily add a philosophy lecture to their queue. They do not need to make special arrangements to attend office hours or to log in to an Internet chat room. According to reports from my online students, they have listened to the class podcasts at breakfast, at work, while playing with their children, on the bus, and on their way to surf, ski, or even play professional football.

Distance Learning Beyond the University

While the educational value of half-listening to a podcast on the way to go surfing may be slight, the opportunities for it to occur (virtually anyplace and anytime) are numerous. These opportunities are numerous enough that the incremental benefit of listening to podcasts is enough to motivate widespread experimentation with distance learning. In this context, distance learning is often tied to not-for-credit courses—courses simply for personal education, either for its own sake or perhaps for professional development.

In the past few years there has been a dramatic upsurge in podcasts. 'Podcast' was chosen as the 2005 word of the year by the *Oxford New American Dictionary*: "Only a year ago, podcasting was an arcane activity, the domain of a few techies and self-admitted 'geeks'. Now you can hear everything from NASCAR coverage to NPR's *All Things Considered* in downloadable audio files . . ."[2]

Not all of these podcasts are educational in the traditional sense (and many are not educational in any sense). However this new medium includes many non-traditional contributors and topics.

Traditional education occurs in an institution with walls and regular hours of business. This significantly limits who can be educated and when. Podcasts increase the availability of material and decrease the opportunity cost of education. By stacking podcasts on top of other activities the user can educate him or herself without having to give anything up. Rather than waiting for and then scheduling one's life around a course, one learns something new on the go. For example, while I was writing this chapter in a coffee shop, the graphic designer next to me told me that he uses a variety of video podcasts for professional development. He showed me an animation feature for a website that he had learned about over his morning coffee which he had then integrated into a client's website by lunch.

It isn't just bells and whistles for websites. Physicians are listening to MP3 files of heart sounds to improve their stethoscope training.[3] Many top universities such as MIT, Berkeley, and Notre Dame[4]

---

[2] "Podcast Is Word of the Year," from Oxford University Press, OUP.com (accessed January 15th, 2008).

[3] Eryn Jelesiewicz, "iPods Help Docs Improve Stethoscope Skills," Temple.edu (accessed February 25th, 2008).

[4] *Editor's Note*: Also, the University of Southern Queensland, home to two contributors to this volume.

are making course materials available to the public through OpenCourseWare and other websites and portals. Some, like the Berkeley lectures, are available on YouTube, which makes them accessible to Video iPods. There is high demand for these lectures—there were 1.3 million downloads of one of MIT's linear algebra classes in just six months; many of those were students and instructors at other universities.[5] The *Los Angeles Times* describes the case of Baxter Wood who listens to Berkeley philosopher Herbert Dreyfus's podcasts while he drives his truck. My wife listens to audio books and, sometimes, my environmental ethics course while she edits digital images. My retired parents have yet to integrate their distance learning with iPods, but watch the Great Course series on DVD while they exercise. While no grades or credit is dispensed for the work, this is not necessarily a bad thing. Because users are not worried about grades, they are not constrained by a semester schedule and they are listening to content they are interested in, so they might be more motivated to learn.

Content that was previously available only to those who were admitted to and could afford to attend an elite private university is now available to anyone with a broadband connection. This is possible because both the providers and consumers of this content are discovering the difference in value between the education and the degree. As the director for MIT's open course ware initiative puts it: "If you're going to work as a public health professional, you need the certification . . . If you're working in a community"—say, in Africa—"you don't need the certification. You just need access to the information."[6] As bandwidth abroad improves, the podcast revolution will continue to spread throughout the world and the globalization of ideas will have much greater reach.

There's no shortage of criticisms of the global spread of first world technology and ideas, and given the abundance of non-educational material that is available, more bandwidth for the developing world is likely to bring plenty of unhelpful content. It will be

---

[5] Justin Pope, "Internet Opens Elite Colleges to All," Associated Press, *International Herald Tribune* (December 30th, 2007). Accessed February 4th, 2008.

[6] Pope, "Internet Opens Elite Colleges to All." At the time of writing this chapter, the accessibility of this content for download *in* the developing world is restricted by bandwidth in the foreign country. While MIT's classes are available for free, that knowledge cannot be downloaded without crashing the countries' servers. For the time being OpenCourseWare must be shipped to these countries "the hard way" and placed on their hard drives. This seems to be a temporary problem.

easier for terrorists to find cohorts and to train if they can do so anywhere and anytime. It will be easier for racists to find support for their views. Acquisition of new skills will be possible but so will an enhanced "ability" to be distracted. This capacity to share ideas will undoubtedly have mixed results.

Yet, to the extent that this global spread of ideas is inevitable, my intention would be to highlight some of the positive features of global learning that could be emphasized. Denying terrorists access to podcasts seems like a doomed project, and our goal instead should be to encourage the spread of good information. A more educated populace would be a better one. As Justice Brandeis said, "Publicity is justly commended as a remedy for social and industrial diseases, Sunlight is said to be the best of disinfectants; electric light the most efficient policeman."[7] It was once believed that ignorance about voting issues was not a serious problem because this ignorance resulted in a random distribution of votes—canceling one another out, leaving an election to be decided by informed voters. However as Bryan Caplan persuasively argued in *The Myth of the Rational Voter: Why Democracies Choose Bad Policies*, people are often ignorant about issues in a systematic and consistent way. As a result, ignorance can conspire to trump an informed view, as illustrated by a satirical column in the Onion titled: "Yee Haw, My Vote Cancels out Y'all's!"[8] A more educated democracy would be less prone to systematic error.

Another related benefit of having podcasts available worldwide is that it can improve the quality of the content. If a lecture is heard not only by the students (subject to evaluation) that one sees in the classroom but is available for scrutiny to a worldwide audience then the instructor may pay more attention to his or her lectures. I was surprised when an instructor in Israel who had listened to my class on iTunes emailed me. He was curious about some claims concerning the nature of value I had made; questions that would

---

[7] Justice Brandeis, "Other People's Money," *Harper's Weekly* (December 13th, 1913), from Library.Lousiville.edu (accessed January 22nd, 2008).

[8] "Yee Haw, My Vote Cancels out Y'alls!" The Onion.com (January 21st, 2004). Dylan Wittkower has asked me to include a note that, while the *Onion* column is quite funny and reflects a very real trend in the result of ignorant voters, the reference here is not meant to nor should be taken to assert that systematic voter ignorance is limited to persons of Southern descent. I might also add that I am secretly anticipating the day when the colloquial use of "y'all" becomes acceptable, rather than the pallid "you guys."

have been unlikely to come from students, but which forced me to think harder and defend my views on the matter.

Memory and Learning

With the rise of anywhere, anytime access to a global buffet of ideas, we are witnessing an explosion in the number and rate at which users can learn. As the technology for recording and editing podcasts improves, so to will the supply, variety, and quality of podcasts. The most interesting effects of the iPod will be the results of making the Web 2.0 revolution, the collaborative web, portable. With anywhere, anytime access to the web, we could see an important shift in education and learning; first, as the wireless iPod becomes a standard device even among elementary schoolchildren, the value of teaching kids a body of facts will decline. Instead of teaching content acquisition, we could see a new emphasis on teaching critical investigation of these facts, as well as the interpretation of their significance and reflection upon values. And, as the need for personal knowledge declines, the value of teaching kids effective collaboration skills will increase.

At least in some elementary schools in Boulder, iPods are pervasive, and by middle school cell phones are common as well. A friend of mine who teaches fourth grade reports that using her iPod to play music for her class was a valuable way to bond with the students. Moreover, both she and her students make ample use of the web in class. To explain an "isthmus" she quickly found an image on the web and projected it for the class. When given the choice to use library books or the web to write reports on a country in South America, every child chose using the web.[9] As iPods and the web become more integrated and these devices become cheaper, it will become standard for kids (and everyone else) to have them.

The vision of elementary school kids wired up to their iPods might strike some educators as dystopic. Educators will bemoan "the loss of innocence" that accompanies youths equipped with iPods instead of protractors. The iPod might be perceived as serious disruption to education—actually, some schools have already banned iPods because of their potential as cheating devices.

---

[9] Kim Kleinman, personal communication, March 5th, 2008.

Students have used audio recorders to record test answers as well as downloading notes and stashing them in lyrics files.[10]

While the educators appreciate the potential of these devices to replace memorization, they have missed the big picture. While the cheaters are wrong for taking an unfair advantage, they are demonstrating insight into the world to come. Rather than seeking to deny students access to iPods when taking tests, schools should look for ways to ensure that all students have access to them. To educate students apart from these technologies is to educate them in a way that would leave them ill-equipped to deal with the world outside of their classrooms. We shouldn't oppress tomorrow's students with Dickens's Gradgrind. If we continue to emphasize the value of memorizing facts, these students will have less to contribute to the world than those students who have learned to do something interesting with facts.

When highly portable access to the Internet becomes pervasive, this will mark the end of an era in which people valued the acquisition of knowledge. It's common today for people to be anxious about their ability to assimilate content. However this is changing. No one is anxious about being able to memorize the phone book, because no is expected to memorize it. We're often unfamiliar with the phone numbers of even our closest friends and loved ones. We're reaching this same point with a *much* broader set of facts that we once thought it was essential to know.

Philosophers will tell you that to know something we must (at least) have a justified true belief about it. As Plato argued in the *Meno*, we can lose knowledge through forgetfulness. We can forget what we believe. The glory of an inexpensive, portable device connected to the world of ideas is that we can easily retrieve things we might have forgotten (if we remember that we have forgotten them). The result is that the value of memorizing information is dramatically reduced.

Obviously, the most important invention to liberate learning from memory was writing. When facts and ideas could be recorded, mental energy could be devoted to new problems. Exchanges in the marketplace could be facilitated with cuneiforms rather than mere exchange of words. It was not as important to

---

[10] Rebecca Boone, "Schools Banning iPods to Beat Cheaters," *Associated Press* (April 27th, 2007), from abcnews.com (accessed February 26th, 2008).

memorize the story of one's ancestors if one could read it from a text. One could then focus more attention on reflecting upon its significance. Nonetheless, humans still depended upon memory since one needed access to the written material and such access could be precious. The vast contents of civilization's thinking could not be stored in one's home, or rarely even in a single library.

With wireless, portable Internet, the need for memory, for learning facts, is vanishing. The storage and connectivity of these devices makes vast libraries of content (such as music, movies, and books) readily accessible. Far more content than we could ever expect an individual to learn throughout a lifetime of education is quickly available. The increase in access creates a valuable renewable (and ever expanding) public resource. As such, educating students in facts becomes training to compete on shows like *Jeopardy*, but little else. The answers (or rather the answers in the form of questions) are at anyone's fingertips. If I can quickly look up the tallest peak in Ecuador on an iPhone, it is functionally equivalent to being able to remember it—at least outside a contrived game-show environment. To exclude this technology from the learning environment is to educate students for a bygone era.

The skeptic may point to the possibility of an Internet crash that would cut off the user's access to facts. No doubt it is *different* to have something stored in one's head than on one's iPod, but it is not obvious that it is always better. Concerns about the reliability of such external memory are nearsighted. If not currently, then in the near future it will be more reliable to have something stored on a remote server than to have something stored in one's head. Having knowledge located in one place—the organic server of one's brain—is much more vulnerable than if it were located in various servers around the world accessible through redundant paths. Yes, the server could crash, but so could I.

The Rise of Philosophical and Artistic Education

While the future offers a public stock of knowledge, this knowledge will not necessarily be transparent. Finding an answer to a factual question is rarely as simple as typing the question into Google. What my fourth grade teacher's class discovered was an abundance of answers. The project deadlines needed to be extended. It's not just the amount of information but the reality that one is confronted with a variety of results, many conflicting, some with vested interests in being chosen. Traditionally the learner was in the position of lacking answers to questions and so needed a reasoning process to be able to reason from whatever evidence could be found. Now the problem is having too many answers to the question and not knowing which one is best. Either case requires critical thinking, but the challenges are distinct.

In part, the present (and future) predicament is a much more bottom-up process. Confronted with data on a question that might be true how can one assess its truth-value? For example when researching this article I did what many academics rarely admit to: I consulted the entry on the iPod in Wikipedia. There I found the claim that Apple's iPod held a ninety percent market share in the U.S.[11] I knew the iPod was popular, but a ninety percent market share was implausible. When I followed the footnote I found that the author and collective editors had indeed misread the data. What the original source claimed was that ninety percent of the market for portable stereos still remained.[12] Similarly, we will need to learn to be more critical of images we see that are likely modified by Photoshop or similar software. Neither seeing nor hearing is or ought to be believing.

In addition to assessing the accuracy of data, educators should place an increasing value on the ability to interpret and appreciate the significance of content. Once one has arrived at the best data, it is important to appreciate what it means. This requires more than analysis but, as the philosopher John Dewey held, reflection and artistry as well.[13] The artist works with the meanings of society to express something new—to see and then show the world in new ways. What was previously a more advanced skill should be emphasized earlier. In general, this post-factual age will be one that values what one can do with information. What will be valuable will be the creation of more valuable syntheses of information, not mere combinations of information but philosophical and artistic creations. Skills that now must wait for an ample body of facts to be internalized could begin to be cultivated much earlier.

---

[11] Various, "iPod," *Wikipedia*, http://en.wikipedia.org/wiki/IPod (accessed February 5th, 2008).

[12] Katie Marsal, "iPod: How Big Can It Get?," Apple Insider, www.applein-sider.com/articles/06/05/24/ipod_how_big_can_it_get.html (accessed February 5th, 2008).

[13] See for example John Dewey, *Art as Experience* (New York: Perigee, 1980).

To free learning from memory is also to free it from a focus on self-reliance—the value of knowing it yourself. When facts were dispersed in peoples' minds and in various libraries, it was far more important for the learner to demonstrate his or her self-reliance in being able to produce those facts. This skill was developed through individual assignments (for example, *my* country report) and exams in which wandering eyes were severely punished. Although it's worth noting that the example of the fourth grade class's report mentioned in this chapter was in fact a collaborative project. However in a highly connected world where a vast pool of knowledge is publicly accessible, who cares which of those facts the student can produce on their own? It will be actually be unhelpful to instill in students a guarded view of knowledge. The student who conceives of learning as a private activity will be less likely to become an avid collaborator. As Wikipedia has demonstrated, millions of small intentional contributions can quickly produce achievements that dwarf what an individual can accomplish. Whether within a company or through informal voluntary arrangements we are likely to see greater individual success to those who can cooperate.

As I have already mentioned, there has been an explosion in podcasts. We should hope for greater emphasis in the future on more collaborative creation of these by educators. Furthermore, it is likely that the iPod of the future will not just be used for consuming content but for generating it as well. Because it receives its content from its hard drive or flash drive the iPod has up to this point been a mostly passive device; allowing people to consume audio and now video content. The release of the iPhone, which integrated a full-featured web browser with a music player, may mark the start of a switch to a more active role. While Wiki-style content is still largely produced and consumed on desktops, this constraint may soon disappear. Of the top ten novels in Japan in 2007, five of them were originally composed on cell phones."[14]

Aside from the dystopic fear one kind of concern that might arise from educators worried about iPod education is simply the practicality of evaluating students. How will we test students—how will we give them individual grades with all this emphasis on col-

---

[14] Norimitsu Onishi, "Thumbs Race As Japan's Best Seller's Go Digital," *New York Times*, January 20th, 2008, www.nytimes.com/2a08/01/20/world/asia/20japan .html (accessed January 28th, 2008).

laboration and sharing? I don't know, but the need for individualized testing raises the question of the goals of learning. If the goals are not mere acquisition of content then we will indeed need new modes of evaluating.

Another kind of criticism might be grounded in a general suspicion about collaboration. The traditionalists might roll their eyes at the idea of education that emphasizes group projects, or consider it some form of communist conspiracy. The reality is quite the opposite. As authors of *Wikinomics* note, the collaboration of individuals that we are witnessing is distinct from autocratic systems because it is not orchestrated from the top down; this collaboration arises instead from individuals making unique contributions.[15] The point of collaborative education is to prepare individuals to have the sorts of skills that will be most valued in the marketplace.

After Forgetting

The iPod has already expanded and will continue to expand the opportunities for people to learn, continuing to liberate people from a variety of constraints of traditional education. The result may be not just more information but more creative and philosophical potential being expressed and enjoyed. Yet this liberation will come with a new limitation: to reach these new heights, we will have to accept that who we are as human beings is in a significant way integrated with technological devices. I suspect that the transition to this dependency has already occurred, yet selective realms of technological deprivation make possible the continuation of the myth that we are essentially biological beings.

While I take this transition to be inevitable, we might still wonder whether something valuable is lost by depending so heavily on a technological object as part of learning. I suppose it depends on what one values. Most of us never learned the skills to survive off the land that were, at one point in human history, necessary knowledge. However, the quality of most lives is probably better for *not* having learned it. That is, we have benefited from the scientific discoveries and artistic innovation because we do not require students to master these skills, but rather focus on the development of new

---

[15] Don Tapscott and Anthony D. Williams, *Wikinomics: How Mass Collaboration Changes Everything* (Penguin, 2006).

knowledge. We trust that society will be there. I suspect that the integration of the iPod into education will follow a similar arc. There will perhaps always be nostalgia for those people who could remember a wealth of facts. Yet, the vast majority of people will forget that there was a time when remembering mattered but will take delight in the range of new discoveries.

8

iPod Therefore iAm

CRAIG A. CONDELLA

Though it by no means ranks with *Gone with the Wind* or *Casablanca* as one of the most iconic films in the history of American cinema, *Saturday Night Fever* does capture a time, place, and culture in a way that is memorable if not remarkable. Even if you've seen the film only once, and not since the time of its release roughly thirty years ago, you would be hard pressed to forget Tony Manero self-assuredly strutting down the sidewalk to the tune of "Stayin' Alive" in the opening scene. *Saturday Night Fever* would be about the music, a fact made known to the audience at the very start. The soundtrack for *Saturday Night Fever* would actually become more popular than the movie itself as it remains the second highest selling soundtrack of all time.

There's nothing unusual here since music has always played an important role in film-making. Does anything, for instance, transport us to the Civil War South better than Max Steiner's sweeping score from *Gone with the Wind?* And what could possibly surpass "As Time Goes By" when it comes to capturing the feeling of unrequited love and heroic valor in *Casablanca?* Music taps into human emotion like nothing else, a fact well known to film-makers from the time of the first motion pictures up until the present day.

There is, however, something very different about the opening scene of *Saturday Night Fever.* While Tony initially strikes the viewer as the essence of late 1970s cool, an impression fortified—if not altogether formed—by the music that seems to mark his every move, we soon realize that he is doing little more than delivering a can of paint, a task as mundane as it is *un*-cool.

That Tony must complete such a task, however, does little to undo the image of himself that he has cultivated in his own mind. What defines Tony are not the menial tasks that he must perform at his job all week, but the moves that he executes on the dance floor at week's end. The music of the Bee Gees thereby transforms an otherwise trivial task into something that sheds light on who Tony truly is, or at least who he thinks himself to be. Unlike films of the past, the music is used not so much to *capture* the mood as it is to *alter* it. Tony would rather be elsewhere and, given the music, we know exactly where he wants to be.

Tony Manero provides us with a mirror of ourselves in a world increasingly shaped in our own image. We, like Tony, seem inclined to alter our immediate environment, but no longer feel compelled to rely on our own imagination to do so. Who, after all, needs an imagination when I can simply dial up a tune on my iPod mobile digital device and interject meaning into an otherwise insignificant act?

Need some motivation to get through that workout? Imagine yourself as Rocky Balboa while running on the treadmill to the beat of "Eye of the Tiger." Feeling a bit rundown while riding home on the bus after a long day at work? A little "Mrs. Robinson" by Simon and Garfunkel can transform your whole experience. Perhaps while shopping for groceries you find yourself in the mood for love. What could be better than immersing yourself in Etta James's "At Last" or "Let's Get It On" by Marvin Gaye? Such are the wonders of the iPod, whose size, portability, and ease of use afford us constant opportunities to alter our reality with the mere click of a button. Tony Manero, born too soon, never had it so good.

Acknowledging the iPod's many virtues—not the least of which is providing us with a soundtrack for our everyday lives— I feel compelled to give fair voice to some of its potential vices. Having lived in the city of New York for nine years, I can certainly sympathize with the subway rider who wants to escape her surroundings as quickly and thoroughly as possible. In such instances, the iPod presents itself as nothing less than a godsend. That granted, is there anything troubling here? Are there implicit dangers involved with escaping our environment and, in many cases, disabling our imagination? Even with the greatest of inventions, there are inevitable problems that, quite often, proceed unnoticed. Given his preoccupation with modern technology, the German philosopher Martin Heidegger can prove helpful here, in spite of the fact that the iPod itself would not become popular until some thirty years after his death.

Some Thoughts about Thinking

For Heidegger, the most basic and important of all philosophical questions is the question of being. What does it mean to be? How do I make sense of my own existence? Why is there something rather than nothing? Throughout history, different thinkers have responded to these questions in a number of different ways, which is not to say that anyone has proven successful in answering these questions once and for all, or to even think that any definitive answers are possible in the first place.

Heidegger, like Socrates, believes that philosophy is more about asking questions than providing ready-made answers. To think that we can conclusively answer the question of being not only reveals a certain kind of arrogance on our part, but a certain kind of ignorance about the nature of philosophical questioning as well. Students, when first exposed to philosophy, often criticize the discipline for raising questions that do not allow for objective answers in the same way as, for example, a physics problem, where there can be no doubt about the correct answer. Far from counting this as a strike against philosophy, Heidegger views such criticism as a mark of distinction. The most important questions in life refuse to admit of easy answers. Unfortunately, in an age predisposed to the straightforward answers offered by science and technology, such questions become evermore difficult to see.

Philosophical thinking is precisely the type of thinking that is becoming something of an endangered species in an age dominated by modern technology. For Heidegger, the question of being, though timeless in and of itself, must be rethought at every point in human history, since the world around us unfolds in different ways as we move through time. Whereas religion dominated most people's understanding of the world during the Middle Ages, science and technology have come to rule the day in the modern period. As Heidegger writes in *The Question Concerning Technology*,

> Everywhere we remain unfree and chained to technology, whether we passionately affirm or deny it. But we are delivered over to it in the worst possible way when we regard it as something neutral; for this

conception of it, to which today we particularly like to pay homage, makes us utterly blind to the essence of technology. (New York: Harper, 1977, p. 4)

The question of being thus amounts to the question of how science and technology shape our entire worldview, which presently includes everything from the way we think to the way we relate to each other to the way we treat the natural world.

As Heidegger sees it, the question of modern technology is not one question among others, but *the most important question of our time.* As such, we should not expect any reflection on the essence of modern technology to yield any simple solution to the problems which modern technology newly creates (be it global warming, the threat of nuclear weapons, or the debate over stem cell research, to name but a few). And yet, if we wish to uncover the truth of our age and see modern technology for what it truly is, we must devote ourselves to such reflection regardless of what, if anything, results. "Thinking," as Heidegger writes, "is a deed. But a deed that also surpasses all *praxis.* Thinking towers above action and production, not through the grandeur of its achievement and not as a consequence of its effect, but through the humbleness of its inconsequential accomplishment."[1] Thinking, for Heidegger, is its own reward, an idea that we tend to find unsettling given the emphasis we typically place on offering solutions and producing results. Such uneasiness takes us back to the iPod and the essential distinction that Heidegger draws between *calculative* and *meditative* thought.

Thinking Outside the Pod

If we were to characterize the difference between calculative and meditative thinking, we could say that, whereas the former was and continues to be used in the creation and manufacturing of the iPod, the latter tends to be stunted in those who buy and perpetually use it.

Whereas calculative thinking is interested in producing results and manipulating things to our own advantage, meditative thinking considers the true nature of reality, the forces behind the forces that propel us forward through time, the way the world *reveals itself* and the place we occupy in such revealing. In short, meditative

---

[1] Martin Heidegger, "Letter on Humanism," in his *Basic Writings*, p. 262.

thinking wrestles with the question of being. As such, it requires time, it requires concentration, and it requires a certain amount of silence, as prohibitions on noise in libraries can certainly attest.

To the extent that modern technological devices such as the iPod interfere with these requirements, invading our inner space and directing our attention elsewhere, they become obstacles in the way of meditative thinking. For Heidegger, the potential effects of this are dire.

Stressing the fact that meditative thinking requires time, focus, and a good deal of effort, Heidegger emphasizes that such thinking remains a distinct possibility for each one of us. "Anyone," says Heidegger, "can follow the path of meditative thinking in his own manner and within his own limits. Why? Because man is a *thinking*, that is, a *meditating* being."[2] In issuing such a declaration, Heidegger makes a not-so-subtle reference to seventeenth-century philosopher René Descartes, who essentially defined human beings as "thinking things," a conclusion that quickly followed from his well-known pronouncement: "I think, therefore I am."

While "thinking" and "meditating" may initially strike us as synonyms, we must overcome this immediate impression. Far from reaffirming Descartes's definition of human beings as thinking things, Heidegger is criticizing Descartes and the subsequent academic tradition (philosophic and scientific alike) for understanding thinking in terms that are far too narrow. The thinking that Descartes has in mind and the thinking that drives our modern technological age is what Heidegger refers to as *calculative* thinking, the thinking employed in both the scientific study of nature and technological production. While such thinking certainly has its place, its sheer dominance over the last three centuries has put us in a precarious position. Understanding why can shed light on the need for meditative thinking, however difficult such thinking increasingly becomes.

Drawing our attention to the pervasiveness of calculative thought, Heidegger argues that "our whole human existence everywhere sees itself challenged—now playfully and now urgently, now breathlessly and now ponderously—to devote itself to the planning and calculating of everything."[3] Such planning and

---

[2] Martin Heidegger, *Discourse on Thinking* (New York: Harper, 1966), p. 47.

[3] Martin Heidegger, *Identity and Difference* (Chicago: University of Chicago Press, 2002), pp. 34–35.

calculating reduces all decision making to a cost-benefit analysis that comes to pervade our entire life. When choosing a major in college, for example, students (and their parents) tend to think primarily in terms of the financial security which different majors will eventually provide. The college experience, in other words, is not seen as being intrinsically valuable in itself (that is, as a place where meditative thinking can take place), but as a stepping stone to a future career that will prove as lucrative as possible. In this sense, even philosophy needs to be "sold" as a major, the attractiveness which philosophy majors hold for law schools being an oft-used selling point.

For Heidegger, to think about everything in these terms is not only to sell ourselves short, but also to do damage to the world around us. As we well know by now, the thinking that places a priority on our individual needs, and that emphasizes speed, comfort, and prosperity above all, has taken quite a toll on the natural world. From the notion that science and technology can pave the way to a happier life

> arises a completely new relation of man to the world and his place in it. The world now appears as an object open to the attacks of calculative thought, attacks that nothing is believed able any longer to resist. Nature becomes a gigantic gasoline station, an energy source for modern technology and industry.[4]

In a particularly moving passage, Heidegger bemoans the transformation of the Rhine River in his own homeland. Formerly a source of beauty and inspiration, it has become reduced to an energy source with the introduction of a hydroelectric plant.[5] The reign of calculative thinking thereby distorts our own nature and threatens the fate of the natural world. The only hope lies in a different type of thinking—a meditative thinking—that allows us to step back and take stock of the world in which we find ourselves. Standing as it so often does in the way of such thinking, the iPod, from a Heideggerian perspective, proves as dangerous as any technological device invented to date.

Genuine reflection, simply put, requires a certain amount of intellectual breathing room. Few of us, I presume, have happened

---

[4] Heidegger, *Discourse on Thinking*, p. 50.
[5] See Heidegger, "Question Concerning Technology," p. 16.

upon a great insight when watching *Desperate Housewives* or playing *Halo 3*. Conversely, how many of us have had an important revelation—or have at least sorted out our thoughts—while taking a shower? Speaking for myself, I can say the experience is quite common, and it's not difficult to understand why. Assuming you haven't installed a radio in your shower (or waterproofed your iPod!), it's one of the few remaining places where we find ourselves alone with our own thoughts. Here, for Heidegger, is where meditation is born. The problem with the iPod—a problem essentially related to everything that *otherwise* makes the iPod great (namely its size, portability, and ease of use)—rests in the fact that it threatens to annihilate the few potentially meditative moments that we are still afforded. The iPod, therefore, is not only a product of the modern technological system, but an instrument by which the system reinforces itself. By providing us with constant wonders while simultaneously shutting down thought, modern technology, in effect, becomes the new opiate of the masses.

Homelessness Is Next to Podliness

If the iPod indeed proves problematic, the problem lies not only in what it *prevents* us from doing, but also in what it *allows* us to do.

A feature of modern technology that Heidegger returns to again and again is the feeling of homelessness that it tends to engender. In many cases, the loss of a homeland is quite literal, as many of us are driven away from the places of our birth (which naturally includes our family and friends) to seek employment or opportunities that otherwise cannot be had. It's not that we want to leave, it's that we have to, particularly if we want to realize the "American dream." In such cases, it's easy to see how a sense of homelessness can creep into our lives, a longing for where we come from, for the people we identify with, for who we really are. Homelessness, however, not only infiltrates the existence of those who have moved away from their homeland. Speaking of his own people, Heidegger illustrates how homelessness, in an age of modern technology, is becoming a more universal experience:

> Hourly and daily they are chained to radio and television. Week after week the movies carry them off into uncommon, but often merely common, realms of the imagination, and give the illusion of a world that is no world. Picture magazines are everywhere available. All that

with which modern techniques of communication stimulate, assail, and drive man—all that is already much closer to man today than his fields around his farmstead, closer than the sky over the earth, closer than the change from night to day, closer than the conventions and customs of his village, than the tradition of his native world.[6]

Modern technology, in effect, eradicates the differences that once existed between people, places, and things. Distances in time and space become increasingly nullified to the point where the sense of a homeland—any homeland—is all but lost. As any one place begins to look and feel like any other, we cannot help but notice that the world, as Thomas Friedman would tell us, has become *flat*. And while Heidegger identifies the television as "the peak of this abolition of every possibility of remoteness,"[7] the more recent inventions of the World Wide Web and iPod would certainly force him to rethink his position.

How, exactly, does the iPod perpetuate the modern feeling of homelessness? We need look no further than Tony Manero to find our answer.

Just as Tony imagines himself elsewhere and effectively alters his environment when delivering that can of paint, the iPod affords us the opportunity of escaping our present context and, by doing so, contributes to the overall flattening of the world. It doesn't matter where I *actually* am, as the place around me can be essentially ignored. By simply listening to my iPod or, better yet, watching a video, movie, or television program on the LCD screen that fits so easily into my pocket, I not only provide myself with a seemingly inexhaustible source of entertainment, but—perhaps unknowingly—perpetuate the feeling of homelessness that has come to define our age.

Technologies like the iPod tend to render all places more or less the same because I can transform any place into whatever I want it to be. Place is thereby eradicated and, with it, any sense of a homeland, since a true home requires the sort of idiosyncrasies and nuances that are lost in a modern technological world. In short, the iPod moves me that much further away from the world in which I find myself. Should we put this in terms of Plato's Allegory, the iPod puts us pretty far down in the Cave, so far, in fact, that it becomes

---

[6] Heidegger, *Discourse on Thinking*, p. 48.

[7] Martin Heidegger, "The Thing," in *Poetry, Language, Thought* (New York: Harper, 1971), p. 163.

difficult if not impossible to see technology for what it is. Since the question of being cannot be so much as raised today without considering the impact of modern technology, Heidegger would consider the iPod to be a threat to our very essence as meditative beings.

Thinking *In*side the Pod

In a highly engaging and readable book entitled *Technopoly*, Neil Postman alerts his reader in the first chapter of the approach he has chosen to take in considering the impact of modern technology. Acknowledging the extent to which technology has truly made our world a better place, Postman informs us that he will be dwelling on the negative since there are more than enough people willing to accentuate the positive.[8] Likewise, I have focused, till now, on the more negative aspects of iPod usage. In so doing, I'm almost certain that I have not persuaded a single iPod devotee to abandon her use of the device, re-gifting it to some unsuspecting family member or committing it straightaway to the nearby trash compacter. Even Heidegger, however, does not expect us to do away with modern technology and curse it as "the work of the devil."[9] What Heidegger ultimately wants us to do is reflect on the way in which technology impacts our lives on a daily basis, especially since this impact often goes unnoticed.

If we remain mindful in this way, we open up the possibility of becoming something more than the tools of our tools, who "push on blindly" within the modern technological system (p. 25). We can achieve what Heidegger calls a *free relationship* with technology, a relationship that is depicted in the following passage:

> We can use technical devices, and yet with proper use also keep ourselves free of them, that we may let go of them any time. We can use technical devices as they ought to be used, and also let them alone as something which does not affect our inner and real core. We can affirm the unavoidable use of technical devices, and also deny them the right to dominate us, and so to warp, confuse, and lay waste our nature. (*Discourse on Thinking*, p. 54)

Heidegger often uses the German word *Gelassenheit* to express the sense of calm that accompanies a free relationship with technology.

---

[8] See Neil Postman, *Technopoly* (New York: Random, 1993), p. 5.

[9] Heidegger, "Question Concerning Technology," p. 26.

He borrows the term from German mystics like Meister Eckhart who stressed the importance of not becoming overly attached to anything in the world since any temporal good (which is to say any good other than God) is ultimately fleeting.

Taking this one step further, I would argue that we can use technology in a way that not only leaves our "inner and real core" unaffected, but actually helps us to hold on to this core in the first place. A simple example can illustrate how.

We often associate meditative thinking with Eastern philosophy, and not without reason. Whereas Western thinkers have been more preoccupied with scientific achievement and technological progress, Eastern schools of thought place great value on spiritual growth and an inner sense of peace and harmony. That many people in our decidedly Western culture have become interested in yoga suggests—to me at least—that meditative thinking can indeed help in coping with the alienation that many of us experience in a world that, at times, just moves too fast.

Here enters the role which technology can play in slowing that world down. Before each yoga session, my wife's instructor mentally prepares for class by listening to the meditative chants that he will play for his students that evening. Important to note here is that he listens to these chants on his iPod while riding on a crowded city bus that slowly winds its way down Fordham Road in the Bronx. So while his iPod does alter his immediate environment and remove him from reality, the reality he finds himself in is so invested with modern technology that meditative thinking in its midst would prove impossible were it not for such removal.

In such cases, the iPod does not prevent meditative thinking so much as it opens up the very possibility of it. The problem of modern technology, therefore, does not so much concern the technology itself as the way in which we allow it to affect us. This is not to say, however, that I do not have reason to be suspicious of the quality of studying my students are achieving when I see them plugged into their iPods while sitting in the library. But I must admit that it all depends on how you use it. Though iPods *tend* to stand in the way of meditative thinking and contribute to the annihilation of place and the corresponding feeling of homelessness, *they do not necessarily do so.* Even Heidegger, who often strikes us as among the most pessimistic of philosophers, would have to admit that the iPod, in the final analysis, is not all bad. Imagining Heidegger grooving to the musical stylings of the Bee Gees, on the other hand, may be taking things a bit too far.

IMAGE

9

The Unbeatable Whiteness of the iPod

JON AUSTIN

I've just arrived home with my latest music gadget purchase. Two of them in fact: a nifty 80 gigabyte iPod Classic mobile digital device and a mini-sound system with iPod dock for turning the private into the more public performance of my self-selected, ordered, and sound-equalized repository of whatever it is that I think is groovy at present.

I really can't remember the day I brought my previous iPod purchase home, but it wasn't long after the release of the very first iPod in Australia and I'd bought a 20-gigabyte model. It's now called the Classic, in order, I suppose, to differentiate what was at the time something of a marketing risk and gamble from the current stream of "models" that are indicative of the success of the gadget.

My first iPod was relatively simple by comparison with my new one: certainly no mention of video storage and playback and definitely no hint of the programmatic package that was to grow out of and take its name from the iPod—the podcast. But the one thing that really stood out as "new" with my 2007 must-have was the change in the most essential marker of the iPod—its color. My pure white 2003 model has become a sleek black number. But there was something that struck me for the first time about the iPod; the one consistent and seemingly constant feature: the enduring centrality of the whiteness of the iPod.

Inside my new iPod box—all matte black with some very minimalist color graphics on the front—is an equally black environment, and delving into it is almost like engaging in an archaeological dig (a Whiter Shade of Paleontology?). Lift out the trays constituting the surface stratum and we discover deceptively simple and simplistic instruction manuals. It's almost as if the iPod is such a ubiquitous part of life that there really isn't any need or reason to provide detailed operating instructions. After all, no other items of the everyday come with instructions. When was the last time you purchased cutlery and were issued with an instruction manual? The message sent by the very thin level of operational detail in itself presents as a statement of the extent of the colonizing of the lifeworld by the iPod, its ubiquity and, thereby, its relatively mundane nature—but I'll come back to that later.

The next stratum contains the Object; that which I was really in search of: the iPod, the gadget itself, along with its associated cables and Apple stickers. And, of course, the earphones. I had successfully negotiated the extraction of my much-prized cultural artifact. It had been exhumed from its black box, and lay waiting for the final step of assembly.

Thankfully, most of the real assembly had been completed by my fellow proletarian workers in the People's Republic of China, and all that was left for me to do was to connect myself to the iPod, because for the iPod experience to really work, I need to be assembled and aligned with the artifact as well. And therein lies what I have come to understand as the core component of the iPod experience. It's all about the earphones, or buds as I know I should be referring to them.

Let's Hear It for the Buds

If there's one thing that stands out in a crowd, it's the iPod earphones. They signify the cool, hip, now-ness that brings the wearer the type of cultural and lifestyle cachet that only money can buy. Might not buy me love, but it sure can buy me style, social position, and the envy and admiration, if not the adoration, of the In Crowd (and, more vainly, the wannabe Ins). What a clever idea from those Apple people: make the product really stand out from the Others in the mobile music gadget crowd—here black has been the standard of art school cool, and variously, fluoro shades, red, purple and the 1970s orange and lime green have had their time as the color of the really in-group. Now the stark whiteness of the iPod stands out with icy distinction.

When the iPod was launched, it was almost a case of whether the wearer actually needed to have those white wires that were running under their jacket or up their sleeves connected to anything. Just the sight of the white wires was sufficient for the cognoscenti to Know. As a marker of identity, and in particular youth identity, the iPod is second to none in contemporary pop cultural capital terms, but it is through the whiteness of the earphones that the cultural power of the iPod flows.

In fact, the whiteness of the iPod is its most defining feature. The first few models were nothing but white—albeit with a silver back, straight black carry case and the green-grey LCD screen—but it was the whiteness that stood out. And it was more than just white—it was an almost translucent, radiant white that you would swear glowed. Angelic almost, or at least other-worldly. And I guess that to its many users and admirers, the iPod did promise something never before experienced and seemingly not of this world, promises of the literally fantastic: the capacity to store entire record collections in a gadget the size of a very thin cigarette packet, thereby supplanting a previous era's physical marker of youth hip-ness.

(I don't think it's totally a coincidence or merely a far left-field reading of the semiotics of the growing range of sports armbands designed to hold the iPod of your choice to suggest that the visual effect of strapping an iPod to your upper arm very closely replicates the James Dean look of youthful White rebellion represented by the sight of a cigarette packet rolled into the sleeve of the t-shirt.)

With the iPod you could replay your whole music collection in pristine, digitally clear formats, a sound quality previously not experienced in a mobile music player (and you didn't suffer the likelihood of developing emphysema). All of this in a privatized consumption environment where no one else need intrude upon or be annoyed by whatever the iPodder was listening to. It could be Black Flag, Neil Young, Kylie Minogue, Hayseed Dixie or Perry Como, it didn't really matter.

In practice, the iPod allowed for simultaneous consumption of as many different tracks as there were iPodders in a room without detracting from the musical experience of any one of them. This feature of the mobile music gadget market led to the phenomenon of silent dance parties, where whole hordes of party-goers could switch on their mobile music player, insert the headphones and dance and party to their personalized rave soundtrack in complete auditory isolation from their fellow ravers, sharing only the experience of physical proximity and cultural occasion. And what was it that most partygoers inserted into their ears? Those white iPod bud-style earphones connected securely to that glowing white magic music box on their belt or wrapped around their upper arm, looking for all the world like a lifestyle-transfusion apparatus.

And that's where I started to think about the real connections between hegemonic lifestyles and cultural sustenance via the iPod, and I came to realize that it isn't so much the content of those MP3 files—all ten thousand or so of them that sit so conveniently (but mostly unplayed) in my 'first edition' 20 gigabyte iPod—but the color of the gadget that makes it such a powerful reminder, reinforcer and visible marker of everything that is connoted by the word "white."

Since its launch in the United States in October of 2001, the Classic (as the original iPod is now suffixed) has undergone a number of revisions, but one thing has remained constant: all iPod classics from the first to the fifth version (October 2005) are white. The release of the latest version (six, September 2007) saw brushed aluminum and black replace the whiteness of the main body of the gadget, but the controlling mechanism—the click wheel—retains the centrality associated with whiteness. And, of course, the constant of the whiteness of the earphones. There's nothing more "classic" about the iPod Classic than its Whiteness.

Subjecting the iPod to critical scrutiny opened up for me a way of exposing and explaining the centrality of whiteness in the contemporary global political and cultural context. Aided by recent philosophical understandings from postcolonial theory, whiteness studies and critical race theory, I approached this task with the intention of what critical pedagogue Ira Shor terms "re-experiencing the ordinary," where the purpose is to make those taken-for-granted aspects of everyday life the subject of a fresh viewing and critical conjecture.

This requires, as others have described it, making the mundane, strange. As Bertrand Russell said in his "The Recrudescence of Puritanism" (in *Sceptical Essays*, 1928), "in all affairs it's a healthy thing now and then to hang a question mark on the things you have long taken for granted." Is there anything more commonplace, taken-for-granted or mundane now than the iPod? Inhabiting the mundane typically puts the object out of conscious consideration.

So let's take the iPod out of its everyday innocuousness and make it a little more strange. In a broader political and philosophical sense, this re-viewing becomes part of Richard Dyer's project of making whiteness strange, particularly to those who are white.

Orientalizing the iPod

The iPod is one of the best examples of a global commodity. Apart from its multinational technicalities—designed in the United States of America (more specifically, California); manufactured in various localities around the world, but typically somewhere in the Asian region; assembled at present in the People's Republic of China and marketed to everyone everywhere—the iPod is one of the most ubiquitous contemporary cultural artifacts. When one focuses on this feature of the item, it's easy to locate the iPod in the realm of the invisible and dominant center around which much of post-colonial theory and philosophy (and, happily in my view, social action) has developed.

Palestinian-American postcolonial theorist Edward Said is probably best-known for his work on the concept of Orientalism, and is considered to be one of the founding and most significant theorists or philosophers of what has come to be known as postcolonialism. Said's book *Orientalism* and to a lesser extent its related follow-up (*Culture and Imperialism*, 1993) present his basic ideas about how representations of the non-European and the non-Western world came to be promulgated. These works addressed the question of how cultures, and the individuals who inhabit and construct these cultures, come to conceptualize, name, and assimilate those who are different; those who constitute the Other. Said's particular interest was in how the West, the Occident, had come to conceptualize and name the Middle East, the Orient, in such a way as to both justify and maintain a self-proclaimed superiority that, in his view, thinly disguised a intensely exploitative relationship.

Orientalism was Said's conceptual and philosophical vehicle for exposing and exploring the "ideological suppositions, images, and fantasies about a currently important and politically urgent region of the world." In so doing, he explored the power of imaginative geographies that operated to mask the human and social, as opposed to the natural or divine, origins of the line that divides Center from Margin.

Said himself acknowledges the long-standing field of Oriental studies (he traces the existence of such a field back to Vienna in 1312) and did not coin the term 'orientalism'. His major contribution resides in his exploration of how such a field of study had developed and how the discourses it offered and sustained have come to operate on such a global level as to effect a hegemonic view of the nature of those who are located in the Orient.

Said explored the application of a politics of representation, particularly as such representations were constructed and embedded in global consciousness through various literary forms and practices. From Said's perspective, the dominance of orientalist views has justified colonial projects over a number of centuries, such projects continuing up to the present day in the Middle East.

The Orient was construed in the popular Western imagination as reflecting the precise opposite of what the West valued and lauded in itself. Where the West constructed images of itself through its cultural practices as being strong, masculine, rational, intellectual, technologically-advanced, civilized and progressive, the Orient—the exotic Other to the West—had to exhibit binary-oppositional characteristics (weakness, "inscrutability," physicality, untrustworthiness, barbarism, and the like).

And the single most powerful line of demarcation? Race, and its main signifier, Color. The West, and all of its attendant characteristics of desirability and superiority, was and remains constructed and represented as essentially White. The rest, the Other, was not. Such a schematic compartmentalization of cultures requires the production of widely accepted notions of identity, and it from this point that Said's work leads me back to the iPod. And those white earphones.

The iPod and the Invisible Default of Whiteness

The iPod has become the industry standard: it has achieved that degree of iconic stature, functionality, and quality against which all others are measured and, typically, found wanting. In much the same way, white culture, white epistemologies and whiteness generally serve as the political and social "standards" of performance and behavior, that against which all Others are named and ranked and, in this case, found wanting. At least with the iPod, the position of supremacy is acknowledged and lauded. It's the very invisibility of the "industry standard" of whiteness that makes for a very insidious aspect to the lived performance of white ethnicity.

The iPod presents itself as the embodiment of the cultural and political traits Said and other postcolonial philosophers like Gayatri Spivak, Homi Bhabha, Leela Gandhi, and Chandra Talpade Mohanty identify as an unthinking assumption of superiority claimed by and ascribed to the white West. Screen critic and critical media theorist, Richard Dyer, argues that "white people create the dominant images of the world, and don't quite see that they thus construct the world in their image; white people set standards of humanity by which they are bound to succeed and others bound to fail."[1] As such, "white" anchors the positive end of the binary scale in the Good-Bad split framed by the work of Said and others.

So, what does the color white represent to those who operate within a Western epistemological (and cosmological, perhaps) frame of reference?

White Is . . .

It is white that brushes goodness and morality. It is the color of the angelic and the pure. The great repository of authority on the English language, the *Oxford English Dictionary*, conveys just this connotation of the term. As an adjective, "white" means "morally or spiritually pure or stainless; spotless, unstained, innocent." Further, "white" means "free from malignity or evil intent; beneficent, innocent, harmless, esp. as opposed to something characterized as black." So, 'white magic' is the innocent and positive version of 'black magic', which clearly is sinister, evil, and destructive. And no one really worries about the 'little white lie', do they? And remember, the good guys always wear white hats, performing 'White-Knightly' acts.

White is also the color of the pristine, clean, and pure. Doesn't the domestic-sphere obsessed hanker for the whitest wash and the cleanest house, courtesy the bottled White Tornado? And inside that spotless house—the white goods. Domestic appliances might well come in a range of colors, but the serious items—the basic, essential-to-life items like refrigerators, washing machines,

---

[1] Richard Dyer, *White* (London: Routledge, 1997), p. 9.

dishwashers—these are the White goods. The others—the television set, the DVD player, the home theatre system—are of the more frivolous kind. The serious items needed for the essential maintenance of the everyday conduct of the domestic sphere are the white goods. In recent years, the iPod has become another of these core items, and the first such item to travel beyond the confines of the domestic sphere.

White is the color of scientific authority. We have been impressed and influenced by the presence of the white lab coat—even perhaps intimidated by its wearer—into accepting all sorts of claims to scientific endorsement (some highly spurious) of all sorts of products, including nuclear weaponry. The iPod generates the same sense of confidence inspired by its connection to the World of Science, technological sophistication and (almost guaranteed) trouble-free operation.

White reflects a sense of refinement, as in flour and sugar, and it's only a short conceptual step to parlay such notions of high refinement to the cultural sphere. All the best that is human is construed as emanating from the invisible white cultural core. By way of example, Richard Dyer explores the embodiment of whiteness in Christian iconography:

> I am not arguing that Christianity is of its essence white . . . Yet not only did Christianity become the religion, and religious export, of Europe, indelibly marking its culture and consciousness, it has also been thought and felt in distinctly white ways for most of its history, seen in relation to, for instance . . . the gentilising and whitening of the image of Christ and the Virgin in painting; the ready appeal to the God of Christianity in the prosecution of doctrines of racial superiority and imperialism. (*White*, p. 17)

In 1970, a book of illustrations of what being White meant was published,[2] and it included what is to me probably the most evocative image of whiteness and its self-denial. The image was a very stereotypical caricature of an African-American man, complete with flared pants and a 1970s afro hairstyle. The caption for this image

---

[2] Preston Wilcox, *White Is* . . . (New York: Grove). The book consists entirely of caricatures, one to a page, with short captions completing the sentence "White is . . ."

was: White is . . . a flesh-colored band-aid, for there stuck across his shiny black forehead was a white-ish Band-aid.

If there was ever a representation of the ubiquity and universalization of whiteness, it was this single image and caption. Most whites would not think twice about using a color approximating their skin color to describe a universal, despite the fact that a much larger majority of the world's population is enveloped in a skin tone that would not come close to matching what would be largely understood as "flesh colored."

Here is the importance of understanding the capacity whiteness has to transfer its own characteristics onto all humanity. Whatever White is, everything is, or should be. If it isn't, then it is, obviously, failing to meet the standard expected. I was taught throughout my schooling that white, as a color, is the product of the presence of all colors. It's not a huge step to take to then accept the logical extension of this scientific fact to the cultural arena: white culture really indicates the presence of all cultures.

The iPod similarly displays the universalization of the specific that whiteness has managed to achieve. The iPod stands for all MP3-based mobile music repositories. Its very name is synonymous with the whole range of these types of gadgets. Many of my students will talk of the music library they have stored on their iPod, even when the machine is a Sony, or a Samsung, or a Sandisk Sansa. The term "iPod" has colonized the world of MP3 players to the extent that whatever iPod is, all mobile music players are. Or should be.

Increasing awareness of, curiosity about, and imperative to explore whiteness as a social, cultural, philosophical and political phenomenon has led to the development of the fields of critical race theory (CRT) and whiteness studies. In the case of the iPod, the current volume is one step towards working through some of the curiosities evoked by a more philosophical consideration of the white music machine phenomenon.

In the field of whiteness studies, such critical inquiry is based upon an acceptance that the importance of uncovering the invisibility of white ubiquity and consequent power and influence upon racialized views of the world cannot be underestimated. The iPod provides an excellent provocation to track through these theories in an attempt to understand something of the power of dominant to become so ubiquitous, so mundane, that its influence and hold over the market, culture or world operates unnoticed, but certainly not unexperienced.

Whiteness and White Ethnicity

One of difficulties for Whites in talking about and reflecting upon their whiteness is that the very novelty of the concept for many of us is such that we don't have a familiarity with an appropriate lexicon of race from which to draw in formulating even a sketch of what it is that the term 'whiteness' circumscribes. This is reflected in the inordinate amount of anxiety and struggle many Whites apparently experience in trying to describe themselves. Indeed, as one study demonstrated, the very experience of coming to see themselves as White was in itself a novelty for the participants. Non-Whites, on the other hand, have little difficulty in either conceptualising or articulating what whiteness is.

The irony of this White flailing about in search of the language of identity is that, more than any other group, Whites inhabit a powerful position of identity-naming and Outing; as Dyer put it, "white people have had so very much more control over the definition of themselves and indeed of others than have those Others" (*White*, p. xiii).

It is the central location of dominant White culture within the spheres of production of image and identity that leads to an unthinking capacity to name others while avoiding any responsibility to name oneself. The continual act of naming and re-naming the Other forces an outward fixation of the gaze with the result that the White self becomes unfamiliar, strange and almost unknowable. This is part of the root cause of the self-alienation philosophers of the postmodern era identify as a key characteristic of the contemporary.

In very similar ways, the iPod, a very specific brand of technology, has come to colonize and name the whole world of mobile music players. Its features define what constitutes a complete mobile music player. Its style articulates a cool aesthetic chic that others can't possibly achieve (I'm sure there are some copyright and trademark lawyers just waiting for someone to give it a try, though). And the market applies its brand name to a whole category of distinctive and diverse—that is, different—items and conflates the whole kit and caboodle into a single, universalized class.

Whiteness Studies

As a relatively recent focus, whiteness studies and Critical Race Theory have attracted a curiously wide range of interests and perspectives belying a considerable diversity of political location. Before returning to the iPod, let's look briefly at the primary ideas in the Whiteness studies movement.

In the field of Whiteness studies and Critical Race Theory, the gaze of the oppressor has been turned back upon itself. Kobena Mercer talks about whiteness's violent denial of difference as a strategy for sustaining its own unearned privilege. He calls for the exposure of the exploitation of things not-white attendant upon the myth of the invisibility of whiteness as a color—in fact, *the* color of privilege. bell hooks, as a further example, challenges white theorists to turn the critical gaze upon their own ethnicity:

> One change in direction that would be real cool would be the production of a discourse on race that interrogates whiteness. It would be just so interesting for all those white folks who are giving blacks their take on blackness to let them know what's going on with whiteness. (*Yearning*, p. 54)[3]

The end result of these types of concerns over the misdirected nature of critical interrogations of the relationship between race, ethnicity and advantage is captured in AnnLouise Keating's summation of the effect of the unquestionable privileging of whiteness:

> "Whiteness" serves a vital function in masking the social and economic inequalities in contemporary Western cultures. By negating those people—whatever the color of their skin—who do not measure up to "white" standards, "whiteness" has played a central role in maintaining and naturalizing a hierarchical social system and a dominant / subordinate worldview.[4]

Critical reflection on what it means to be white is by no means a recent phenomenon. G.S. Schuyler's 1931 novel *Black No More* explored the social and economic consequences of the elimination of the black race (through the application of a process of changing "Negroes" to whites) as a means to laying bare some of the threads of privilege that attached to whiteness. Ralph Ellison's *Invisible Man* (1952) similarly presents a construction of white identity

---

[3] bell hooks, *Yearning: Race, Gender, and Cultural Politics* (Boston: South End, 1990).

[4] Ann Louise Keating, "Interrogating 'Whiteness', (De)Constructing Race," *College English* 57:8 (1995), pp. 901–918.

through the chronicling of aspects of the life of its main character, an African-American man. The main effect is to show that "whiteness is produced through the operation of marginalizing blackness." As something of a parable of the production of whiteness, the narrator in Ellison's novel describes the secret of the Liberty Paint Company's prime paint product, Optic White:

> During his stint as a worker in the paint factory, the narrator must add ten drops of a "dead black" liquid into each bucket of "Optic White" paint, thus producing "the purest white that can be found," a paint "as white as George Washington's Sunday-go-to-meetin' wig and as sound as the all-mighty dollar" according to his white supervisor Kimbro, who adds, "That's paint that'll cover just about anything."[5]

What's both common throughout and striking about this historical body of literature that attempts to draw images of dominant white identity is that it does so from and through the perspective of those who are not-white—it's through encountering what it means to be not-white that one comes to see what it means to be white. Images of whiteness to date have come largely from the margins of the predominant Western dualistic notions of difference.

Turning up the (White) Heat on the (White) Light

Said's notion of the construction and rationalization of difference and Other, as but one influence, provides a useful means of viewing this identity of whiteness, but is not necessarily in itself sufficient. Toni Morrison's 1992 work, *Playing in the Dark: Whiteness and the Literary Imagination*, is often cited as a crucial point in the emergence of Whiteness studies, particularly in the United States (although anchor points to the area were laid down during the previous thirty or so years). In this work, Morrison explains that

> images of blackness can be evil and protective, rebellious and forgiving, fearful and desirable—all of the self-contradictory features of the

---

[5] Harryette Mullen, "Optic White: Blackness and the Production of Whiteness," *Diacritics* 24:2–3 (1994), p. 74.

self. Whiteness, alone, is mute, meaningless, unfathomable, pointless, frozen, veiled, curtained, dreaded, senseless, implacable.[6]

Amongst the many attempts to track the "floating signifier" that is whiteness, Ian Haney López has documented the legal construction of whiteness throughout the history of the United States of America, demonstrating that the issue of "whether one was 'white' . . . was often no easy question." He shows how, in pursuit of the United States Congress's 1790 dictate that naturalization be restricted to "white persons," the legal system of the United States of America has had to grapple with defining this particular descriptor. At various times, for example, Syrians have been considered white (1909, 1910) then not white (1913, 1914), and then white again (1915). Similar experiences of legal classification have confronted Japanese, "Asian," and "Arabian" people, as well as the Irish.[7]

A similar situation has been evident in Australian history through the operation of the White Australia policy. This policy, which operated from 1901 until phased out during the 1960s, authorized the use of procedures of selective and restricted immigration for the purposes of maintaining a pretence of a homogenous—white, Anglo-Saxon—population in Australia in the face of a growing realization of the reality of the country's Asian geographic location. At various points through the twentieth century, the Irish, Germans, Spanish, Greeks, and Italians were legally considered to be, if not non-white, then at least not-quite-white-enough for admission to the country as citizens.

The point here is that, even in the more formalized legalistic social codes, "race," ethnicity, or color is demonstrably a social rather than a biological construct, and, as such, requires a sociopolitical analysis, not a biological one. The ways in which race is constructed, signified and lived warrant serious interrogation.

The field of "Whiteness studies" has split on the question of the reconstruction of White identity and identification. One branch exhorts Whites to eliminate Whiteness as a socially constructed category in order to overcome racially coded systems of disadvantage. David Stowe, for example, talks about "the race traitors of the

---

[6] *Playing in the Dark: Whiteness and the Literary Imagination* (Harvard University Press, 1992), p. 59.

[7] López, *White by Law* (New York University Press, 1996), p. 1.

Nineties" as "a small but growing vanguard resolved to battle racism in America by renouncing the privileges of whiteness." In a society where "only white people have the luxury of having no color" Peter McLaren maintains that "Whites need to ask themselves to what extent their identity is a function of their whiteness in the process of their ongoing daily lives and what choices they might make to escape whiteness." This is not an easy task.

Eugene Wolfenstein describes the whiteness of domination as the one fixed point of America's many racisms and argues that whiteness is a social designation and a history disguised as biology. He links white racism to what he calls "epidermal fetishism"—that process that reduces people to the color of their skins and renders them visible or invisible depending on the adjudication of the color judges.[8]

The second main branch of Whiteness studies calls instead for the reconstruction of a non-oppressive identity for Whites. David Roediger believes that the White signifier, though able to be self-consciously renounced, is too strongly embedded in systems of power and privilege to be ignored or shed:

> Whites cannot fully renounce whiteness even if they want to. Whites are, after all, still accorded the privileges of being white even as they ideologically renounce their whiteness, often with the best of intentions. Choosing not to be white is not an easy option for white people, as simple as deciding to make a change in one's wardrobe.[9]

A fork in the road of whiteness has arrived, it would seem, whereby one can either reject and jettison whiteness and embrace Otherness, or re-work the essence of white identity into something less exploitative and exclusionary.

The iPod as Cultural Industry Standard

The iPod presents itself as yet another embodiment of the features of whiteness described above, and is probably the quintessential contemporary White good. In its glowing whiteness, it oozes cleanliness and purity. It has pure, clinical digital sound that mirrors the scientific and technological wizardry associated with the white lab

---

[8] Wolfenstein, *Psychoanalytic Marxism: Groundwork* (Guildford, 1993).
[9] *Towards the Abolition of Whiteness* (New York: Verso, 1994), p. 16.

coat, even though some argue that this cleanliness empties the music of the soul, the warmth, the aural dynamics and the idiosyncrasies that characterize music played from vinyl. (Compare music recorded to and played from black vinyl—with all the deficits and problems proponents of digital sound highlight and deride—with non-White cultures, which similarly endure despite the derision and devaluing heaped upon them by dominant White cultural practices.)

The process that has seen analogue (vinyl) supplanted by digital (iPod) in many ways replicates the incorporation of black music into a White mainstream. During the days of "blackface" minstrelsy—where white performers made an art (literally) of lampooning and generally deriding black racial stereotypes ostensibly for the entertainment of their largely white audiences but more subliminally for the embedding of respective White racial superiority and its concomitant, black inferiority—Edison's wax phonograph cylinders were progressively replaced by vinyl pressings played variously at 78, 45 or $33\frac{1}{3}$ revolutions per minute. Despite some straying for the purposes of commercial differentiation, vinyl recordings remained essentially black. (One of the many prized items in my personal vinyl collection is a reddish-pink vinyl pressing of Captain Beefheart's "Safe As Milk " album. Did it sound any different pressed into red vinyl? Probably not.)

Vinyl music's iPod-equivalent was the jukebox, but whereas the iPod necessarily privatizes the consumption of music, making it a solitary pursuit, the jukebox of course was the center of a social experience. It's not difficult to contrast the iPod and White obsession with privacy with the Jukebox and black sociability.

Essentially, in the pre-digital era, the color of music was black. Now it's white. And I'm not only referring to the medium of carriage here. In the United States, the basis for almost all contemporary popular music can probably be traced back into Black musical forms and traditions. While the Otherness of black music made it initially fearsomely strange, the passage of time saw its novelty and rebellious attractiveness to white youth provide an impetus to its sanitizing and incorporation into "mainstream" (read "White") culture. Now that the dangerous Margin has been safely steered into the neoliberal reaches of White Culture Bay, music is again White. And physically embodied as such in the whiteness of the iPod.

In its more recent versions, the iPod mirrors broader social concerns to moderate the more visible presence of white cultural dominance. Just as the culture industry attempts to massage some of the more visible yet innocuous aspects of previously marginalized cultures into the white exterior, the evolution of the external appearance of the iPod reflects a dilution of its phenotypical whiteness as well. The addition of a range of colored skins—now, there's a dead giveaway—has been intended to add color to the standard iPod whiteness.

These allow for a consumer to try on a bit of exotica for a while, to add a touch of color and contrast to their everyday experiences with the iPod. All the while knowing that at heart, the iPod just isn't the iPod unless it's white. Changing its external colorings fail to mask the white heart, epitomized by the click or control wheel, and the earphones. Even though its contemporary packaging presents a far more exotic face to the purchaser, it doesn't take too long before those outer layers of blackness and mystery are negotiated to expose the White core of the product lying within.

As industry standard, the iPod remains unchallenged by non-iPod wannabes. Just as Diane Jeater describes the embarrassing effects of the adoption of a black wannabe identity (described in some places as a "Wigger") as a possible location for the development of an alternative, non-exploitative White identity, the non-iPod challengers—almost all of which are non-white—try to be what they can never really be: on a level pegging with the white centre. In global cultural terms, whiteness is the industry standard equivalent of the iPod.

Playlisting the iPod: White Soul

If I were to create a playlist about the iPod itself, what I include? Clearly the genre is white soul because that's essentially what a focus on white cultural domination is all about: the infusion of everything with the soul or essence of whiteness. Or maybe it's world music, since white culture has become synonymous with world culture.

Which specific tracks might find a place in the iPod and Whiteness playlist? Well, for a start, Incubus's "Clean" would feature, especially with a lyric that goes something like "You could never offend, your dirty words come out clean." The pure, angelic white iPod could sift anything even slightly nasty and make it sound good.

There are two songs that I know of that carry the title "The Universal," one by the Small Faces and the other by Blur, and with that title, I couldn't pass either of them by in building this playlist. The iPod is as universal a cultural artifact one could hope to find these days, and if you're aren't sure about this, just have a look for the whiteness of the earphones wherever you happen to find yourself.

Given the iPod's ubiquity and synonymy with MP3 players generally, The Comeback Kid's "Industry Standard" is an unquestioned addition, even if only because the Kid ask us to "turn it up so I can hear 'cause it's reassuring when I can hear it." Surely they're referring to the iPod here.

Photograph courtesy of Photography Department, University of Southern Queensland

And I'd certainly add two tracks by Skunk Anansie: "It Takes Blood and Guts to Be This Cool" (because the iPod is the epitome of aesthetic coolness) and "Intellectualize My Blackness." Any song that carries the lyric "he tried to intellectualize my blackness to make it easier for his whiteness" deserves a prime position in the whitest of white goods.

Just as it seems impossible (and improbable) that Whites can shake off their white ethnicity, it would seem similarly unlikely that the iPod would be the iPod without its white characteristics. A rose by any other name might well smell as sweet, but an iPod without its whiteness just wouldn't be an iPod—it wouldn't be right, or natural, would it?

10

iCon of a Generation

ANDREW HICKEY

The iPod mobile digital device is an iconic expression of the digital age. It informs and carries along the identities of those who use it and those with whom it comes into contact. What I'm suggesting relates to how we express ourselves in this current era of late capitalism and the ability people have to assume their own sense of self against those presented to them in our global world.

We live in an era in which the image assumes ever more currency and the real increasingly follows behind; at a point in our technological development where the manufactured dispersion of images has become the primary medium with which we communicate. Jean Baudrillard made this point as he viewed the Gulf War via CNN from the safe distance of his living room in the early 1990s:

> Simulation is no longer that of a territory, a referential being, or a substance. It is the generation by models of a real without origin or reality: a hyperreal. The territory no longer precedes the map, nor does it survive it. (*Simulacra and Simulation*, University of Michigan Press, 1994, p. 1)

Baudrillard's interest was our growing distance from the real "territory" of the world and, subsequently, from the humanity that resides within it. It was difficult to consider that, under the computer-game graphics of carefully edited footage of green-grey fireworks CNN night-visioned to us from the Gulf, actual, real, flesh-and-blood people were being blown up, *live and in real-time*, every time our TV screens flashed and throbbed with light. For those of us who were merely viewers, this war was entertaining, captivating and—by the magic of global communication networks—kept safely behind the glass of our TV sets. To us, the war was a television experience with all the nasty, messy, inhumane bits carefully cut out.

Images inform us about who we are and provide the context of our understanding—a structure upon which we develop our senses of self and the outward identities we present to the world. In an era where image is everything, to borrow the slogan from another pop cultural icon, the formation of self is often achieved at the expense of real, corporeal experiences; we are mediated beings, actively shaped by the image networks that we simultaneously design and live within. This is life in *the now*, life saturated with television and video, billboards and signs, maps and other simulations of the real. Supermodels are retouched images in magazines, computer games simulate actual activities without the attendant physicality,[1] and lives can be lived in cyber-space, as in *Second Life*. Welcome to postmodernity.

The iPod Image

Though it's not a device designed to do harm like a night-vision equipped missile, thankfully, the iPod is an extension of this same state of being. A product arguably for young people in particular, the iPod offers an epistemological point of reference indicating the nature of its owners. You become an iPodder by virtue of your iPod and join those others who similarly have an iPod as owners. But ownership also suggests affluence and cultural and economic access. iPods aren't cheap, and the different models and prices suggest something about your relative wealth. Since they are complicated devices, they say even more about the owner's connection to digital technologies, or more grandly, the global information networks we necessarily negotiate in the now.

Like selecting the upgrade options available on new cars or even splashing out on a super-sized McDonald's meal, buying a 160 gig top of the line iPod Classic says something about you that the purchase of a Shuffle never will: you didn't compromise; you

---

[1] Slightly differently to older games machines, Sony's new *Wii* actually uses a remote hand control that allows participants to play tennis and other activities but with virtual competitors, the hand control taking the place of the racquet. I'm still unsure as to why you just wouldn't go and play 'real' tennis.

wanted the biggest and the best; you're affluent. Similarly, having an iPod with its small but readily identifiable headphones plugged into you says '*I am here, I am a member of the now and understand how technology works*'. It's a statement of tech-savvyness that no CD Walkman could ever make.

Of course, pragmatic questions come into play whereby the decision to purchase one model or the other will also be based on a perceived 'need' for a particular size, shape or style of iPod. But in a market where a hierarchy of models is presented and valued according to their size, functionality, and subsequent price, various ideas of prestige and affluence are wrapped up in iPod ownership. You get more than just an MP3 player with an iPod. You also get a whole range of social assumptions about who you are.

The iPod in this case is like an item of clothing, but one that also works on a larger scale by telling us where we are collectively in our technological march forward. And much like our chameleon identities in our ever-changing postmodern environs, the iPod also regularly refreshes itself with new models and new versions, all fashionably ready for consumption by those continually refreshing people into which its headphones are inserted.

The iPod therefore speaks much about our identity and who we have become in the product-saturated West. As consumers, citizens, audiences and individuals in all aspects of our lives, we are—in part—what we reflect back at ourselves, what we manufacture in our image, and how we adorn ourselves according to these simulated identities. We configure ourselves to appeal to the outside world and the world indeed relates back to us through this image.

What develops here is a dialectical relationship between the image and the real, in which the imagery of the self and the reality of existence intertwine to the extent that a *simulacrum* of identity is formed. The "simulacrum" is the copy, the image of something, crafted to represent but not entirely replicate. Postmodernity and its conditions—conditions such as the saturation of mass communication into all aspects of life, the increasing domination of global economic systems, and those more personal feelings of disconnection (*ennui*) living in the now sometimes brings—has blurred our understanding of what is real to the point that it is largely *images* that we interact with. These images, however, are devoid of substance and no longer refer to an underlying 'real'. As with Jean Baudrillard's television-mediated viewing of the

Gulf War, it is the simulacrum that now matters, for in our world the real has given way to the image.

Yet images are often blurred, messy, and ephemeral. The current fascination internationally with 'reality television' stands as an example of this state of being. Here we are presented with a 'real' that is entirely fabricated, that exists (like the Gulf War considered as Media Event) as a series of images that we take as real, but with which we have no immediate physical connection. All our hopes, fears, assumptions and desires are applied to the screen—the image that just *is*. A simulacrum of reality that we fill with meaning according to what we both know and want it to be, and what we have learnt to expect. We don't know, and most likely never will know personally (*corporeally*) the people we see in these television shows, yet we still "know" them according to the manufactured lives they play out for our entertainment. Here our experience is manufactured—a façade with no substance, but from which we take our cultural cues.

The iPod is both symbolic and symptomatic of this existence. The simulacrum of the iPod is one derived broadly from ideas of 'youth,' in which I suggest an experience of digitally derived coolness and youthful tech-savvyness is bound up in this cultural product. This also implies that those who have one *are* similarly implicated in this image of cool, youthful tech-savvyness; either through intentioned desires to connect with this latest expression of the digital age, or by the requirement to own and use an iPod that various aspects of our lives mandate. In this regard, it is a simulacrum of what it means to be human (albeit, young-human). Both a symbolic representation of the concerns and logic of the now, and a mediating influence over what the experience of the now is.

The iPod as Cultural iCon

The seeming ubiquity of the iPod would suggest that this portable digital audio player is, due to its *everywhered-ness*, in fact experienced by everyone. Or at least those who are *now*. As a recent addition to the arsenal of products the contemporary individual requires (like the mobile phone or networked computer), the iPod has quickly developed its own logic and cultural significance. Unlike the mobile phone or computer however, whose manufacturers are many, the iPod is both product and type, often used as a collective name for digital audio players generally. Imitators of the iPod abound, but it remains supreme in our cultural logic as both a product and a type. Think about the way we consider "the PC"—several *products* exist here according to the many manufacturers who produce them, with not one single brand being entirely symbolic of the PC. The iPod in contrast is representative of digital audio players with iPod standing for the product *and* type.

Besides the ubiquity of the iPod and the accessory-industry that cashes in on it, we can see from this small, battery powered device how products and their images draw on other discourses in culture to eclipse 'the real' and become integral to our vernacular. To listen to an iPod, to download from iTunes, and to podcast are Apple-branded actions of everyday people.

Or consider recent academic and medical studies arguing the perils of deafness faced by the current generation of iPodders whose hearing may be shot by the time they're roughly thirty years old. (This is perhaps the contemporary equivalent of stadium rock concerts by bands such as The Who—talking about *my* generation, indeed.) I don't in any way wish to suggest that the iPod isn't problematic for hearing; at high volume any device placed directly into the ear is. My point is that what the iPod has successfully managed to achieve is the identification of a generational identity, grounded in this specific instance in seeming medical 'fact' and, blandly enough, the deafness of those young, active and hip folk who have one. By this reasoning, to own an iPod is a youth experience, with the youth experience being a potentially deaf one. The discourses of medicine say so.

Myriad similar arguments also point to the iPod as a simulacra of youth. Reports about the sterilisation of social interaction from the shielding-off of the world via plugged-in headphones carry age-old fears of youthful rebellion (the same ones attached to Sony's original Walkman in the 1980s)—How will young people listen to their elders and voices of authority when their heads are plugged with headphones spewing music and podcasts from sources that most likely should contain an explicit content warning (well, that's what we'd love to imagine anyway)? Others suggest that the iPod can function as a tool for renewed pedagogical dynamism; a learning tool to sharpen the minds of young learners, and similarly as a means of connecting to Gen Yers 'on their turf'. Whether it's as apocalyptic tool representing the means of social disintegration or revolutionary entertainer and pedagogue, the iPod features as an intermediary in our understanding of youth, and as such implies an idea of youth in our collective consciousness whether we own one or not.

It's the construction of the discourse that surrounds the iPod that is significant here. Apart from the youth angle—in which the very meaning of youth is facilitated by the iPod as an intermediary between us and our worlds (that is, it is a 'simulacrum' of youth)—the iPod has seamlessly made itself an indispensable tool for entertainment, learning, and collective interaction, integral to these pastimes in their postmodern incarnations. As Ludwig Wittgenstein might put it, there is now a *language game* that authorises the iPod according to these activities and the people who take part in them.

For Wittgenstein, a language game consists "of language and the actions into which it is woven," and that social processes become mediated by the language used to describe them. These language games form a cultural logic that makes sense of these processes and authorises them as part of our existence and normal day-to-day operations. These language games may relate directly to those actions involved in using an iPod, or to the imagery of iPod ownership. To listen to your iPod, to podcast, to download from iTunes and all the associated actions connected with iPodding are part of the game. Even jogging and cycling with an iPod strapped to your arm is now part of the experience—as the line in the *Nike + iPod* section of the Apple web site notes,

> *You don't just take iPod nano on your run. You let it take you. Music is your motivation.*

As a type as much as it is a product, the iPod is representative of portable digital media players because it is part of our experience of life. But more than this, it also symbolically stands for and defines those individuals who use it. As I noted above, this is largely a definition bound up in ideas of youthful tech-savvyness. Supporting this experience is the language game of the iPod, which introduces into the vernacular new concepts and new interpretations of old ones that attach meanings and symbolism to youth-ness to configure the iPod (and its brethren of 'must have', digital age accoutrements such as the mobile phone) as central expressions of this existence. In this 'condition,' everyday lives and real existences are played out in terms of the iPod.

The iPod Is Us

The iPod has lept from mere cultural icon to representative of actual people—a jump into a symbolic cyborgism that variously alters the look, feel, and experience of being human. Zoologist, feminist and, later, philosopher of technology Donna Haraway helps to explain this leap. She suggests that the essentialisms presented in some branches of feminism—essentialisms that argue that *all* women share certain characteristics or modes of behavior or attitudinal disposition—deny opportunities for difference within this category of 'woman'. Haraway argues that we should think about associations rather than categorical, biological determinations, and she uses the metaphor of the cyborg to open opportunities for considering difference outside of preconceived and biologically framed descriptors of women. The cyborg throws open the opportunity for reconsidering identity outside of our biological limitations; something new, undefined and relational in its connection between the biological and technological.

Consider the advertisements for the iPod that represent desire for technological connectedness, at least as expressed by its makers. The original 'silhouette' advertisements black out the identity characteristics of the iPodder (a major point of interpersonal recognition, the face, is obscured, leaving only the striking but anonymous silhouette of the iPodder) with this shadowy human set against the stark white detail of the icon itself. Are discernible identity characteristics relegated only to those cyborg attachments to flesh in the current era? Who would these people be without the discernible iPod included in this image—Platonic shadows alone, perhaps, devoid of any connection to the real?

But just enough of the iPodder is left in the imagery of these advertisements to decipher the suggestion of the pre-iPod identity. We still see that these iPodders are primarily young and slightly eccentric, with their hip hairstyles and clothing just able to be made out via the silhouetted outlines. The poses these generational archetypes hold stand variously dancing or adjusting the brim of an oversized baseball cap, all the while suggesting activity and youthful energy. We might assume that the iPodder is active, young and 'cool'. iPodders understand trends and fashion and know that the iPod is a hallmark icon of a contemporary state of being.

This is what Apple sees its iPod user as being. The user isn't (in these ads) old, out of fashion or 'stuffy'. They probably won't be downloading anything much prior to 1980 (*like, as if . . . like, pop culture and stuff existed then anyway!*). The iPod is young and hip. Pop culture is young and hip. The iPod and pop culture go hand in hand to create the terrain which young and hip actual incarnations of Apple's silhouettes will traverse.

With the iPod representing a pop-culture-transfusion device, from which youthfulness draws its defining lifeblood, the cyborgism that Haraway symbolically conjures takes on a new meaning. It's almost as though a 'real' cyborgism has been constructed. The "technology dependant youth" is certainly a theme that emerges from the silhouette ads—none of the action, activity nor cool would seemingly be possible without the iPod present. It is the iPod that makes these things possible.

In these ads, all you need to know in detail is the iPod. It doesn't matter that its users are shadows, that they lack the detail of their human characteristics. The iPod speaks for and defines these iPodders, and demarcates clearly what is being presented; a new vision of youth that is in-part iPod. But of course this is marketing hype. What has the iPod got to do with real identity?

Notes on iDentity

No matter which way you shuffle it, the iPod is an über-chic reminder of the now. Like many postmodern objects, it heralds a new age of technological innovation. It celebrates the individual's disconnection from the rest of the world into a self-space that simultaneously brings in selected bits (those selected songs, podcasts and videos). It provides space for individual creativity and expression, but connects individuals with the work of others the world over. It also operates as an object capable of mobilising impassioned responses to world poverty (as per its connection to *Red* and U2's Bono) and becomes an indispensable tool for learning (Duke University in the United States, as one high-profile example, currently utilises the iPod as a teaching and learning resource).

This marks the identity of the iPod itself. A complex marketing mix that has seen the iPod grow from entertainment device for young hipsters, to being a fully fledged member of the technological stratosphere deployed in those most serious of learning institutions: universities. Like all good postmodern chameleons, the iPod is and can be what you need it to be when you need it (and this will presumably only continue with new models containing extended functionality).

Or is it perhaps, more accurately, that the world now *requires* (at the very least for 'coolness') us to connect with products like the iPod? As I have argued above, the iPod is connected intimately to the experience of the world its user has in this digital age, and it is this requirement for connectedness that indeed makes the iPod a desirable object. Through this incorporation of the iPod into our lives (like the computer, and plasma screen television before it) it functions as an intermediary between the user's self and the physical realities around that self. It is a very real component in the experience of many people's lives, with everything from sheer entertainment value to podcasts of university courses connected with it. This is no simple gadget.

As individuals who negotiate virtual spaces with increasing regularity, how we both present ourselves and make sense of each other involves the digitally networked aspects of our selves as much as it does our the 'real' corporeal bits. We no longer have just our physicality to draw on, and establish our understandings of the world digitally as much as much as we do physically. This is an experience where technology actively mediates the connections we share with each other and the world. Virtual reality becomes as important as 'real' reality. A world where life without digital communication is almost unthinkable. Where relying simply on physical proximity for contact with other people is just about impossible.

While I steer away from arguing that the iPod is *the* central icon of the digital age responsible for fundamentally altering our connection to the world (it clearly isn't solely responsible) it fulfils a role both as representative icon and hallmark object of postmodernity and our postmodern identities. It stands as symbolically representative of our desire and requirement for technology and operates as the medium upon which our connections are launched.

Identity, however, is fluid, changing and contains multiple aspects. Ultimately any individual presents varying applications of their identity depending on the social context they find themselves in. So for instance, my professional identity at work will present aspects that are different from the identity I present with my family at home, from the identity I present in a sporting club and so on. While there may be certain traits that constitute a core to your being, the responses you make within specific locations will be intimately connected to them. This in itself is nothing too startling (of course, most folks would realize that they are different people in different locations), but what is worth noting, and is central to postmodern views of identity, is that there is no *essential* you.

You are, by virtue of being in the world, constituted according to the contexts you find yourself in. You are made sense of in terms of how you correspond to the physical, emotional, spiritual, psychological and social mediations your 'location' prescribes. Your identity then, is connected to this being-in-the-world and can be read against the dynamics and constraints of those locations you find yourself within.

This immediately poses a significant conundrum: if identity is indeed formed and read against the contexts individuals find themselves in, does this ultimately mean that individuals have limited, if any, ability to influence their contexts and affirm their 'will to power'? Of course they do. We know in the real world that individuals exert their will, or *agency*, quite regularly and to varying degrees of success, dependant on who they are and where they are located. How you come to be who you are is the product of a negotiation between will and context; between what you want and the limitations your locatedness prescribes.

My experience, my approach to the world, my epistemology, is ultimately formed and framed by the context of living in the society I do, with all the social and underpinning interpretive responses I have to this context derived out of how my world view has been formed in this location. Alternatively, if I had grown up and lived in central Africa as a woman, or as a wealthy land-owner in the South of France, my response to the world would be different, and would reflect the nature of this context. But within this I still have the ability to exert my agency, to chart my own life course. This is the interplay of 'structure' and 'agency' that Anthony Giddens talks about. An interplay that operates as a negotiation between the structural conditions of existence you find yourself in and the desires you have to express a certain identity.

Now to return to questions of the iPod in this era of multiple identities. The iPod is one of those markers in our social contexts that contributes to our structural conditions of our world. It is a marker of the logic of our age and as such defines us immediately by the act of wearing and owning an iPod, suggesting attributes of affluence, coolness, tech savvyness, student-ness and much more depending on the situations in which it is worn. It defines us more collectively by suggesting things about the way we deal with enter-

tainment and information flows. It also defines us through the interactions we have through it. In short, the iPod is an intermediary in
our experiences.

Pedagogies of the iPod

I'm suggesting here that discourses of identity are built from the
consumption of products like the iPod and their associated language games. It is from these identities that framed visions and
responses to the world are formed. As such, the connection we
have to icons like the iPod and the imagery of the world they present fulfill a pedagogical role. We learn collectively who we are
from objects like the iPod.

As much as the iPod *represents* what youthful, tech-savvyness
is, it also *defines* it. iPod-transmitted ideas of networked youthfulness present themes and imagery that permeate the actual situations it draws its logic from, to the point that its imagery transcends
the image alone—the simulacra—to also inform the operation of
those real locations it mirrors and supposedly "represents." The
imagery of the iPod, and all it suggests about its location in the networked now, become hallmarks for a reconstructed social landscape that configures the iPod and its owner-user's identity within
its binds.

A colleague (Jon Austin, author of Chapter 9 in this volume) and
I recently took part in a discussion with a group of students, during which it emerged that the iPod was, far more than other types
of MP3 player, bound up with suggestions of style, social status,
and other similar semiotics. There was desirability attached to the
iPod specifically that intending owners wanted to connect with.
The iPod indeed carries its own discourse and it is one that seemingly conveys much to us publicly, particularly when the identity of
its owner-user is in question. My colleague and I noted that
responses to the questions we asked of the iPod drew heavily on
the appeal it had as a 'youth item' (several had received their iPod
as a gift from family members who had understood the street cred
such a gift would generate). Again, it is a simulacrum of youth, but
more so, one that has been learnt by us, and subsequently understood and applied to reinforce this same youth experience.

While we might worry about the dominance the iPod holds in
determining contemporary definitions of style and youth, the iPod
also has some important positive and empowering identity-prompts.

Just as it is used as a source for what counts as youthful hip-ness, formal applications of the iPod, most notably the use of the iPod as a learning tool by universities, suggest equally important things about our current social context. It isn't the first time an icon of popular culture has entered a formal learning environment, but what this shows is the iPod's ability to transcend pop appeal alone to become something *important.* A veritable shift in the market to include legitimate activities of youth (like formal study) is now available in conjunction with those traditionally and archetypally less desirable past-times of youth (like listening to the music that drives their parents mad). Youth is again in question, with this addition to the iPod's arsenal of functionality now including a formal, institutionalized appropriation of the youth experience.

Youth and the Image

A paradox of teenage individuality and mass consumerism is generated by the iPod. The advertised and mass-produced identity of the iPodder has been carefully crafted by Apple using themes of individuality and difference. Various identifiers give us clues to who the iPodder is, but it is the overarching category of youthfulness as an expression of hip "now-ness" that stands as the key identifier of what the iPodder *is* and what the iPod is about.

Youthfulness is more than a simple age demarcation in this imagery, and suggests something more akin to a disposition towards consumerism and digital technologies. The actions of youthfulness (outside the very act of purchasing an iPod) are demarcated by movement, youthful trends and a general vibrancy in these ads. The iPod is young and hip, and that's about all we seem to see in the imagery. A discourse of identity is developed, out of which entire personalities, lifestyles and approaches to the world are mediated. This applies as much to those who don't own an iPod as it does for those who do—it draws both that which is presented and that against which it is defined into the equation.

Think again about what the silhouette ads suggest to you. It doesn't matter so much whether we agree with the semiotic specifics (that is, whether the silhouette of the baseball-cap-wearing iPodder is a homie gangsta or pro basketball player) than it does that they actually depict *something* to you. You have 'read' and themed these images with a particular set of identity characteristics. Attach to that process the desire that advertising by its nature is constructed to create, and you have an excellent mechanism for generating a vision of identity that we crave and see reflected in the product advertised.

But I don't want to suggest that the iPod and these mechanisms of postmodern consumerism and identity have a demonic hold over us, as if we have no alternative but to play out our identities as consumers of the digital now. Far from it. Michel DeCerteau's influential book, *The Practice of Everyday Life*, helps make my point clear:

> . . . the analysis of the images broadcast by television . . . and the time spent watching television . . . should be complemented by a study of what the cultural consumer 'makes' or 'does' during this time and with these images. The same goes for the use of urban space, the products purchased in the supermarket, the stories and legends distributed by the newspapers and so on. (University of California Press, 1998, p. 484)

While the images which form our world are founded within very specific racialised, classed, gendered, and aged perspectives, we do not necessarily become brainwashed into thinking as the images prescribe. We do have agency available to us and can in fact resist the imagery of advertising by switching off, not buying, or actively refusing it. Better yet, we can *re-appropriate* it. As Certeau notes, we can look beyond the message of the images and take note of what individuals do with them.

In the light of this agency we have, we can start to approach more basic questions, such as why we lust after the images that function much like Platonic shadows in the caves of our desire. Why are we content to operate on the level of the simulacra and take our cultural cues from things that aren't actual? It may be that these images present the *Zeitgeist*—the logic of our age—through which we think and exercise our agency. As such, the iPod presents a suggestion of 'youthness' as a category of human social organisation. *"These are young people, and this is what young people do"* is what is subtextually suggested here, with the underlying questions being how we as society determine, contain and present our identities. Identity in this imagery is about being switched on, networked, tech-savvy and digitally cool.

These are images that make sense to us, because we see young people similarly presented this way in other images from popular culture. From this iPod-specific visioning of youth is added the iPod-specific discourse of youthness which connects directly to larger narratives of youth elsewhere in our post-modern, late capitalist, and globalized world. Together, these icon-specific narratives tell us something significant about how we consider each other and the categories of identity we each fit into. The iPod doesn't just entertain and teach us; it tells us who we are.

11

You Are Your iPod!

DELIA DUMITRICA

Ever wondered what the person next to you is listening to on their iPod mobile digital device? Ever tried to guess what type of person hides behind the earphones? I have.

Every time I take the bus, every time I go to the gym, every time I'm walking on the street. Even in class, when the guy sitting in the very back slips his earphones into his ears, believing I don't see him. What is it that we are listening to and what does it say about who we are? How do we create ourselves through our iPods?

The French writer Michel Foucault has something interesting to teach us about this. Trained as a philosopher, Foucault was mostly concerned with how thought changes throughout history, an activity he labeled as both philosophy and history. However, as he himself has emphasized, this activity was placed under the bigger aim of understanding "how the subject constitutes itself in an active fashion, through practices of the self."[1] It is from this perspective that Foucault's work may make us look in wonder at our cool, little gadgets, the iPods, and ask the unimaginable: What do you have to say about who I am? How do I make myself through you and how do you make me in return?

"I Lost My 80G Black iPod and I Feel So Empty!"

So, we've started talking with our iPods. What could they have to say?

---

[1] "The Ethics of the Concern of the Self as a Practice of Freedom," in *The Essential Foucault Reader* (New York: The New Press, 1984), p. 34.

Consider this woman, complaining in one of the over five hundred Facebook groups on iPods: "I lost my 80G black iPod and I feel so empty!"[2] What was the iPod to her so that its loss provoked such a feeling? Maybe the emptiness comes from the silence: one cannot hear the sound vibrating in the ears anymore. Or maybe it comes from the sadness of being separated from a part of you. But just how are we to think about our iPods as parts of ourselves?

Departing from the question of 'what' is identity, Foucault proposed we switch to asking "how an individual acts upon himself"[3] and "how do we come to think of ourselves the way we do?" This is an important shift, because it moves us from thinking about identity as something inside people, already formed and patiently waiting to be discovered, to thinking about identity as something that is always in the making. In fact, as Foucault himself put it, the how-question—how do we construct our own selves?—introduces suspicion that the concept of self even refers to an existing reality.[4]

"Identity" is a muddy concept. In everyday life, we take it to refer to who we are—some stable core of values, beliefs, ideas, feelings, experiences that make us. Yet we also change: we are different today than we were ten or even five years ago. Take me for instance: I confess to being a big Michael Jackson fan in my teen years. But check my iPod now, and you won't find a single Michael Jackson song on my playlists. I still like his music, but I've moved on to, well, whatever Top 40 gives me. I'm no longer idolizing Michael Jackson or any other singer for that matter—no more posters in my room, that's for sure. But I am still the same person.

As we know from experience, who we are also depends on the context and the other people there with us. I've quickly learned not to express my teenage crush on Michael Jackson around, say, death metal fans. At least, not if I want to avoid a conflict! And my grandma was definitely not the right audience for elaborating on the many details of Michael Jackson's look, moves, and life. As we grow up, we quickly learn when to show which side of our selves. Yet, in most cases, this doesn't mean we are distinct selves inhabiting the same person. Foucault makes us think about identity as

---

[2] Like this one, many of the other section headings in this chapter are taken directly from these discussions on Facebook.

[3] "Technologies of Self," in *Technologies of the Self: A Seminar with Michel Foucault* (Amherst: University of Massachusetts Press, 1982/1988).

[4] "The Subject and Power" in *The Essential Foucault Reader*.

both something that we create and as something that society forces us into:

> . . . if I am now interested in how the subject constitutes itself in an active fashion through practices of the self, these practices are nevertheless not something invented by the individual himself. They are models that he finds in his culture and are proposed, suggested, imposed upon him by his culture, his society, and his social group. ("The Ethics of the Concern of the Self," p. 34)

Take the woman who lost her iPod and now feels empty. We can easily imagine her accessorizing her iPod: a shiny skin, a colored case to match her mood that day, and a long list of songs she loved, carefully selected or randomly thrown together. She has constituted her self, in relation to her iPod, according to her own preferences. Maybe she even discovered new preferences, or she started building some precisely because she had the iPod.

Yet at the same time, however she constituted herself, her ideas about what it means to be 'cool' or to have an iPod, her music preferences, even her choice of colors for the iPod's skin—all of them are part of a wider context, where she finds herself at the intersection of the music industry, ideals of beauty, models of the successful teenager, and so on. Even more: the way in which she thinks about technology in relation to the self is partly inspired by the way in which our society has come to relate to technology.

Technologies of the Self

Foucault aptly called these processes through which we construct ourselves "technologies of the self." Technology, derived from the Greek *techné*, meaning art, skill, refers here to both material tools and ideas about the self which are predominant in a particular society:

> . . . technologies of the self . . . permit individuals to effect by their own means or with the help of others a certain number of operations on their own bodies and souls, thoughts, conduct, and way of being, so as to transform themselves in order to attain a certain state of happiness, purity, wisdom, perfection or immortality. ("Technologies of Self," p. 18)

When he says 'technology' Foucault means a bit more than just your iPod. The idea that the iPod is all about you; your choices and preferences; the presence of an iPod community out there, with its values and images of happiness and satisfaction—all of them are also part of these "technologies of the self." Although we might not pay much attention to them, they are influencing our way of being and our ideals.

Let's look closer at two of Foucault's examples of "technologies of the self." For the Ancient Greeks and Romans,[5] the idea of taking care of yourself was a main principle of social life. To take care of yourself meant to develop the art of living by constantly contemplating your way of living in relation to the principles of just and virtuous behavior and action. It meant being mindful of diet, of exercise, of thoughts and desires, and so on. The care of the self was a way of thinking and a personal goal that any respectable male member of the community would set for himself. It was also the basis for being a political member of the society, because only those men who were exercising this activity were able to reach an understanding of political justice: "the effort of the soul to know itself is the principle on which just political action can be founded" ("Technologies of Self," p. 25).

If the purpose of the technologies of the self in antiquity were to enable individuals to lead an exemplary life deserving respect, the purpose of these technologies in early Christianity changes. The Christian focuses on the self in order to purify it and ensure it achieves the promised immortality. The Christian views the self as constantly corrupted by sin. Thus the self has to be given up, by confessing its deepest secrets and perpetually monitoring its desires and feelings, which are always suspect. The main method through which the self purifies itself is confession. By following the rules of behavior described by the Christian doctrine, the individual makes the self better: "It is a sacrifice of the self, of the subject's own will. This is the new technology of the self" (p. 45).

Different understandings of the self characterize these two periods. One is based on better knowing yourself, while the other is based on giving up who you are, because the self is corrupted by sin. The question that Foucault raises is, what type of self are we dealing with today? What understanding of the self motivates our practices and forms our ideas of what it means to be an individual

---

[5] Foucault discusses Plato's *Alcibiades*, but also mentions Xenophon, Epicurus, Stoics, Pythagoreans, Plutarch, Seneca, and Marcus Aurelius.

who makes her own choices? And in this highly technological society of ours, how do the gadgets of our everyday life relate to us, to who we are?

"I Love My Lime Green iPod Nano!"

Lime green? Well, it's all about choices when it comes to the iPod: your choice of accessories, your choice of colors, your choice of content. The identity constructed by the iPod is a customizable and mobile one. It's constructed through our preferences. Our iPods are the material technologies enabling us to self-customize ourselves. So how does this happen?

For Foucault, material technologies have an important function in the creation of identities. His analysis focused on writing in two historical periods, antiquity and early Christianity, but his insights can be easily applied to interrogating the role of iPods in our modern conception of self.

Writing did the same thing in both periods: it recorded the self, it provided a material inscription of who you are, which could then be read and used to reflect upon the self. If you keep a diary, you'll know what I'm talking about. Flip back the pages, and you see yourself in a different light. Promises to be kept, lessons to be learned, questions to be answered—the diary is a material reminder of them.

Yet the diary doesn't tell you how to evaluate them: should you try to seek more in-depth knowledge of yourself? Should you rejoice in your inner thoughts, even the awkward and embarrassing ones? Or should you incriminate them, renounce them and free yourself of them? This is precisely where we find the difference between the two periods that Foucault tells us about. The particular purpose of writing in relation to identity differs with the way in which identity is understood in an age: in antiquity, people were writing the things that were said, the things that impressed them, or the events that took place. The self was formed by re-reading those collections and meditating on them. In early Christianity however, the purpose of writing the self changes: it's about confessing your deepest desires and thoughts, it's about a constant interrogation of your soul. The goal here is to purify yourself: "this new Christian self had to be constantly examined because in this self were lodged concupiscence and desires of the flesh. From that moment on, the self was no longer something to be made, but something to be renounced and decipher."[6]

What about the modern self? Foucault's own work on this subject is spread across various works, including books such as *Discipline and Punish* and *The History of Sexuality*. With modernity, a new form of political power—the state—was on the rise. The state is based on individuals, from whom the state derives its strength. As such, individuals become the central resource of the state: a state needs strong individuals, able to work and thus generate wealth. The state thus attempts to shape individuals; this is achieved by expanding government to all spheres of the individual's life and prescribing their 'right way'.

> This form of power that applies itself to immediate everyday life categorizes the individual, marks him by his own individuality, attaches him to his own identity, imposes a law of truth on him that he must recognize and others have to recognize in him. ("The Subject and Power," p. 130)

From how the family members should behave with each other, to what it means to be healthy; from the police patrolling on your block, to the schools you went to: the state intervenes in all spheres of our everyday life and provides rules according to which these spheres should work. This doesn't mean the state controls each and every aspect of our life, but rather that it creates and controls the general framework of the society in which we live. Yes, the state doesn't regulate your choice of songs in your iPod playlist, but it does create a framework for defining 'appropriate' music. Think of the case of rap music, where lyrics have been widely debated in terms of their effect on young people. Or think of the different roles that music is given by the state: in democratic societies, it's mostly about entertainment, but in a totalitarian state, music is tightly controlled by the state and serves propagandistic purposes (Nazi Germany easily comes to mind).

The peculiarity of modern identity is precisely the conflict between internalizing these rules and rejecting them. I am pretty sure that many people living in totalitarian states are finding ways of listening to Top 40 instead of the patriotic music aired on local

---

[6] "On the Genealogy of Ethics: An Overview of Work in Progress," in *The Foucault Reader* (New York: Pantheon, 1983/1984), p. 366.

radios stations. Yet, at times, an occasional propagandistic song may similarly captivate them. The most interesting iPod playlists I've seen are the ones of people who have been living and traveling around the world: they mix together folk music from their previous home-lands with the hit-of-the-day from their current homeplaces.

Such playlists are all about the individual and her life experi-ence. The modern individual, argues Foucault, is obsessed with her own identity. She constantly surveys and alters herself in relation to the social rules and legal frameworks. It's because of this process that Foucault calls our modern society a 'disciplinary' society, in which surveillance and punishment are constantly being employed. We care about what our friends will think of our new iPod skin or of our clothes. We want to be trendy and liked by some particular groups. And we try to follow those models and rules which we think will help us achieve that. But, as Foucault would say, this is precisely the way in which we comply with society and its rules. We model and survey our identity in relation to these perceived rules and models, and we are punished by the group with exclu-sion or mockery if we fail.

Can we look at our iPods as technologies enabling this "model self"? As technologies through which we buy into the social expec-tations of our times, but at the same time intervene, and alter them to our own preferences?

"Which iPod Are You?"

Which iPod are you? Maybe you've got thousands of songs in your music library. Maybe you have just a few. Maybe you like watching video on the go. Maybe you just wanna grab some tunes and run. No matter where or what you want to play, there's an iPod made for you.[7]

We may think of our iPods as state-of-the-art material devices ful-filling a simple function in our lives: that of allowing us to listen to music or watch a video wherever we are, whenever we want. But we may also start from noticing precisely the flexibility of this device that the Apple iPod website boasts: one device which can be molded on every personality. Is the iPod just a receptacle of our many iden-tities? What understanding of identity are we talking about here?

---

[7] "Which iPod Are You?" Apple.com, http://www.apple.com/ipod/whichipod/ (accessed January 12th, 2008).

For Foucault, material devices are precisely the site where we can study the relation to ourselves.[8] These devices talk about what we deem as important and in what contexts, about how we view identity and its expressions. Take iPods: their context is that of entertainment, which has become so central to our everyday lives. The iPod fits nicely within this environment of entertainment. But at the same time, the iPod is also different from, let's say, your laptop—just how many girls have you seen working out on the treadmill with a laptop in front of them? iPods allow us to make entertainment mobile; and more, they allow us to transform waiting or travel times, which for some were previously boring and empty, into something more interesting. With this also came disconnection from the people with whom you are squeezed in the bus, as well as the deafness and blindness to the sounds and sights of life around us.

Foucault argues that to examine technologies of the self, we need to look at three areas: What aspects of our behavior are to be evaluated morally? What rules do we use to evaluate our behavior? And what goals do we pursue when we behave morally?

What Aspects of our Behavior Are to Be Evaluated Morally?

For instance, we tend to believe (along with Kant) that the goodness or badness of our intentions needs to be evaluated in order to judge an action to be moral or immoral. In our modern societies, feelings are central to our evaluation of human action: to be 'true to ourselves', we are encouraged to explore what we *feel* and act upon these feelings ("Genealogy of Ethics," p. 351). iPods emphasize personal choice: listening to or watching something are individual options to be evaluated only in relation to the individual's preferences. The self is seen as a collection of likes and dislikes which we need to pursue or avoid, if we are to be true to ourselves. Because it is a collection, these preferences can change without causing any major disruptions to who we are.

What Rules Do We Use to Evaluate Our Behavior?

Western societies no longer derive their rules from divine law or scripture. Instead, we rely on a mixture of scientific and legal prin-

---

[8] Paul Rabinow and Nicholas Rose, "Introduction," in *The Essential Foucault Reader*, p. xxi.

ciples such as human rights to evaluate behavior. When it comes to the iPods, the major rules we employ to guide our behavior have to do with the ability of coming to know what you like and dislike from an array of options provided by various industries. Yet, these options are always connected to particular lifestyles. Think of heavy metal—it is not simply a style of music, it is a life-style! It is as much about how you present your body as about your thoughts and states of mind.

What Goals Do We Pursue when We Behave Morally?

In Christianity, moral action is necessary if we ultimately want to be redeemed from sins which constantly erupt into the self. Redemption is the goal to which we should aspire and which can be achieved only by behaving according to a Christian morality. But in our contemporary Western societies, what's good or bad is defined by law and not by religion. Morality is no longer 'given' by God, but decided by law. What goals are we aspiring towards? In the case of our iPods, being true to ourselves through an awareness of our own preferences contains the promise of happiness. Carrying with you your entire collection of songs, photos, and videos is almost like having an external memory of who you are, which you can access at any time, depending on your mood.

The individualization embodied by the iPod is part of the understanding of the self which we share today. The iPod is about me, about my experience, my time management, my preferences. It separates me from the social world in which my body is present. It signifies a state of being to this world: *I am present, but I am with myself. No intrusions, please!* It also represents an obsession with doing something: time is no longer wasted, but it becomes used for a purpose. As we become lists of preferences, filling in all our time, we should also ask, where do these preferences come from, and what do they signify in our society? What cultural models do the iPods connect us to, and what type of power they subject us to?

"I Can't Imagine Life Without My iPod"

With your iPod, who you are seems to have become who you choose to be. But the choices in question are, in this case, linked to an entertainment industry, selling lifestyles more than anything else. Implied in these lifestyles are ideas about what we should aspire to, and what parts of our behavior are morally relevant. These ideas legitimize particular forms of power relations in society, meaning particular types of relations through which people influence the actions of other people. Take your own iPod: you do not build it, you have little ideas about what goes on inside the little box, but you want what it has to offer. To get it, you have to buy it. To buy it, you have to have the money for it. The act of owning your iPod places you within a network of economic power relations. From your point of view, you indulge yourself in your own preferences. Yet from the industry's point of view, you consume: you consume technology, you consume accessories, you consume music, you consume ideas and values, and the list can go on.

Granted, this consumption is not passive. And, as in the case of illegal downloading, there is also resistance to this pay-to-own model. In charge of your own identity, through your iPod, you may well be reproducing Foucault's now famous vision of what 'power' is: you accept the social models, while at the same time transforming them, making them your own. Foucault claimed that "there are no relations of power without resistance."[9] But what exactly did he mean by that?

Modern identity is not built within an empty space: while it is true that we construct ourselves, it is equally true that this construction is influenced in many ways by the models around us. Parents, teachers, favorite singers, and movie stars all represent and speak for models of identity which we embrace fully or partly. Beyond those individuals central to you, and which you can name, lie more complex models, ideas and values. For Foucault, there are three main processes through which modern societies operate on our identity ("The Subject and Power," p. 126): dividing us from others, classifying people according to scientific principles, and each of us forming our own selves.

Dividing Us from Others

Foucault calls this process 'dividing practices'. Think of how the sick are isolated, or the criminal confined: the material boundaries of the hospital or the prison separate us from those whom society

---

[9] "Power and Strategies" in *Power/Knowledge* (New York: Pantheon, 1977/1980), p. 142.

deems unfit, for one reason or another. The unfit are removed from society, isolated until cured. In this way, divisions between good and bad are being created.

When it comes to iPods, identity, and lifestyles, these lines of division are less drastic. We are not put in prison for our choices. But we are judged on the basis of the lifestyle to which we adhere. The mere act of owning an iPod is taken as a means of dividing 'us,' the owners who are in control of our own identities, from 'them,' the others, those who—in the words of a Facebook iPod fan—use Apple earphones but hide in their pockets "lame MP3 or CD-players." "They make me so angry," complains the fan—echoing long-standing tendencies in our society to judge others according to their material possessions.

Yet it's not only the iPod fans judging. The reverse of the coin is that, whether a fan or not, sometimes the mere fact of owning an iPod may be sufficient cause for some to dislike you—or at least get annoyed with it. "What's an iPod? Sounds pretty gay to me!" protests a Facebook user, member of the "iPod Sucks!" group. Rejecting the hype around the iPod, contesting its aesthetics, or simply disliking the rather pricey cost, those who define themselves in opposition to the market dominance of the iPod are equally building and reinforcing the division line. And whether you like it or not, outside the group of those enamored by the iPod, your little identity gadget is no longer a symbol of your choices and self-construction, but rather the proof of your enslavement to the market and of your utter ignorance in technical matters. Things don't look that bright from the other side of the barricade!

Classifying People According to Scientific Principles

The role of science—both natural science and the social sciences—is central in our society. Science informs government. Science informs our understanding of our bodies. Science compartmentalizes every aspect of our lives into a field of study, and promises to return a universal recipe for it.

For Foucault, this is an aspect of modern power, the state, as mentioned above, and its attention to the individual. Since all aspects of the individual's life are important to the state, and therefore need to be monitored, particular social science disciplines emerge. Psychology, hygiene, statistics, criminology, and others emerged in relation to the social problems raised by the state. Each of them classify individuals according to particular features: for example, psychology sees us in terms of personality patterns; medicine sees us in terms of healthy bodies; and statistics transforms all of us into numbers—fifty percent of this kind, forty percent of the other.

The classifications which social sciences produce are hierarchical. Some personalities are better than others. Some features—like for instance body mass—make us more or less desirable or able to perform certain tasks. In our daily lives, we do not think of how these classifications relate to our own identity. We may take a slim body to be beautiful today, but that was not always the case (think for instance of Renoir's famous paintings). And this is certainly not the case in many African cultures. Our preferences and ideals are very much influenced by the classifications predominant in our societies. And we try to fit our identity into the categories of these classifications: we obsess with weight, we are addicted to new gadgets or we buy into particular lifestyles.

While we may opt in and out of lifestyles through the lists we make on our iPods, the classifications behind these lifestyles should be acknowledged. We opt for hip-hop and not heavy metal. We choose comedies over dramas. The context of these choices is also important: I might listen to a happy song when I am down, and I may avoid listening to love songs when I'm heartbroken. Our preferences are always connected to what society deems as acceptable or rebellious, positive or negative, good or bad.

Each of us Forming Our Own Selves

Also called 'subjectification', this process consists of an active involvement of the self in deciding who she is. We've talked about the various techniques through which people constructed their selves throughout history. Foucault's work on this was primarily focused on sexuality, starting from the question of how we come to see ourselves as sexual beings, and how we come to think of our own sexuality. With Freud and the emergence of psychoanalysis, sexuality becomes the locus of the true self: our self is unknown to us, but revealed through its sexual impulses, desires, and frustrations. It can be accessed through introspection and a modified form of confession—modified from the Christian one discussed above—the confession of the patient to the psychoanalyst.

These processes of self-formation are intrinsically connected to the wider social sphere which deems something as acceptable or good behavior. We come to understand ourselves as sexual beings in relation to the prevailing discourses about sex in society. In Christianity, sex is a sin, and therefore everything inside us connected to sex has to be renounced. In psychoanalysis, sex is the essence of identity, and therefore everything connected to it has to be scrutinized.

With our iPods, we form ourselves in terms of our preferences. It's an act we do for us, because we are concerned with being authentic, being true. But it's equally an act we do for others, for our peers, for our families, for the unknown people with whom we intersect in our daily lives. Our iPods have something to say to each of these groups: *I'm one of yours, I'm part of this group, I'm different from that one.* Through our iPods, we separate ourselves from society and rejoin the groups with which we identify. And the more we invest in our iPods, the more we ask ourselves, how could we have ever lived without them?

Become a Work of Art!

What knowledge of ourselves do we get through our iPods? And what do we lose? Amidst Facebook iPods fan groups, magazine articles, scholarly research and so on, what is it left to say about the role of these little gadgets in our lives?

> But a new pole has been constituted for the activity of philosophizing, and this pole is characterized by the question, the permanent and ever-changing question, 'What are we today?'[10]

The question of identity is central to our social lives: it is the source upon which we build social relations. Our iPods allow us to create ourselves not only in terms of sounds, but also visually and aesthetically. Wired through our white headphones, we make technology a part of our own bodies. But the ways in which we may do this remain open: some may listen to music, others may be reviewing the lectures for today's exam. Whether taking your family videos along in your travels or motivating yourself while doing your training, your iPod is there, bringing along a consumption-

---

[10] "The Political Technology of Individuals," in *Technologies of the Self*, p. 145.

based industry and an individualistic culture into your project of self-construction.

Maybe it's time to take the iPod on a different level and think about our own identity beyond these models. Foucault was keen on rejecting all pre-established identity models, because he found them too narrow. Instead, he wondered, couldn't we just regard our identities as works of art? To move outside the realm of the pre-established lifestyle that the iPod proposes, and to reclaim the iPod for something else, for something that does not freeze you into a stereotype, how about that?

I recently showed my iPod to my father, and he liked playing around with it. I showed him the pictures I uploaded from my last holiday. Insisted on showing him the calendar, so that he could finally see for himself how busy I am. And I felt happy, not by plugging the earphones and plunging into my own, self-enclosed world, but by sharing all those things with my dad. That's who I am, and this is my work of art: I like my iPod not because it's posh or sexy, but because I can transform it into moments of happiness just like this one.

COMMUNITY

12

Listening with the Other; Listening to the Other

DONALD L. TURNER

Look out! Whoa—unplug those white wires from your ears for a minute!

Okay. Sorry to yank you backwards so roughly; I didn't mean to scare you, but you were so absorbed by your iPod mobile digital device that you didn't see my wild gesticulations or hear me yelling your name, and you almost walked right in front of that bus. Now that I have your attention, I think you should slow down and consider the awesome and dangerous powers of that little machine, which is transforming the way you listen to music in both valuable and problematic ways.

It's not just the headphones that almost led to your injury. These have been dangerous since Walkman cassette players became popular, but the iPod age brings newer ethical challenges. The Walkman held a single album at a time, but the iPod holds thousands. Serving for storage as well as delivery, the iPod has not only replaced the Walkman I carried; it has also removed from my daily experience both massive elements of my previous music arrangement: the stacks of electronic components (receiver, cassette decks, CD player, turntable, and more) and the shelves full of albums, tapes, and CDs to play on them.

This means that iPods are often shared. Previously, my wife and I, who have some overlapping but largely different musical tastes, maintained separate CD collections in our living room, but now we share an iPod. For the first time in our household our collections are stored together on one unit, and while iTunes recognizes which content belongs to whom, our iPod doesn't. When I listen by genre to the hip-hop content, ninety-five percent of which is mine, I still periodically get samples of French rapper MC Solaar and British artist M.I.A. from my wife's small but international collection. And when she listens to the mostly G-rated bluegrass genre, which is almost entirely her domain, she is occasionally faced with rude cuts such as "Sharon Needles" from my Earl Lee Grace *Blackgrass* CD. When we listen together, the random play feature produces a mutually agreeable soundtrack that would have taken much more thought and effort before we switched to the iPod. Sometimes we're pleasantly surprised to enjoy one of the other's favorite songs, but even when I'm gnashing my teeth through a Bette Midler cut, I know there's something better on the way.

Ethically, this relationship requires numerous considerations. Caring for my wife, I must remain mindful of ways my collection might cause her harm: I must not demand more than my duly decided share of memory, I must be willing to cede space sometimes if she needs it, I must allow pre-emption of a Motörhead cut if she is in a vulnerable psychological state. Sharing an iPod forces numerous questions of musical justice, requiring new and different lines of negotiation involving allocating memory space, constituting joint playlists, determining what listening option (artist, genre, playlist, random) will best fit our different moods, the legitimacy of "veto power" when listening together, and other factors. The iPod necessitates these and other new considerations, complicating our shared musical life.

Why You Should Care about Ethics

Why, you may ask, longing to tarry in your iPod's hypnotic sonic embrace, are we obliged to think along these lines? Philosophy helps answer this question.

We might look as far back as Ancient Greece. Back around 360 B.C.E., Plato wrote a famous story about denizens of a cave, tied immobile to posts, able to recognize and esteem nothing but the play of shadows on one cave wall. Thus he depicts ignorance among people who lack philosophical insight into questions about values and virtuous living. In contrast with such a life, Plato's writings also portray the hero Socrates, who was executed by the state—a martyr to an ethical vision in which the pursuit of wisdom about virtue was paramount.

Socrates used to walk around Athens bothering people about fundamental moral questions about the meaning of justice, virtue, etc., and he characterized this activity as a service to God and state. In these encounters, Socrates often ironically purports to learn something from someone who supposes to have wisdom about such matters, but conversation with Socrates usually illuminates his interlocutor's ignorance or confusion. Eventually, Socrates's behavior angered enough influential people to earn him the death penalty.

Socrates believed that pursuing ethical questions was his divine calling. In his defense at trial, he famously insisted that "the unexamined life is not worth living" and, paraphrasing a less famous but equally important thesis, that one's virtue is more valuable than one's wealth or worldly power. (Socrates presents both of these ideas in Plato's *Apology*.) Plato and Socrates thought that we have a duty to think and that thinking about these kinds of ethical questions is crucial, and they were right. As Plato's student Aristotle described, the good life requires developing various forms of virtue. Too often we fail to adequately reflect on morally significant aspects of our lives, damaging our ability to promote important ethical values, and our iPod experience is no exception. Only by considering ethically significant aspects of iPod phenomena do we exit this particular cave.

If you find ancient writings off-putting, perhaps my favorite single source for inspiration on such matters, including those involving iPods, is twentieth-century French philosopher Emmanuel Levinas. Levinas was a phenomenologist. He saw philosophy's first task as patiently and faithfully describing our conscious phenomena—philosophy's job is to help us understand our experience. Key figures of the phenomenological movement have brought this orientation to questions on diverse topics, including mathematics, embodiment, death, and time. As part of this tradition, Levinas's individual mission is to describe the ethical encounter between a self and an Other, which he sees as supremely important and as crucial for understanding most other philosophical questions.

In this encounter—the "face to face" as Levinas calls it—a relatively secure self meets a suffering Other. The Other's suffering disturbs the self, provoking a corresponding pain of conscience in the self and inspiring in her empathy and desire to help. (Levinas's poetic descriptions are much better than this basic clinical account.) This drama is both the *primary* philosophical event, as Levinas believes that even self reflection begins with the realization that one is under another's gaze, and also the *most important* philosophical event, a claim he supports by fusing theology with ethics, casting "God" as an exclusively ethical concept and inspiring moral philosophy with airs of supremacy.

In Levinas's lofty discourse, I see the trace of God in the face of the Other, whenever the Other's worldly powerlessness wields ethical power and his suffering afflicts me, dominating my consciousness whether I like it or not, awakening me to my responsible status, inspiring me to action, and elevating me to a more noble state of being.

Back to the Family

I agree with much of what Levinas says, so I think we should begin by asking how the iPod impacts our relationships with other people. How do we hurt the Other with our iPod, and how do we help the Other? My iPod most immediately involves my relationships with my wife, so my own considerations begin there, but life changes and further considerations reveal additional obligations.

Once my son was born, thinking along Levinasian lines required attention to his welfare as well, as I am responsible to and for him as to no other Other. Previous portable devices like Walkmen were almost always tied to headphones and were rarely hooked up to speakers. Our iPod's docking station makes my whole musical collection available for my son's three year old ears, and I love this, because I think it's helped him develop a wide ranging appreciation for different musical styles. He's been a huge Wiggles fan and a huger Wheatus fan, and though I prefer the latter, I am fascinated by his developing tastes, and I like the way the iPod facilitates breadth and diversity of the family listening experience.

But this power is dangerous, too, and the iPod era requires heightened vigilance compared with previous arrangements. In pre-iPod days, pondering future children, I rested comfortably knowing that I would be intentionally selecting albums or CDs, so I could easily avoid anything inappropriate for younger ears. The iPod easily allows one to construct prescreened folders and playlists, but sometimes this feels limiting. Sometimes I want to be able to expose the boy to a random listening experience drawing on the whole collection, but this has required heightened vigilance. When he was a fragile infant who could be frightened by aggressive metal or industrial music, I had to take measures to constitute softer playlists and to quickly skip offending songs when they come up in random mixes.

As he nears his third birthday, with a growing tendency to remember and repeat lyrics that he likes and a sometimes uncanny knack for focusing on words we would rather he not adopt, this vigilance has spread to all genres. I love that I never know what song or artist he'll take a shine too next, but I have to be always mindful of ways anything from my collection could cause him harm, and I imagine this dynamic will involve more complex considerations as he matures and begins paying more attention to lyrical meanings.

Render unto Sony BMG that which Is Sony BMG's

The iPod's ethical impact also extends far beyond my immediate familial relations. Consider the Other as starving artist. The iPod is part of a system in which many people illegally obtain music without paying. Because it was created to store and provide access to the kind of small digital files that people download illegally and because it serves this purpose so well, iPod proliferation may indirectly promote some of this downloading.

Might there be ways to justify such behavior philosophically? According to utilitarian ethics, the best choice in any situation is whatever promotes the greatest happiness for the greatest number of everyone involved. An action is morally justified if the happiness it causes exceeds the pain it causes. Many people justify illegally downloading music this way, maintaining that the happiness of having free music exceeds the unhappiness caused by depriving a major record company or millionaire entertainer of a few dollars. Alternatively, contractualist ethicists argue that ethical relationships should be reciprocal, and illegal downloaders might claim that record companies don't meet their end of the bargain because they ask for unreasonable sums of money for small amounts of quality music. (This argument has lost force with the return of the "single," or individual song purchase—a phenomenon common in the days of vinyl, rare during the ascendancy of the CD, but returning in this iTunes age.)

Opposing such theories, Levinas references the seventeenth-century French philosopher Blaise Pascal in describing the beginning of immorality as the self's declaration of possession: "This is my place in the sun!" Thus begins unethical egoism and living at Others' expense. For Levinas, morality begins in hospitality, when I cede my place for the Other, "tearing away of the mouthful of bread" from my mouth "that tastes it in full enjoyment" and giving it to her.[1] Levinas undermines any utilitarian preference for one's own happiness at the Other's expense, even if such a preference is the most efficient way of providing the greatest happiness for the greatest number. A viewpoint where the Other's suffering counts for everything consecrates altruistic gifts, but it declares food taken from the mouths of Others, such as musicians, producers, and salesmen, to be *treif:* not kosher.

Eschewing contractualist ethics, Levinas insists that the ethical relationship is non-reciprocal. The initial moral responsibility is all mine; I may hope that another person might reciprocate or recognize my own suffering as a source of obligation, but such initiative is up to her. Fundamentally, ethics does not involve trading beneficence with the Other, doing good for her on condition that she does good for me. Such egoism may be a necessary part of our lives, but it does not exemplify fundamental moral behavior. The primary ethical encounter is not a "You scratch my back and I'll scratch yours" situation, but a one-way gesture of response to the Other's need. One must scrutinize one's own behavior without initially expecting or requiring reciprocation.

Can a fabulously wealthy artist or record company executive face me as an Other whose suffering commands my response? Certainly artists' psychological suffering has struck me this way, when I've learned of some artist's biographical tragedy, but here these people needed psychological, not economic support, and I do not feel morally required to give them money. Still, thinking along the rather demanding and uncompromising lines that Levinas describes, their suffering is certainly ethically relevant, and taking their property because I think they are greedy could not be ethically justified. Helpfully, there are alternatives to the choice between paying what one believes are exorbitant prices or going without music, and a Levinasian who wants to faithfully meet obligations to artists might seek more direct ways to pay musicians for recordings, such as supporting independent music, buying CDs at concerts directly from artists, or dealing with bands such as

---

[1] *Otherwise than Being, or Beyond Essence* (The Hague: Nijhoff, 1981), p. 74.

Radiohead, who recently—in a widely publicized and very Levinasian move—offered an album without making price demands, allowing procurers to pay as little or as much as they liked.

Owed to the Madding Crowd

Beyond those with music producers and purveyors, what do iPods communicate about other social relationships, and what are their implications for ethics here? Effective advertising campaigns show hip and exuberant dancing shadows of individuals so rapturously attuned to the spirit of music that connections to other people seem unnecessary. And when I'm rocking out with headphones on, I feel a bit this way, too. But other forms of cyborg life strike me with dread, such as the woman I saw whose hair *almost* managed to conceal her white earbuds one day during a philosophy class discussion, or the man I saw who wore a beeping cellular earpiece to an ostensibly silent meditation session.

(If you're in a public place, you'll probably not have to look far to find a "cyborg" or "cybernetic organism," defined as a "hybrid of organism and machine," distinguishable by iPod ear buds, vibrating pagers, and cell phone headgear. Take a look at Donna Haraway's "A Cyborg Manifesto," from which these quoted phrases come, for a classic philosophical discussion of these beings.[2]

iPod headphones can hinder ethics by isolating the listener in her private soundtrack, inhibiting attention to others and to the ethically significant realizations that might come from cultivating silence and mental calmness. To employ Levinasian metaphors, headphones sometimes communicate this: "Here I am, but I am deaf to your appeal." Large-scale headphoned solipsism is at least as old as the Walkman, and it continues with those iconic white ear buds. (Not that headphones are all bad; eliminating auditory distractions, they can sometimes intensify one's listening experiences and enhance artists' ability to communicate with the listener.)

Headphones are not necessary to the iPod experience, however, and iPods might promote more dialogue than they discourage. Here the differences between the iPod and the Walkman are more obvious, and Levinas's philosophy is helpful here, too. Acting ethically

---

[2] In *Simians, Cyborgs and Women: The Reinvention of Nature* (New York: Routledge, 1991), pp. 149–181.

requires listening to what the Other says about her existential situation, and the iPod serves extraordinarily well as a means for learning about the Other, speaking volumes more than previous portable music devices. Observing someone's Walkman or Discman, which carries one audio cassette or CD at a time, one can tell relatively little about the owner—for example, that he might enjoy a particular artist or genre. But hand me your iPod, and I can behold the entire contents of a vast collection, learning numerous nuances. The memory is fully occupied, so I deduce that music is a key interest for you. You have thirteen genres populated, so you have ranging tastes; four of these are rock-oriented, so you enjoy certain instruments and beats (drums/guitars/vocals, up-tempo). The various playlists you've created tell me about the kinds of moods you find yourself in. This depth of information about the Other that in the past required a lengthy conversation or long home visit one can now obtain by rapidly scanning the contents of a handheld unit—and this information could be very ethically significant. It might help me select a musical gift that the Other will love. Or I may see that she has six versions of one song, the lyrics of which might give tremendous insight into her biography, suffering, or values.[3]

Levinas's ideas about language also illuminate another aspect of the iPod experience: in addition to functioning as a bridge that brings people together, language *maintains separation* between speakers:

> Language precisely maintains the other . . . The relationship of language implies transcendence, radical separation, the strangeness of the interlocutors . . . Language is spoken where community between the terms of the relationship is wanting or is yet to be constituted. (*Totality and Infinity*, Nijhoff, 1969, p. 73)

In other words, ethically attuned language mediates the two-party relationship while maintaining the Other's "otherness" or, as Levinas's puts it, her *alterité*. This kind of discourse frees me from solipsistic self-involvement and, when it helps me recognize moral obligations to Others, makes me more human. Along these lines,

---

[3] Everything I've said about learning about the Other via the iPod also applies to the way the Other might learn about me: my iPod speaks truths about my life, my inspirations, and my values. But such considerations are ethically secondary in the ethical philosophy I'm describing, in which the Other is most important.

iPods create new types of communal experience and social discourse. There are now iPod-themed cafés where people share the contents of their iPods with each other, beyond the one-to-one encounter. Some cafés have their patrons connect their iPods to its PA system and take turns playing DJ for periods of time, creating a mix together. In others, listeners network their iPods and a DJ draws from different units to direct the communal listening experience. In these ways, patrons present themselves for the Other's hearing and open themselves to hearing the Other, but in a way that preserves their individual separation. This kind of communication not only brings people together—it also maintains distance, upholding the individuality and strangeness of participants to each other as they create their shared experience. We're all still strangers at the café, though we get glimpses and traces of one another's musical lives. Fostering such discourse, these institutions extend music as a communal activity beyond the traditional model of artist as purveyor and audience as recipient.

Other Others?

Extending our ethical focus, we might look for other Others, beyond the human realm. Might animals, or the earth itself, qualify as sources of significant ethical obligations? How would a Levinas-inspired iPod ethics consider these obligations?

How, with our iPods, do we hurt and help other beings, including non-human animals and natural bodies such as rivers and the atmosphere? The iPod's impact here is mostly positive. Though some users purchase tangible media and upload the content to their iPods (including not only the music but the associated cover artwork, and also, if one takes the trouble, the liner notes and other documentation), many iPod users make the computerized version their primary purchase, never obtaining any tangible object. This means less packaging, requiring fewer trees for boxes and inserts and fewer barrels of oil for plastic cases. Obtaining iPod content via the Internet means less transportation of music industry goods, reducing petroleum consumption and air pollution, which is good for the earth and all who inhabit it.

On the other hand, iPods do leave problematic environmental footprints. Planned obsolescence, by which computer hardware manufacturers ensure continued revenue inflow, means that outdated units will end up in landfills. Greenpeace claims that the iPod's batteries (which, unlike standard batteries that power most small electronic devices, are not easily accessible and removable for recycling) and headphone cables contain toxic, carcinogenic compounds.[4] Environmentally speaking, the iPod may be have a net positive effect, but it still presents problems that need to be addressed.

Putting the "I" Back in "iPod"

Levinas clearly dismisses ethical egoism, the idea that one's only or fundamental obligations are to oneself. But other philosophers have been readier to discuss one's duties to oneself, including some of the biggest names in moral philosophy, such as Aristotle, who described the moral life as the cultivation of personal excellence, embodied in effective manifestations of virtues such as courage and fortitude, and Kant, who insisted that one must respect the inherent dignity and value of one's own status as a rational agent. If Levinas is right that ethical relationships happen to me regardless of whether I want them to or not, then, after considering other possible candidates for ethical obligation, it seems reasonable to ask whether I might discover duties to myself. If so, then I am obliged to ask how the iPod helps or hinders fulfilling these duties.

Philosophy offers several ways to approach this. For example, utilitarian theory defines an action as morally good to the extent that it promotes overall happiness, including my own, and bad to the extent that it promotes unhappiness, including my own—and the iPod undoubtedly promotes my happiness by extending my mastery over my music. The iPod's small size and huge capacity let me carry thousands of instantly accessible songs in the palm of my hand, without requiring shelves of CDs or boxes of records. Its portability and battery power give me access to this vast miniaturized collection anywhere I go. Its cataloging and programming functions allow me to control my listening experience in previously difficult or impossible ways, such as listening to a random mix from a particular genre in my collection, drawing from hundreds of albums. This unprecedented control over my music col-

---

[4] Brad Cook, "Apple Gets Poor Marks, in Greenpeace Report," *Mac Observer*, http://www.macobserver.com/article/2006/08/25.12.shtml (accessed March 10th, 2008).

lection leads me to think the thoughts that Levinas places in the mouth of the egoistic self: "Everything is here, everything belongs to me, [and] everything is comprehended" (*Totality and Infinity*, pp. 37–38).

Or, when I want to relinquish the reins and *not* set any parameters at all, then I can employ the random feature. This single function alone makes the iPod revolutionary and extremely exciting. Before, most people were limited to a CD player that could randomly play cuts from a single disc, or, at best, a small number of discs loaded into the machine. My 60GB iPod will play me a random train of cuts from a collection fifteen thousand songs deep. It unearths cuts that, because I've hitherto been left to consciously select individual CDs, I haven't heard in ten years. This promotes what the German philosopher Martin Heidegger called "openness to mystery:" a valuable existential orientation that is less calculative or instrumentalist and more reflective and meditative. As I refrain from consciously engineering my experience by choosing the albums I'll hear, my iPod brings forth these long, long dormant voices, enhancing my experience as previous listening arrangements could not.

The iPod also detracts from my experience, and the very features of the iPod that promote my mastery, and thus my happiness, also involve limitations and drawbacks. Classic utilitarian theorist Jeremy Bentham, whose stuffed nineteenth-century body we can still view at University College, London, suggested quantifying happiness in terms of what he called "hedons," or "units of pleasure." While it provides a listening experience that makes me happier than I was before the iPod, the device arguably also reduces the amount of hedons I can accrue, thus countervailing morality. For example, many people claim that compressing a recording into a small digital format compromises the sound quality, producing a shallow and impoverished listening experience, leading some purists to reject the iPod in favor of analog vinyl records or the larger digital files such as those on standard industry CDs. Because I can hold thousands of albums in my iPod's memory, I've uncluttered my living space by storing my CD cases in boxes in the garage—with the drawback that I no longer enjoy the pleasures of holding the album's artwork in my hand or reading the accompanying literature and lyrics. My shopping experience is similarly impoverished, because now I often purchase intangible digital files from home via iTunes, staying out of record stores and eliminating discourse with other customers. Rarely do I spend an hour thumbing through obscure musty shingles in milk crates, discussing the merits of Badfinger or Black Oak Arkansas with an eccentric shop owner.

Gotta Serve Somebody, or You Owe Your Soul to Rock'n'Roll

What of other sources of ethical obligations? Do abstractions such as "art" or "being" have moral relevance? Heidegger thought so, and his writings illuminate numerous ethically significant aspects of iPod life. For example, in *Being and Time*, he writes:

> When curiosity has become free, it takes care not to see in order to understand what it sees . . . but only in order to see. It seeks novelty only to leap from it again to another novelty. The care of seeing is not concerned with comprehending and knowingly being in the truth, but with possibilities of abandoning itself to the world . . . Consequently, it also does not seek the leisure of reflective staying, but rather restlessness and excitement from continual novelty and changing encounter. In not-staying, curiosity makes sure of the constant possibility of distraction. (Harper and Row, 1962, pp. 37–38)

So, novelty and distraction foreclose certain revelations. Perhaps the iPod's random feature, vehicle of an "openness to mystery," might also function this way by rarely allowing me to settle for longer than a few minutes into any one mood. Before iPods, most people intentionally selected individual CDs to play, often all the way through. The allure of novelty and the ease of switching to or away from any track in one's collection lead listeners decreasingly to listen to entire albums, preventing the longer works from developing characters, themes, and plots. The Who's *Tommy* does not get two hours to unfold its ethical drama—it gets three minutes to hit me with the "Pinball Wizard" riff.

Beyond this, my iPodded mastery silences other musical voices, as an analogy with Kant might help me illustrate. Earlier philosophers had viewed understanding as the result of the human mind's properly adapting to experiential data. Kant instead showed how the data must conform to the ordering principles of my mind in order to be recognized, because sensual and cognitive capacities set limits on our possible experience. As Kant explains, time and space are not things that I perceive but conditions for experiencing whatever I experience, in that I could not perceive an object that exists outside of space and time. It could be that there are things that really exist, but do not take up space; but since all my experience is experience of things in space, if things like that *did* exist, how would I ever know?

In a similar way, because the iPod is the prime content deliverer in my living space, all my music must conform to certain conditions. Mainly, it must be digital. Today in my house, because of the difficulty of converting analog vinyl records and cassette tapes to digital formats, I never hear any music I only possess on such media. (Such conversion is possible, but it's a pain in the neck with the average consumer's current technological toolbox.) This silences many great works in my music collection, including classic but obscure LPs that never made it to CD, cassette recordings of spectacular Grateful Dead concerts obtained through complex trading networks, and numerous meticulously crafted "mix tapes" that encapsulate important biographical narratives and speak profound psychological truths. (Before the recent development of easy "ripping" and "burning" CDs, such mixes had to be compiled on cassette.) Even after the ascension of the CD, my old cumbersome stack of components was also hospitable to multiple other formats, and these media had a voice. My unobtrusive iPod demands conformity to the universal code of zeros and ones, and recordings that do not meet this basic condition do not even qualify as possible musical experiences for me.

Cataloging the Flux

The iPod's cataloging and classification functions also strike me as ambivalent. As I indicated above, the iPod allows me to assign each song a genre label, allowing me to listen to long, randomized strings of similarly-mooded songs, but this same capability also prevents certain song strings. If I listen by artist to Aesop Rock, I will not hear any of the many tracks he performs on other artists' albums. If I listen by genre to hip-hop/rap, I will not hear great cuts from the *Judgment Night* soundtrack, filed under metal, in which hip-hop artists pair up with metal bands. Levinas's phenomenology describes the individual's status as "refractory to every typology, to every genus, to every characterology, to every classification," and perhaps assigning a genre label to a piece of music in some way violates its singularity (*Totality and Infinity*, p. 73).

Recently deceased French philosopher Jacques Derrida helps illustrate what I mean here. Derrida repeatedly describes the way conceptual categories—especially binary opposites such as "human" and "animal" or "literature" and "philosophy"—obscure differences, and such generalizations conceal the fact that what we lump together under, say, the "animal" umbrella is actually a huge diversity of beings, from snails to dolphins, ants to elephants. Classifying an artist, album, or song as a member of some genus risks obscuring the uniqueness of the person or the piece.

Furthermore, certain individuals challenge the categorical schemes that marginalize them, and Derrida shows that when we employ binary oppositions we sometimes fail to recognize that each category contains traces of that which it purports to exclude— that each category is infected by traces of that against which it defines itself. Animal ethicists compare so called "marginal cases": the adult gorilla who possesses subjective richness normally located among humans and the brain damaged person whose phe- nomenological possibilities seem much closer to those that we call "animal." And as Nietzsche, Freud, and Darwin showed, our animal nature links us more closely with beasts than many prefer to admit.

Along musical lines, I have many songs, albums, and artists on my iPod that inhabit the margins of certain categories or embody characteristics of multiple categories. A complex song or artist that employs elements of multiple genres may not fit neatly into any of them. Do I file *Highway 61 Revisited* under folk or rock? Do I clas- sify my album of the San Francisco Symphony playing Metallica songs as classical or metal? What of Luther Wright and the Wrongs' bluegrass version of Pink Floyd's *The Wall*? Where the hell do I put Urban Dance Squad's *Mental Floss for the Globe*? These marginal artworks beautifully challenge my categorical conventions, but I must choose in these cases, and whichever choice I make, I pre- clude certain songs from being heard when I listen to a random mix from the other genre.

The Verdict

So before you cram those white plugs back into your cyborg ears, let's review. You use an iPod a lot, and this use is ethically significant for others, for yourself, and for the world of music.

You're obliged to think through all of this and do your best to live appropriately.

To the possible consternation of readers seeking closure, I will not conclude with a clean final answer to the question of the iPod's ethical value. Instead, I invoke a mysterious line that Heidegger lifts from the poet Friedrich Hölderlin:

> But where danger is, grows
> The saving power also.

Heidegger includes this citation in an essay about modern technology, which he sees as problematic because people under its sway see only the basest economic and crassly self serving values of things: the river is seen not as the subject for a painting or a poem but only as a machine for producing hydroelectric energy. In Heidegger's philosophy, this kind of calculative thinking stands opposed to more reticent and meditative ways thinking, including those involved in artistic revelation. Because both modes of thinking reflect the same fundamental human power to reveal and shape the world, Heidegger's essay on technology ends with the note of hope lifted from Hölderlin.

I would sound a similar optimistic note regarding the revolutionary and powerful iPod: a device by which we channel both technological mastery and artistic creation. An extremely powerful machine and a complex social phenomenon, the iPod serves both crass economics and aesthetic revelation, solipsism and community, egocentrism and responsibility, obfuscation of alterity and openness to mystery.

All of these potentials are real and powerful, and I hope that people will increasingly promote the trends I value in their iPod use.[5]

---

[5] Thanks to Dylan Wittkower, Ford Turrell, and Rachel Dresbeck, whose input and insight helped to strengthen this chapter.

13
Don't Talk to Me

JOSEPH C. PITT

The iPod mobile digital device is one of the pernicious developments of recent technological innovation. It, even more than electronic gaming, has fostered what seems to be the ideal environment for the social solipsist. Electronic gaming, once the scourge of mothers and fathers trying to communicate with their kids, has now evolved into a social phenomenon, where groups participate. But iPod owners revel in the splendid isolation provided by a hand-size player and a couple of earphones.

One of the more joyful sounds is that of people engaged in conversation. Talking to one another is the most exhilarating form of human activity. The lilts, the accents, the rhythms, the modulation of sound is more complex and more rewarding than even, for example, a Mahler symphony. The sound of the human voice is a joy and it brings joy. The iPod, however, has managed to do what even Big Brother could not: silence that voice. Worse, it has turned iPod users into antisocial beings, those who avoid human interaction. The spontaneity of the social has disappeared and the silence of the anthropoid now rules.

Lest you think I exaggerate, take a look around you. The subways are silent. In a recent issue of *Wired*, a reader wrote to ask if it was okay to tap another subway-rider on the shoulder whose iPod volume was turned up so high he (the iPodder) couldn't hear his cell phone ringing.[1] It used to be the case that the most vibrant

---

[1] Brendan I. Koerner, "Earth to Rocker: Reality Calling," in *Wired* (March 2008), p. 50.

place in our department was the end of the hall where the graduate student offices are. If you got bored with what you were doing and wanted to liven up a bit, you would wander down there and you could always find a good, loud, animated philosophical argument in progress. Today, there are few sounds down there, only drones sitting at their desks plugged in and staring vacantly. If you interrupt one of those reveries, you are met with surly stares and impatience.

Walking down the sidewalk on a college campus you used to hear students greeting one another, yelling to friends, arguing, making plans for the evening. Now: silence, walking slumped over, staring at the ground, plugged in. iPod users avoid eye-contact. They don't want to engage in conversation. They want to listen to their music. Their entire body language signals avoidance of human interaction.

Consider the following situation. We all love to go to the beach. There's something primordial about the pull of the ocean. Then there are the sounds of the waves, the birds, children laughing and parents yelling at them to be careful. But the beaches have been invaded by the brainsnatched; the iPodders. They walk the beach heads down, listening, not to the sounds around them, but to their music. Why go to the beach if you are going to avoid everything that's there? An early morning stroll amid the sounds of gulls and pelicans calling, with the waves lapping at your feet is one of the more relaxing things to do. What makes it relaxing are the sounds, the ambience of the waterfront, the feel of the sand between your toes. But can you have that experience when you're plugged in? I doubt if you even feel the sand.

So what's so wrong about all this? It might be argued that it is I who has missed the boat. What the iPod does, it will be argued, is provide people the opportunity to disengage from the roar of contemporary living, to collect their thoughts and even to meditate. There is, it is said, simply too much noise in the world today, and the iPod provides a means for limiting the impact of that noise on our fractured and stressed being. It helps create a haven wherever we are and for the most part in whatever we are doing. What is wrong with that?

Well, nothing, as such. That is, there is nothing *wrong* with it. The iPod itself is a piece of technology. As a piece of technology, it's neither right nor wrong, good nor bad. In another place, I argued that it is the use to which individual technologies are put that gives us the context in which to say a technology is good or bad.[2] Here, I would like to extend that somewhat and argue that it's not just the use to which a technology is put that allows us to make value judgments regarding it, but the consequences of its use as well. It's the consequences of using the iPod as an escape mechanism that are so bad.

In *Brave New World*, Aldous Huxley offered us *soma* to achieve the desired state of bliss and state control. Who would have thought that the contemporary version of an imagined science fiction drug would arrive in form of a music player? But it has. The iPod is our form of soma. And the reason it's so successful is that each one is individually programmed by its owner. We, or should I say, Apple, has found the way to achieve the perfect isolated state of bliss by having iPodders program their own version of musical heaven. No need to worry if this or that version will fit all. Furthermore, the iPod has overreached even Linus's blanket as the ultimate comfort giver. We now have iPod stations and special speakers so that when you unplug you can keep the music going. But what happens when two people who share an abode each have an iPod? Do they usually share the station, or does each have his or her own and do we then have iPod station wars? I doubt it, since the whole point of an iPod is to avoid the social and conflict is social—my guess is that in most households one or the other will simply plug back in and avoid conflict.

So now we have come to the set of iPod consequences that are most pernicious. As I just mentioned, the iPod is an antisocial tool. By that I mean that the consequences of using iPods to create your own haven, into which you can retreat and ignore the world around you, are dangerous. The ubiquitous use of the iPod may be one of the final nails in the coffin of social skills.

So what's the big deal, what's so important about social skills? Social skills are the means one has to interact with others in a productive fashion. The ability to interact with others in a productive fashion is the key to technological innovation and to a successful democratic government.

Technological innovation in our high-tech world is a product of lots of brainstorming, group projects, feedback loops and team

---

[2] *Thinking about Technology* (New York: Seven Bridges Press, 2000), and available at http://www.phil.vt.edu/HTML/people/pittjoseph.htm.

building. Even Steve Jobs had a co-inventor working with him. Technological innovation is not the product today of single individuals working alone in backrooms. It's the result of ideas being tossed around by people willing to try something new, something they may not have invented, and work with it and others to improve, modify, and convince others to build and market the gadget. Good ideas do not speak for themselves. They need advocates, and they need advocates at all levels of their development, from the first glimmer of a thought to the polished thing in front of you. The ability to articulate your ideas and to be an advocate for them also calls for different types of skills. Articulating your ideas requires that you have the ability to express clearly your thoughts using readily understood means such as clear language, obvious diagrams and useful metaphors.

Being an advocate for those ideas requires all of the above and more. The 'more' is the ability to successfully interact with others—to know how to read body language, the ability to present yourself as open and approachable. To develop those skills requires experience and lots of work. These skills will not come to you when are you slouched over a desk, lost in the world of your iPod.

What worries me about the lack of argument in the graduate student offices is that it is during those informal discussions that philosophy students develop their skills at argumentation—skills that require more than rigorous logic; skills that require command of rhetorical strategies and knowledge of how to make eye contact and good use of body language. These students may know the details of Kant's transcendental arguments, but if they can't defend their interpretation in person, on the hoof, then their futures as successful philosophers will be severely limited. Likewise their futures as teachers and, more importantly, as productive members of society at large.

Good teachers must be able to interact with their students in ways that draw students into the discussion and help them expand their own skills. You might object that to be a philosopher you don't have to be a teacher. Okay, then—except for the very rare individual like Martin Luther King or Ghandi, the real philosophers of the twentieth century—philosophers are professors. How are you as a professional philosopher with a Ph.D. going to make a living? There are no more patrons today.

Now, this argument does not apply only to philosophers. There are so few jobs available today that don't require social skills that anything that impedes their development ought to be carefully scrutinized.

Above, it was also claimed that social skills are necessary for one to be a productive *member* of society. I would like to take this one step further. Social skills are necessary for there to be a productive *society*. Today we are experiencing an America in which social skills apparently are not deemed important. How can it be that we tolerate the rantings of radio shock jocks and TV talk-shows in which interlocutors scream at each other and show no sign of courtesy and respect? A society in which intolerance for the differing views of others and a fundamental lack of respect for the other is considered entertainment is a society in which the value of social skills has been lost. The ability to interact with others in a respectful and productive fashion is essential for a democracy to function. If we no longer think democracy is a good thing, then why not scream at someone you disagree with instead of entering into a civil discussion? Why not stick your earplugs in and tune out the world when taking to people becomes such a burden? Why not tell everyone else "Don't talk to me, I'm listening to MY music!"?

14
Mobile Clubbing: iPod, Solitude, and Community

RUUD KAULINGFREKS and
SAMANTHA WARREN

The iPod mobile digital device has often been criticized because it engenders a new egoism—even autism—in public life. Visually, the wearing of earphones signals to others that social contact with this person is not possible; whilst plugged in to the iPod, so the argument goes, the user is simultaneously *un*plugged from society. In a society of widespread iPod use, then, we might expect community to be lost, along with any possible sense of 'being together'.

Following the contemporary French philosopher Jean-Luc Nancy, we claim that this 'lost' community never existed in the first place. The idea that in past eras people enjoyed a strong community is a romantic myth used to portray our *existing* society as something centered on an identity once held and now lost. However, as we'll explain in this chapter, the dynamic of society is, surprisingly enough, the *lack* of a central identity. In other words it's in plurality and in difference that our society evolves.

The iPod embodies a deep need in all of us—a couple of deep needs, actually. The desire to be alone, and yet be part of a group, is perhaps one of the most primeval human attributes and we find it fascinating that this tiny technological wonder is at one and the same time a way of shutting oneself off from the world (either in real or imagined solitude) and a way we can find ourselves in the company of like-minded others, sharing experiences as part of a community. When we use an iPod, we are brought into relation with other iPod users even if this relation is not made explicit and so the iPod *promotes* community.

Of course, the idea of one's own personal musical soundscape is not new. Since the Sony Walkman was introduced over twenty-five years ago, we have enjoyed the delights of losing ourselves to a favourite tune on say, a crowded train or during a long and boring hike home, and even before that, ghetto blasters were carried around on shoulders blaring out the soundtrack to its porter's life. Or, even before *that,* stereo headphones have been used since the middle of the last century, enabling a complete immersion in music without the sounds of daily life. So what makes the iPod different?

With the iPod, nothing is new and yet everything is new. It's an iconic site where high quality digital sound enabled by smarter file formats; high speed connectivity through the Internet; and personal, customisable music on-the-go converge, and so for us it is the perfect place to think about how and why people come together or remain alone. We're not suggesting that it is the iPod *alone* that conjures up these effects—the iPod is only a possibility because of the development of connective technologies, new file formats, storage capabilities and processing speeds—but we do suggest that the iPod, as an artifact, provides a vantage point from which we can think philosophically about community and solitude. Furthermore, the more general role of sound, music and silence in social life is an inextricable factor in how the iPod works as a technology of togetherness and aloneness. We will argue that the iPod enables togetherness in a very individual way.

All by Myself: Soundscapes and Solitude

The idea of a soundscape is not new—the ability to choose what one listens to and shut everything else out of aural reach—has a long history. Many fundamental elements of civilization are built on our capacity to hear and produce sounds.

Take work, for example. In the early European Middle Ages monks in the cloisters introduced clock bells to mark the beginning and ending of prayers. The silence of religious work was encapsulated in two acoustic signals marking the beginning and end of prayer. Later the clock was used to mark the beginning and ending of work for each of the crafts guilds, producing a cacophony of bell-ringing. Sound was the precondition for organizing, and organization and labor was something to be done between sound signals: bells and later sirens. By encapsulating work in between sound signals, organizations form their own sound identity or soundscape. And in between the *signal's* silence the sound of the work itself is produced and further distinguished from the daily sounds of the city. Of course, in the white-collar environment the opposite applies; work should be done in silence and as little noise from outside should be heard.[1]

Each soundscape marks out the boundaries of where one set of social relations begins and ends—in between sirens the machines produce their noise and work is done in a specific soundscape different from free time. *This* soundscape is organized and controlled, as opposed to the uncontrolled street noises, and it's this notion of control that we want to focus on here with regard to the iPod. The mere distinction between 'sound' and 'noise' is a sign of one's *own* soundscape—the pleasant, acoustic signals we want we call 'sound' and the unwanted or dysfunctional ones we call 'noise' and try to reduce or get rid of.

We're continually creating our own personal soundscapes. At home we create quiet 'cosy' sounds and keep loud machines away. The materials we use in our living rooms absorb sound and soften noise. We continually organize the sound in soundscapes of wanted or pleasurable sounds and discard the unwanted noise. Even our bodies seem to have good and bad or healthy and unhealthy sounds. Physicians literally listen to us in auscultations and can determine our wellbeing by the sound of it.

So we might say that when we put on our iPod, we enter a unique aural world, control our soundscape, and enter a kind of 'virtual reality' as an escape from (or change to) the activity or task we are performing. We are using the iPod to organize sound that marks out one form of existence from another. But is this so? In the end the iPod is not much different from reading a book or a newspaper, or watching a film in a darkened cinema—activities we do in the solitude of our own mind.

The idea of escaping reality can be seen as a reluctance to understand the new and in this sense we can compare the iPod to the reactions of laypeople after the introduction of books in Europe. It is said that people gathered around to see monks reading in silence! The novelty of watching people completely imbued in a world of their own, detached from the world around them was a spectacle in itself. So, perhaps the iPod is not an escape from reality and doesn't bring us into virtual reality in any sci-fi sort of

---

[1] See Martin Corbett, "Sound Organization: A Brief History of Psychosonic Management," in *Ephemera* 3:4 (2003), pp. 265–276, www.ephemeraweb.org.

way. It just provides the means to engage in our own reveries and mindful activity—like philosophical thinking, for example.

We could assert that the iPod transports us into a fantasy universe, but music has always done that, and art even more so. We get carried away by the performance of a play or in viewing a painting, we dream in the concert hall, the novel transports us into the magic world of words, and so on . . . and we love it to the extent that we actually search out these experiences. We consider a life without art—without the possibility of fantasy and dreams—an impoverished world, and are shocked when we hear of societies where art has no place. According to the German philosopher Friedrich Nietzsche (in *The Gay Science*), art affords us disconnection from the concrete materiality of our present surroundings, which we *need* in order to understand the world. He reminds us that art gives us the necessary distance to comprehend the world we are otherwise imbued in.

As a result of this 'retreat into art', the iPod closes our senses in an inward world of contemplative sound, but it also forms a visual barrier to social engagement. When we see a person's white earplugs we know that she is not available. But should she be? At this moment, we are writing this and we are not available for our colleagues or friends. If one of our children demands our attention we make it very clear that he should wait till we finish work. In the same way, iPod shuts the social world out and gives the signal that we do not want social contact—but this sounds harsher than it really is.

Download and Shuffle: Between the Individual and the Social

The iPod and its associated technologies also allow a new and different kind of individuation. As well as playing our favourite music, audio books, radio programmes and so on, it allows us to customise its content in ways unheard of in the past.

Instead of passively accepting the decisions of the record label to include certain music tracks in a particular order, we can choose to download and store just the tracks that we actually want from a collection. Then we can store them in a genre-classified group if we so choose, mix them up using the shuffle feature for variety, or carefully order them in a set sequence (playlist) that fits the building momentum of a workout, for example. But to what extent do these activities *really* represent acts of personal, solitary choice? Are we truly able to shape these technologies in ways that mark us out as individuals? The very fact that everyone is doing it means that perhaps the act of owning and using an iPod is enough to connect us in some way to others who we know like doing the same things.

The iPod is meant for personal use—to individually listen to its content and shut off the signals from our surroundings, or at least the acoustic signals. But this doesn't *necessarily* mean solitude. It enables a retraction from the world into a kind of concentration that still is highly sociable, since we are listening to music others also listen to, and even playlists are published on the Internet for others to share. So how individual is personal? The iPod makes a strong personalisation possible and in this sense *is* a kind of individualisation gadget. But it's still an individualisation of arranging existing components. The content is publicly available and, as we have already asked, are we really doing something very individualistic and solitary by listening to it?

And then there's the sheer choice of material that we can listen to on our iPods. Music is a small part of the iTunes website, for example, with podcasts making up a significant feature of iPod culture. Although you don't need an iPod to listen to a podcast, the two are often thought of synonymously and represent another way that customisable iPod content can be downloaded. Podcast programs can be subscribed to, or single episodes downloaded relating to a huge range of interests, on subjects as diverse as gardening tips, 'bedroom DJ' dance mixes, higher level chemistry courses, or spoken novels, for instance.

This leads us to the point where we move away from listening, and nearer to *producing* music and sound and so to acts that are more social than solitary. In order to make music, or produce a podcast program, we need a listener in mind—someone who will incorporate it into their own personal library and use it to shut themselves off from the world in the ways we have outlined above. So we cannot say that the iPod is truly a solitary technology. But what does it mean to be part of the iPod-enabled community, or indeed, iPod culture more broadly?

All Together Now: iPod and Community

So far, we've considered the isolating and individuating characteristics of the iPod, looking at the disconnectedness of personal soundscapes and the customization of content as routes to a separation of the listener from the social. Ironically, this customization and decentralised production capability led us to return to the idea that the iPod might be more social than it first appears. Staying with the idea of podcasts and i-mixes that sowed this seed, we can easily see that a community of listeners can assemble around a particular program, episode, or mix. When we download our episode or buy our tracks, we can see how many others are doing the same—are we alone in our choice, or do we join a larger group of seemingly like-minded people? How does knowing we are making similar choices to others out there in cyberspace make us feel?

Here we begin to see how even in the most decentralised and disconnected milieu of the Internet and digital sound human beings have found a way to share and to build community. Why? Because art always creates community. The iPod is a device related to art. It plays music—popular or classical. It enables audio theater plays and literature, some can play movies, and of course the thing itself has won many design prizes.

According to the German philosopher Hans-Georg Gadamer, art creates its own community in the sense that art invites us to participate. Because a work of art is something outside the functional world and because we can't *do* anything with a work of art besides appreciate or dislike it, we're forced to engage with it. Since we can't integrate it into our daily activities, the work of art invites us into its own realm. Marcel Duchamp's idea to use the *Mona Lisa* as an ironing board illustrates this idea: the painting is not useful for anything other than its own existence (and certainly not terribly suited to being an ironing board!)

Of course we can shut ourselves out and not listen to the music or see the painting, but if we engage with it—that is, if we sense it—we're immediately sucked into it and have to participate in it *for its own sake.* Gadamer uses the comparison with the spectators at a tennis match turning their necks back and forth as they watch the ball.[2] No one can avoid playing along with the game. The work does not accommodate itself in *our* world but it is *we* who are driven into the realm of the work.

This means that art creates its own world and, as had been argued earlier by Martin Heidegger, it brings us to a specific space and time: we forget normal time and are transported into the place of the play or story.[3] This is especially strong with music; it makes us forget our sorrows. If we don't forget them we can't engage or appreciate art or music because we are simply too distracted. Put another way, the rhythm of the music grabs us and we are literally pulled 'out of this world' and the iPod—as a technology of art— helps this to happen.

Art also creates identity and difference. Sure, art grabs us and brings us into its realm but it does not create a uniform world. Everybody swings with the music but each listener reacts differently, everyone sees the same play but we all value it differently and actually we see different things. The work leaves the person who responds to it a certain leeway, a space to be filled in by himself.[4]

This personal space is what we talk about later on, when we discuss our experiences after the film or the play, or when we take our earplugs off . . . we dwell upon the work in the specific way the work demands of us. Art gathers us together and challenges us to make the work our own, that is, to engage with it. All art gives us a sense of belonging in the appreciation of it. We can't argue about personal taste—each to their own preferences—but *shared* taste brings us together and this is especially the case with music. The dancers at a party feel bonded by their love for the rhythms, they dance together and can't stand aside. It's literally ecstasy or stepping outside of ourselves (*ekstasis*). The partygoers *are* dance, they become the music in *communio*, that is—fused together.

So the iPod brings us together firstly in the recognition of a shared passion for music in general. Seeing the white earplugs is already a recognition of this shared attribute. But there is also the bonding brought about by the type of music: listening to John Coltrane or U2 brings us together with all other lovers of those artists. Although in the *moment* there is no physical evidence of sharing, there is always the *possibility* of communicating, more or less—just as we share a favourite writer while we still read in solitude.

But there's more. What we want to suggest from here on seems a little weird but—we think—rings true. Gadamer speaks of a com-

---

[2] Hans-Georg Gadamer, *The Relevance of the Beautiful and Other Essays* (Cambridge University Press, 1986), p. 24.

[3] Martin Heidegger, "The Origins of the Work of Art," in *Off the Beaten Track* (Cambridge University Press, 2002).

munity in the sense of *consciously* sharing a taste or a fascination for a particular work of art. But we maintain that a community doesn't necessarily *need* to be consciously aware of itself; it doesn't need to have an identity and the iPod reminds us of that fact.

Singular Plural?

Jean-Luc Nancy is a philosopher who has received considerable attention in continental Europe in the last decade. He has been writing about communities for some considerable time and, together with Italian thinker Giorgio Agamben and French philosopher Alain Badiou, he is considered an exponent of a new way of thinking about society. According to Nancy there is *always* community:

> Community is given to us with being and as being, well in advance of all our projects, desires and undertakings. At bottom, it is impossible for us to lose community. (*The Inoperative Community*, University of Minnesota Press, 1991, p. 35)

This sounds rather a grand statement, since politicians and social commentators alike seem to be continually worried about community or rather, a lack of community. Surely communities can't be that easy? But that is precisely Nancy's point.

We continually forget the given of the community and make it an object of organization. By doing that we tend to create ersatz communities that can't disguise the fact that they are not *really* communities. If groups of people who are supposedly communities (neighborhoods, work teams, the 'friends' on social networking sites, for instance) are actually artificially constructed ones, then more realistically, all we are engaged in is a discussion about inclusion and exclusion and deciding who is allowed or disallowed in the community. We have *politicized* community, which, according to Nancy, invariably leads to totalitarianism. We have to realize that our existence—our being—is from the outset a *being with others*. We don't exist detached from others and can only *be* because there are others. So we're related from the getgo.

At this point we seem to have drifted a long way from tooling through the tracks on our iPod and shutting out the world while we cycle to work! But for Nancy, individuals are like the atoms in a whole. They exist in relation to each other. We can only realize we are individuals because there *is* another. The very fact that we can customize our iPods, choose our own soundscape and make our own mixes automatically shows to us that other configurations are possible—*there must be others too.* But we don't need to know who these others actually are exactly; just knowing they exist reminds us we are not alone.

This 'being with others' doesn't mean we are all alike. It doesn't mean there's no identity or individuality at all. Being is also (and always) diversity. If we *weren't* different then we'd have no concept of alternative possibilities and therefore no idea of our human connectedness.

We're not all the same, and we take an individual position vis-à-vis the other. But we need the other in order to take that position, and so we are always in a relation (indeed, it is impossible to think without the relation). The other is not a radical 'Other' but already is part of us. It makes our identity. Considering what other possibilities there might be makes us up, since we can consider just what it is that makes us into *us.* We are together or singular, but in alteration or plurality. So Nancy concludes that being is always *singular plural.*

Nancy is not advocating nostalgia and a return to an original community of organic relations, where the community forms a homogenous whole and directs the relations and identity of its members. This is certainly no return to Jean-Jacques Rousseau's idea of humans as happy savages who have been corrupted by society and destroyed by the mechanical relations of the division of labour. Nancy actually rejects the idea of a transformation, driven by a social contract, of a community into a society. That 'lost' community never existed; it is a romantic myth that merely serves to ground our idea of society as having developed from *something* that we do not really remember.

> Society was not built on the ruins of a *community*. It emerged from the disappearance or the conservation of something—tribes or empires—perhaps just as unrelated to what we call 'community' as to what we call 'society'. So that community, far from being what society has crushed or lost, is *what happens to us*—question, waiting, event, imperative—*in the wake of* society. (*The Inoperative Community*, p. 11)

The point here is that, because we exist with others in a singular plural, there is no central identity to society. A common trait to a community or society can only exist as an exclusion. The idea of a community of commonality only makes sense if others don't share the trait that the others have in common. Community should be without identity; it should be inoperative. There is no organization of community. Community means we recognize the lack of communal traits and goals and accept that we always are together in a singular plurality.

Being in common has nothing to do with communion, with fusion into a body, into a unique and ultimate identity that would no longer be exposed. Being in common means, to the contrary, *no longer having, in any form, in any empirical or ideal place such a substantial identity, and sharing this* (narcissistic) *lack of identity.* (*The Inoperative Community*, p. xxviii)

So what does all this philosophical talk lead to? Nancy opens up a way to think about the social in a radically different manner, and we think that iPod is an excellent example of what he means. He asks us to think of inoperative communities: the gathering together of people that have no communal traits but are bonded to each other in the recognition of being with others. Of course, there's some commonality between iPodders in that they all have an iPod (!) but that is where the similarities end. This means we must realize that community is not something to be organized, produced, and segmented into markets, as is so often the ultimate aim, but should be seen as emergent situations that are continually changing.

Being in common or being with others is demonstrated precisely where there is no communal identity, nor organized communality. It comes to the fore or emerges in the unexpected situations of being together in singular plurality. A group waiting in line, for instance, or dancing to their own individual music: moments where we recognize we are together but still separated and certainly not homogenous; we are together without forming a club or organization. All attempts to organize communities, to give them a stable identity, are exactly the opposite of community and negate the being with others that always exists, because these attempts are based on *exclusion.*

Inoperative Community: Mobile Clubbing

We leave you with the strange phenomenon that fuelled our interest in these issues and also serves as a perfect example of how iPod simultaneously facilitates community and reinforces solitariness—

the 'mobile club'. The concept of 'mobile clubbing' was originally borne from the 'silent disco' experiment at the 2005 Glastonbury festival in the UK and the Dutch Parade festival in 2003. Problems with late night noise from the festival tents led to the organisers issuing festival-goers with wireless headphones, which were tuned in to the DJ. Revellers danced as they would normally do—except to anyone else entering, the tent was silent: hence the name 'silent disco'.

The 'mobile clubbing' idea takes this further through the activity of flash mobbing. In 2006 and 2007 groups of several thousand people converged on London's mainline railway stations and the Tate Gallery to dance 'in silence' to music through their headphones—but this time, it was their *own* music on their *own* iPods.[5]

It's hard to convey the almost comical spectacle of the mobile club—a simple search for 'mobile clubbing' on YouTube will reveal several camera-phone video clips of the bizarre scenes for you to see for yourself. It's fascinating to watch each dancer, initially self-conscious and looking around for acknowledgement from other people, begin to lose their feelings of individuality and dance—along with everyone else—*as if no-one else was there*. With Nancy in mind, we suggest that this loss of self is only possible because of the knowledge that as we dance we are not alone. But the clubbers are not part of the whole either—how can they be when they are all moving to a different beat? The experience of taking part is reflected on below by a participant, and nicely encapsulates some of the philosophical points we have made in this chapter:

> Despite many people's attempts to make it a social occasion, the fact that everyone was listening to their own music meant that people kept getting drawn back into themselves, however much they tried to be with their friends and have a collective experience. The dancing didn't only transform the space and stop people in their tracks—it transformed codes of behaviour, not only for the dancers but the onlookers too.[6]

The last words of this quotation capture something of the character of the event as a 'show stopper'; such a strange thing to

---

[4] *The Relevance of the Beautiful and Other Essays*, p. 26.

[5] See www.mobileclubbing.com, or Georgina Harper, "New Platforms for Dance," *londondance.com*, www.londondance.com/content.asp?CategoryID=1629 (accessed March 3rd, 2008).

encounter in many ways. Imagine hurrying through a train station during rush hour and coming across several hundred people wearing iPods swaying, jerking and leaping about to *nothing*. They all seem to be there together yet none are actually interacting—do they even *know* each other at all? How did they come to be there? And what is their purpose?

The phenomena of 'mobile clubbing' seems to us to bring together many of the philosophical issues we have discussed above with regard to human beings' need for community, solitude, music, and soundscape. It also calls into question traditional notions of 'public space' and challenges the kind of activities that are permissible in spaces that are supposed to be freely used by all. It reminds us of the power of people who come together for a shared purpose, and in that sense it is a powerful signal to states and governments that we are active agents and can bring about social demonstrations more easily than ever, given the technologies in our hands today. Of course, this is an eccentric and benign manifestation of power and we might be critical of such frivolity as drawing attention away from pressing issues that *need* our communal engagement and demonstration. But it's not really the job of philosophy to concern itself with the political ramifications of human action, rather to ponder what conditions lead to the desire to do such things in the first place.

What we claim the mobile club *does* do is disrupt traditional notions of what it means to be in community, together, alone and individual—and it does so through the power of art, enabled by the iPod and its technologies. With Nancy in hand, we can see that the iPod serves as a vehicle of combining solitude and togetherness, letting inoperative communities form as a demonstration of emergent power, but without a preconceived political goal. It's this bonding in solitude that makes the iPod such a fascinating device and so much more than just the possibility of listening to our own music so as to shut ourselves out from our fellow commuters on the morning train while we still struggle to wake up. Retracted in individuality we still may be in relation with others. Nancy makes it very clear that a community without identity is a powerful antidote to all those political rhetorics that want us to be part of a strong 'community of freedom' in whatever guise that may take—and that if we are not with it we automatically are against it.

The way to understand the diversity of societies today is to think about what it means to be singular plural. Mobile clubbing may in the end have broader political implications we can see at this moment. And all this thanks to the iPod . . .

15

The Shins Really Will Change Your Life

MATTHEW DEWEY

> There are two sorts of possible worlds in which esthetic experience would not exist. In a world of mere flux, change would not be cumulative; it would not move toward a close. Stability and rest would have no being. Equally is it true, however, that a world finished, ended, would have no traits of suspense and crisis, and would offer no opportunity for resolution.
>
> —JOHN DEWEY, *Art as Experience*

Conversations about aesthetics often focus on attempts to justify our preferences for one work of art over another. Today we've decided it's perfectly natural and okay for different people to have different ideas of what is pleasing to the eye or ear. But this relative acceptance or indifference does not suggest we don't have some kind of standard. This brings us to what is one of the coolest qualities of the iPod mobile digital device.

In Chris Breen's *Secrets of the iPod and iTunes*, he begins to answer the question of what makes the iPod so worthy of our attention by stating, "There just aren't more beautiful and intuitive music players available today." By using the word 'beautiful' along with the word 'intuitive', Breen suggests that in the iPod there has been a perfect mix or harmony of function and design.

This perfect mix of function and design includes what Donald Norman, a researcher in mechanical engineering, calls a user-centered design philosophy: good design takes account of our knowledge of the world—our physical, logical, semantic, and cultural knowledge—and closes the gap between the execution and evaluation of the object's functionality.[1]

Norman describes the way light switches are assigned as you walk into a room—the closest switch turns on the closest light—or the number of ways to indicate which way a door opens without using handles or a verbal sign (for instance using a plate to indicate where to push). Symbols such as arrows and colors (red and blue for temperature), and design features that build upon our experiences with earlier ways of using objects (such as using our familiarity the way that older electric appliances indicated 'on' and 'off') are all mindful of human experience.

Beauty then describes an aesthetic appreciation as an experience in the broader sense, taking into account accepted norms and values, our own knowledge and expectations, and the object's specific purpose. These values also cross over into appreciations of form, like color, light, or even the use of metaphor in painting and film. Fritz Lang's film, *Metropolis*, wouldn't be so desperate and haunting, so beautiful, without the extreme and simultaneous contrast and connection created by shadows and machines.

iAesthetics

These contrasts and connections between ideas and objects are the conditions for the aesthetic—what John Dewey called "consummatory"—experience. But it's more nuanced than simply iconic visual cues and obvious practical uses. The consummatory suggests an experience that ends in the natural completion of a moment, as the literal meaning observes, but whose influence causes in us the creation of a new kind of understanding between ourselves and others; an understanding that gives us not simply goose bumps or a heavy ephemeral sigh at sunset, but an *ontological direction*, a sense of where and who we are with regard to the roles we play in and among each other, and how we are to play them. These consummatory experiences are often ordinary and everyday.

> A problem that receives its solution; a game played through; a situation, whether that of eating a meal, playing a game of chess, carrying on a conversation, writing a book, or taking part in a political cam-

---

[1] Donald Norman, *The Design of Everyday Things* (New York: Basic, 2002), p. 140.

paign, is so rounded out that its close is a consummation and not a cessation.[2]

These experiences are not always grand or epic moments, but they are experiences that can produce new understandings and direction, not simply reinforcements of old or conventional beliefs. Dewey thinks the importance of art, of aesthetic experiences, lies in our potential understanding of them as mind-altering or ideal-altering.

Dewey separates the ideas of the artistic and the aesthetic, associating the *artistic* with *doing* or *making,* and the *aesthetic* as an *undergoing* or *experience.* In this sense the architect and the mechanical engineer are just as oriented to a consummatory experience as the artist because, ideally, each exercises an active attention to the impressions of the human individual or audience. In this relationship, the aesthetic can be separated from a strictly artistic experience, a momentary creative surge, and attached to an experience that explores and expands our cognitive abilities of perceiving and understanding life. In *Art as Experience*, Dewey gives the example of the appreciation of flowers: we can enjoy flowers for their color and fragrance, but to understand the flowering of plants, we learn about their biological and ecological interaction with the Earth.

Historically, definitive answers about what was beautiful and what was not were found in the existing authority of the time, be it the church or the aristocracy, and were brought about through forms of privilege, patronage and political power. 'High-culture' art forms, such as the symphony, opera and ballet, or the 'fine arts' of painting, sculpture, poetry, etc., were distinguished from 'folk' or populist forms. The fact that it cost outrageous amounts of money (and still does) to be able to participate in the consumption of what was considered 'high culture' served as both and implicit and explicit class division.

As Western society switched from a more individualist form of capitalism to a more corporate and administered form, the abilities of mass production and industrialization created a 'flattening out' of the access to the 'finer' things of culture. Though most people could not afford an original Monet, they would spend a fraction of the cost to own a copy that would represent or 'stand in for' a

---

[2] John Dewey, *Art as Experience* (New York: Perigee, 1980), p. 35.

position of taste and refinement that would otherwise be acquired if they had the means.

This 'leveling' through mass-production resulted in a general shift of aesthetic status: the formerly exclusive high culture became entangled with a rapidly emerging pop culture, and assumed an equivalent status. We see this process in kitsch reproductions of Munch's *The Scream*, or Wood's *American Gothic* in every dorm room and museum gift shop across America, and in the price of tickets to see the Rolling Stones, which cost more than seats for the L.A. Opera.

Inadvertently, the universal valuation of money that accompanies the process of capitalism—where all things are valued and reproduced through exchange and through the market rather than by traditional powers, hereditary titles, the church, and so forth—also eliminated the traditional and inaccessible aristocratic hold on definitions of 'good' and 'beautiful', and created an *appreciation* for the tastes of the now neutral and faceless mass. The duty of dubbing what is *cool* and *of value* was then inauspiciously given to the advertising and culture industries; the power no longer hereditary, but found in the market logic of capitalism.

iAesthetic Experience

> There is work done on the part of the percipient as there is on the part of the artist. The one who is too lazy, idle, or indurated in convention to perform this work will not see or hear.
>
> —JOHN DEWEY, *Art as Experience*

So if such characteristics as *cool* and *value* dictate the conditions of a market economy, it follows that our experiences of both material (the iPod, the Internet, and music) and nonmaterial elements of culture (such as tradition, religion, and language) that help create our consummatory experiences are influenced in varying degrees by capitalism. Because a guiding principle of capitalism is exchange—a process that constantly shifts value and capital—the idea of an ever changing and developing individuality fits this capitalistic environment well. The consummatory experience also appears to fit well with this process. An experience is aesthetic, is consummatory, if at its completion we are no longer the same person. Through genuine social interactions we evolve or enhance ourselves in new and different ways, rather than strengthening or reaffirming the same old perceptions.

The idea of constantly reinventing ourselves, on a superficial level, fits nicely with the capitalism's need for continuous consumption, but this process is only sustained if we base our identities *on* material consumption. Dewey suggests that the value of art is not found in the artifact, in the song, movie, or painting itself, but "in the dynamic and developing experiential activity through which they are created and perceived."[3] What Dewey is trying to suggest in the concept of consummation is that identity is not based on the material—not based on what's in our iPods—but in how the material changes our relationships within the processes of culture.

Understanding that we've historically trained ourselves to have aesthetic experiences when we visit museums, or when we watch a play, or download a song for the first time and it makes our heart skip and the earbuds drop, provides a platform for a consummatory experience. These subtle materially-influenced experiences have given art in all mediums a particular power over our consciousness. While these are indeed aesthetic-like, biological reactions to beauty, Dewey attempts to broaden this idea of the aesthetic experience and bring it out of the gallery and the finite framed surfaces we've reserved for art, and into the space of the everyday.

To Dewey, all art has intention, is active, and gets its power from its ability to "clarify and concentrate meanings that are contained in scattered and weakened ways in the material of other experiences."[4] Art creates for us a harmony in meaning. But what's particularly significant in Dewey's view—what differs from many other more abstract and subjective philosophical ideas of art and meaning—is that he believes this moment of clarity is not a merely individual experience. It's not simply that I, the listener to a bitter song, have at the particular moment of hearing it found a solid articulation of what the caricature of a sad, suicidal teenager dressed in all draping black means. It's that, in this moment, in the intersection between who I am and all that I am made up of (the

---

[3] Richard Shusterman, "The End of Aesthetic Experience," *Journal of Aesthetics and Art Criticism* 55:1 (1997), p. 29.

[4] Lawrence J. Dennis and J. Francis Powers, "Dewey, Maslow, and the Consummatory Experience," *Journal of Aesthetic Education* 8:4 (1974), pp. 51–63.

'human' subject), and the song (the object), a higher or deeper understanding of my relationship to everyone else is created. In this depressing song I don't grieve for myself so much as I try to understand what conditions of society, which I am intricately and inseparably a part of, have merged to create and distribute such nihilistic and whiney music.

For Dewey, this could lead to a consummatory experience; an experience that allows our understanding to culminate in a new empathy for our existence. Or I could simply not care, write off the performance as bad taste (which assumes my own taste is better) and go on living my life as if the only things of importance are the ones with the 'I' already included in them. In consummation, the experience ends (for it has to end in order for us to refer to it as an experience) and we are no longer the same person, we can no longer see the world, nor the work of art, or event, or situation, the same, no matter how many times we go back, initiate, reupload, or hit play.

iNew and iNow

Or might we just be the same people using new toys, like the iPod, in virtually the same old ways? Understanding the iPod in this way, either as a phenomenon of 'new' or as simply a happening of the 'now,' has a bearing on how we integrate or assimilate the iPod's meaning and effect in our everyday lives. This involves trying to look at the iPod not as an object or a gadget, but rather as an historical process.

Because the iPod isn't an indiscriminate pile of raw wire or chemical plastics, but a crafted and functionalized human device, there persists in its hardwiring an entire ensemble of historical processes of invention and know-how. These technical and mechanical processes developed, through broader social relationships, such as that between labor and ownership of production or that between ownership and federal law, and alongside the development of traditional and evolving cultural values and ideals. In short, the iPod didn't just ripen on a vine. It's been designed by processes that are not simply explained through technical innovation. Shared customs, social norms, and public law and policy all combined in an epic cultural goulash around 2001 to create the conditions for the production and consumption of the iPod itself.

If we can place the iPod in the grand scheme of things we can understand what it tells us about ourselves as creators of culture. 'New' inventions and ideas leave paper trails, so to speak, and we can trace their histories and implications in similar objects that have come before. Though French poet and critic Paul Valéry was right, in a way, to consider the 'new' a poisonous stimulant that one had to continually have in larger and larger doses until it became fatal,[5] it is a *newness* that leads us to different interpretations of the movement of culture—becoming new was what Dewey considered so important about the consummatory experience. Looking at the 'new' with a historical perspective relieves it of this addictive characterization and grounds the concept into more than just mere immediacy. The 'now' seems to be more of a phenomenon of fad and fancy; it is always in flux and impatient, without a sense of justification or reliance on past experience. The 'now' refers to an impression of being, an irresistible need to be of the moment, one that can only temporarily give us a sense of identity.

As German philosopher and critic Walter Benjamin remarked in his observations of mid-nineteenth-century Parisian streets, architecture, and social character, "there is always a sense of the same in the new."[6] There are many familiar things about the iPod too. The real significance of an iPod is not as an MP3 player; we've seen Walkmans and portable CD players, even portable DVD players, and have a pretty good idea about what a personal soundtrack entails. We're more comfortable with the idea of deciding for ourselves whether or not to listen to music or watch movies, rather than leaving the choice to, say, whether we get reception 'out here' or whether we find ourselves near strategically placed electrical outlets.

The iPod doesn't present a distinct break with the history of music players—it's an ancillary adaptation, or a side note, to a larger process of the digitization of the world. We've also spent the 1990s illegally downloading music and have as a culture—stemming from the make-you-a-tape phenomenon—grown tired and impatient with seventeen-dollar CDs with only one or two songs worth listening to. So, in a sense, the process and concept of programming the iPod was, to say the least, readily familiar to us. With all the nostalgia in place, the iPod conceptually does the same things, and works the same way that older portable music player

---

[5] Paul Valéry, *Analects* (Princeton University Press, 1970), p. 11.

[6] Walter Benjamin, *Arcades Project* (Cambridge: Belknap, 2002).

did, simply in a more contemporary and useful way.

Both concepts, the 'now' and the 'new', suggest an instant in time and the culmination of an event, but the 'now' is infused with the idea of immediacy and, with it, popularity or pervasiveness. 'Now' describes a privilege—it's more in our psyche than in an object. The apparent physical need to have new things, this *arousal*, so to speak, contrived by an appealing idea or object, doesn't require that the idea or object be significantly 'new'. People don't buy new cars because the new cars are terribly different from the older ones, or because driving specifically requires new vehicles. There are other more seductive and culturally-influenced reasons for the insistence on new things, and the hyper-accumulation of material objects can reach a significantly addictive quality when it highjacks the sensation of 'now'.

Fashion, in particular, works in this way when past styles, fabrics, and nostalgic 'looks' are 'reinvented' as a 'retrospective'. Each 'line' of clothing is deceptively different for each season, mimicking a historical evolution of style and homage. We may also accept ideas or customs that have been norms among certain subcultures or groups for decades; tattoos are not new but their growing acceptance is specifically a phenomenon of the now (or at least the past fifteen years). The immediacy or popularity of an artifact—its 'now-ness'—does less to include that artifact in a historical and cultural process than it does to allow us to participate in the contrived social connections of a superficial 'now'. There's a lapse in reflection in what is immediate. We can't place whatever is in the 'now' into our knowledge, categorize its effects, or even perceive its significance without some distance or detachment from it.

The iPod is merely new in that it is a contemporary way to do old things, but as it seeks to create a lifestyle—an 'i' aesthetic above and beyond its obvious and historically pre-established uses—it becomes a product of the now. The new can be now, but the now can never be new.

The significance found in the ideas of the 'new' and the 'now' sets the stage for a consideration of the significance of experience and identity. The iPod is a device that is meant to lend an aesthetic character to one's life—or at least this is what's suggested in those artsy commercials of dancing silhouettes. The interaction with the iPod is not one of merely practical use. We don't purchase iPods to simply play music, and that is not their specific function; the ability to play music is simply a by-product or convenient accessory to the iPod's primary function as a portable extension of the Internet—as an individual link to an elaborate web of information in the digital realm. The iPod creates an ability to aestheticize more of our everyday life helping us to elevate and acclimate ourselves to an ongoing digitization.

The digital i, the individual, and the iPod together can now work—digit to digit, zero to one, 'i' to 'i'—with other integrated software and hardware, to mediate a new experience and sense of identity. The iPod offers an entire sense of the contemporary and its use is infused with an intuitive ability to continually 'upgrade', 'interact', and 'individualize' as soon as it connects to the web. But this automation also comes with other effects of material culture such as subscriptions, copyrights, encoded files, and third party programs. Music's eventfulness is no longer in the record store but in a full-fledged armada of the legal, political, and economic developments of the digital future.

iBeautiful in an iExperience

So, for ease and efficiency of consuming media content today, the iPod is a beautiful device. It both is an experience itself and it allows us to have more traditional aesthetic experiences by engaging with art, music, and video. These are two horizons in the process of cultural aestheticization—one being in the material or 'content,' the other in the fluidity of digital integration that helps the iPod change the way we navigate the world around us.

Dewey might say that the iPod represents a 'new' harmony in the way it brings us into the digital experience of culture, by virtue of not only its ability to play music, but to store months worth of it, along with movies, videos, and podcasts, and to connect to other computers in an interface with the Internet. But he would also ask whether this harmonizing experience comes at the cost of other social advances.

The *consummatory* experience is John Dewey's[7] notion of a truly aesthetic experience—a heightened and intensified awareness and understanding of our orientation to both the material world and to our community. Dewey highlighted this aesthetic experience and its relationship to the social in one of his greatest works, *Art*

---

[7] No family relation, which I know of at least.

as Experience, written in 1934, as well as the ways in which the idea of aesthetic experiences have lost their meaning and association to our everyday experience.

The experiences we have are created by, endure in, and reflect social relationships between our community, the material world, and ourselves. So to consider Dewey's ideas today, we would view the new digital relationships we've acquired, sometimes reluctantly, as important frameworks for understanding the interconnected characteristics that make us who we are today. For Dewey, understanding life-experiences is a dialectic of harmony and discord; culture is one such platform for this relationship of harmony and discord in determining meaning. In education, in our families, in our consumption of material objects, and through the media: these are all social spaces where we create and interpret meaning.

These social conditions situate us in relation to a broader community. Community, according to Dewey, isn't simply the people around you—the schools and churches or the bureaucracies and governing bodies—but an organization of all these elements through an integrated principle.[8] In these interconnected relationships, we're able to determine and enunciate this principle, whether it's an idea of fellowship, of responsibility, or of democracy.

Dewey, one of the founding fathers of the American pragmatic philosophic tradition, believed that the validity of our ideas should also be observed in action, as ideals that guide action in real-world practice. The 'integrated principle' that interconnects a community is found in the general practices, associations, and dealings of its public. For instance, the encrypted music files downloaded from iTunes that cannot be shared with others create an extended version of control and a particular, corporation-centric attitude toward consumer ownership rights. Likewise, the need for third-party software programs to use an iPod on a different computer, and the need to buy a separate device to enable use of the iPod by more than one person, reinforces a sense of highly individualized use.

What guiding principle these practices reveal is a matter of political and economic interpretation. But considering these and other material practices involved in using the iPod as reflecting particular values helps us characterize our experience of them. The main concern: Does the iPod (in both use and programmability)

---

[8] John Dewey, *The Public and its Problems* (Chicago: Swallow, 1954), p. 38.

make it easier or harder to develop a musical experience that is inclusive and brings us into community, one that forms a public?

iPublic

The validation of our identities through material consumption tends to increase social inequality and decrease the general public's ability to define the integrated principles of their communities. Participatory democracy—Dewey's ideal—requires that social harmony and discord find a balance. This was his guiding rule of the beautiful: beauty is not what makes us prefer this or that work of art, but is an appreciation of an experience in which the relationship between the individual and their social and physical environment creates a new and more human understanding of community.

The consummatory experience is one that brings us empathy and gives us a common denominator; through the consummatory, the iPod gives us the option to upgrade to new versions of these old questions. There are no longer acceptable or unacceptable places to listen to music, but agreeable, iPod-friendly situations. There is listening to music, and then there is owning an iPod. The former suggests a traditional passive reception to sound and audible beauty, and the latter, an active, programmable, multilayered interaction of software and hardware, file formats, websites, contracts, and copyrights. Our experiences with new media content will not be strictly of sight or sound but perhaps with the additional impression of speed, immediacy, protocol, and network.

When you bought the Public Enemy tape, *It Takes a Nation of Millions to Hold Us Back*, from the record store in the late 1980s, you took it home and immediately listened to it, probably for weeks straight, while hiding the case from your mom. (I replaced the inserts that had the 'explicit lyrics' warning—and the inserts from every Sex Pistols album I had—with the inserts from less dangerous musicians like Bryan Adams or The Bangles). Buying this album was a defining moment that included travel downtown or to the mall, anticipation and a saved allowance, along with friends and strangers. But iPods don't need local or even physical record stores, and they don't have inserts that get left on top of boom boxes and subsequently seized.

These music places and experiences are of the vintage past. We no longer need to fear the vicious sneers of disapproval from the record-store geeks. Buying music is now immediate and acutely individual, consisting of no more energy or time-constraints than checking email. The clicking motions and security prompts of online bill-pay or buying something on eBay are the same. Buying music has lost its eventfulness for a more direct, online exchange experience. But what this loss means to us, or to our relationships with the non-digital world, is determined as we weigh this loss with what we think the individual and social benefits of the iPod process are. We decide where and how much of our experience music or the iPod gets credit for.

The aesthetic experience in an iPod may seem ridiculous or mind-numbing, but with the rapid evolution in technology, our aesthetic senses have also changed, as they should. We refuse to think our lives are going 'robot', and so the idea of harmony in meanings that reflect the artificial can seem counterintuitive—that somehow, consent here means that we are now agreeing that everything is image and the real no longer matters. But if it makes sense to claim that there's a form of beauty in the streamlined and error-free, non-rebooting function of a Linux server, then there must also be an accompanying sensibility; maybe one of fluidity in multiformats, of capabilities in a multiplicity orchestrated into one function.

Understanding how those aesthetic sensibilities help us understand our relationship to the material and social world, and how they are serving to guide the material and social direction of culture, is how Dewey would suggest we go about deciding how beautiful the iPod really is.

ACTION

16
Quantitative and Qualitative Change

LIBRIVOX VOLUNTEERS

JIM MOWATT: Well, we've had a few enquiries from people about who've seen LibriVox stuff on eBay. "Is this right?," "Can they do this?"—"This is free stuff, how can they sell free stuff?"

Well, when we record these things, we record them and give them to the world as they are. These are public domain things; everything we do is public domain. And we give them to the world free. You can sell them, you can put them in your own recordings, you can make music out of them, you can do *anything* with our recordings! That's the joy of LibriVox; that's the joy of what we record; that's the joy of how we record it, and the license we release it under!

If you see people selling our stuff on eBay, they're usually providing an extra service. They're putting these recordings out in .wav format, which we do not do, and they're putting them out on CDs usually, which we do not do. And it's no problem for LibriVox. You can put our recordings in your own database; you can do anything you want with them. We don't care, we're giving these recordings to the world.

SEAN MCGAUGHEY: That's what "no rights reserved" means: 'Go ahead, it's yours, world!'

JIM MOWATT: Absolutely.

D.E. WITTKOWER: Another famous way of expressing this is that what we're doing is free-as-in-speech, not free-as-in-beer.

SEAN MCGAUGHEY: What we're doing is free-as-in-speech *and* free-as-in-beer!

D.E. WITTKOWER: Yes, what *we're* doing is, yes, but anyone can change that—anyone can take our work and create something that is free in *neither* way, and that's the sense in which what we're giving out is not *just* free-as-in-beer, but also free-as-in-speech.

JIM MOWATT: Where do I get this free beer?

D.E. WITTKOWER: You know, what's funny is that—that's language coming from Richard Stallman, and since writing that, many years ago now, somebody actually came up with "free" beer which is free-as-in-speech: it's beer where the recipe is open-sourced.

SEAN MCGAUGHEY: And in fact there are people all over the world who take that open-source beer recipe and go to their local you-brew-its and make that free beer—although I'm sure there's a cost associated with that free beer.

D.E., what do you think about it? You've done all these philosophy texts, and put them in the public domain. Certainly, if you're doing this as a university professor, and part of your professional activity, you could publish these—put them on CDs and sell them. Why do you choose to release them in the public domain?

D.E. WITTKOWER: Why do academics publish anything? Well, we're not in academia for the money, and we don't tend to be publishing things that make a lot of money to begin with. Now, is it possible I'd be able to make some money out of a recording of Nietzsche? It's possible, but, for me, it'd probably be far more trouble than it would be worth.

Those are practical reasons. The real reasons are my ideological reasons, which I'm sort of not going into.

SEAN MCGAUGHEY: Those are what I'm interested in!

D.E. WITTKOWER: Well, basically my view on it is that copyright, and intellectual property in general, is an artificial monopoly that, it seems to me, *was* justified at points where the means of production of intellectual property was too capital-intensive to be generally held. Printing presses and so forth. But what's happened is that the means of production of intellectual property—copyright in particular—have become so cheapened that any of us is able to buy the equivalent of a full industrial-scale production line to reproduce intellectual goods.

JIM MOWATT: The working man has wrested the means of production from the big man!

D.E. WITTKOWER: Well, the actual specific analysis that I have is that competition has improved technology, and cheapened the machinery, until those means of production came within the reach of, well, the *average Westerner*, I'll say; the average worker is much more difficult to define.

SEAN MCGAUGHEY: When I was eleven years old, I had two very specific dreams: I wanted to have a record, and I wanted to have a radio show. I have produced both in my own basement, using consumer computer gear! And there is one more thing that's really important, that's mind-boggling about this: you can too!

JIM MOWATT: Yeah, but, a lot of our dreams back then, we could have still done them without this technology, but on a different scale. I mean, if you wanted to communicate with a lot of people you could photocopy a bit of paper and do a magazine, or you could get reel-to-reel tapes and just dish them out to people. I think all that has changed is the scale.

SEAN MCGAUGHEY: Yes, when you say that just the scale has changed, that's true—but at some point, a quantitative change becomes a qualitative change!

D.E. WITTKOWER: —Which is by the way from Hegel's *Logic* . . .

SEAN MCGAUGHEY: Right now, we are in three different cities, on two different continents, speaking over the Internet on a free connection, and discussing philosophy for publication and public-domain literature. This is a very niche thing! But the fact is, we've got a worldwide reach and that *does* change everything!

JIM MOWATT: I don't know. Because of the ease of being able to communicate over vast distances, you lose some of the connection of a short distance. The connection of a short distance is important if that's all you've got.

If you want to talk philosophy, perhaps your local university is holding informal philosophy classes that they invite the general public to, so you'll take the special effort to go to those. But, because there is the Internet and you can talk philosophy over several continents, you'll sit at home and do that instead.

So I think the same things would have happened. If you wanted something badly enough, you would have *done it* back then, and it would have been very important to you! You would have gone out and made the effort, you'd have gone to your local university, you would have formed a society if you wanted, and you would have made it happen in your own city, so would have gotten that personal connection.

So I think that all that this technology has done is that it's meant that if you only have a semi-commitment to something it makes it easier to do it anyway—it lowers the bar for entry into things that might interest you just a little bit, whereas before you had to be very interested and make the effort. So the Internet only makes a difference in that it makes it a little bit easier. But I think you could have done all these things before; I don't think there's any difference in that.

SEAN MCGAUGHEY: Again, it's qualitative versus quantitative. I'm sitting in front of a couple of machines—I've got my H4 recorder and my laptop in front of me—these machines are right at this moment doing the work of a professional audio studio, which, in my lifetime, would have required an engineer and several people running around; plus telephony and word processing, which would have involved typesetters and printers. And, yes, I could have done all of these things twenty-five years ago when I was in high school, but the qualitative change is that I can do them all, sitting here.

Another one-liner I throw off now and then is that the technology has made it possible that anybody can produce a CD—and I think that's wonderful, I really do, I think everybody should—but, unfortunately *anybody does!*

D.E. WITTKOWER: I don't know, I think we've seen what happens when we throw large amounts of money and social capital towards deciding who gets produced and what the CDs sound like, and I don't think it turned out all that well.

SEAN MCGAUGHEY: There's an understatement!

D.E. WITTKOWER: So, I'd much rather have anyone produce a CD. It turns out that a lot of the things that I care most about, in terms of my listening, are produced by people who are not appreciated by commercial establishments. Things that are, in a way, narrow-casted, which is of course what we're doing too.

This lowering-of-the-bar—in terms of not just capital investment but investment of time and effort—it allows for quite a bit more narrow-casting, which helps to re-create these local communities based around issues of common concern, where our basic social infrastructure at our local levels fails us, I think, in a very real way. I'm thinking, for example, of a book from a number of years ago, *Bowling Alone.*[1]

JIM MOWATT: . . . Aren't you going to explain what the book is?

D.E. WITTKOWER: Oh—Well, the example that the title comes from is that it's becoming more and more common that people go bowling alone, which is sort of amazing to me, not really caring much about bowling to begin with. The broader claim is that in the United States we've seen a decrease in local community involvement, and a decrease in involvement with social and non-political organizations, like bowling leagues, has gone along with a decrease in involvement in more important aspects of community—a decrease in organizations that involve some sort of common commitment to cause. And along with this increasing lack of involvement, we see a decrease in social trust, a decrease in involvement in government, and a decrease in just showing up to vote.

JIM MOWATT: So a kind of personal isolationism.

SEAN MCGAUGHEY: Funny you should say that, because in the last year that I've really been exploring social media and stuff, I've found that Friendsters don't necessarily equal friends. What that has meant for me, on a personal level, is that I'm considering joining a local service club, through my church. Real, on-the-ground working together to do something for your community—that *says* something!

D.E. WITTKOWER: If people really *committed* to doing something, we would make it happen; we would make it happen locally. Instead of doing it through our online connections, we'd do it on the "Sneakernet"—that is, we'd put on our sneakers and we'd just actually leave the house and go and meet people and do things.

---

[1] Robert D. Putnam, *Bowling Alone: The Collapse and Revival of American Community* (Simon and Schuster, 2000).

The problem is, we don't, and that's for a good reason: our society is set up in such a way that this kind of community-based action doesn't tend to happen anymore, and that's something that we *do* need to combat, that is something that we *do* need to work against. We need to get off our chairs, get out of our houses, go and actually meet people in person, form local communities and to become engaged in real live communities with common *concerns* rather than just common preferences, or tastes, or things in common that we're 'fans of,' or whatever else, but projects—actual action.

And I don't think that in any way decreases the importance of community produced, or individually produced, narrow-casted cultural items, like this podcast, or like LibriVox in general, or like any number of other blogs or podcasts. This is a general movement away from dictated culture, a general movement away from things *standing in for culture*, which are produced for commercial gain.

The vision that makes this concrete for me is, if I imagine just a college student's dorm room—or even more dramatically, perhaps, like maybe a thirteen-year-old girl's room—and just look around and see all of the consumer-training that lines the walls; all of these products that are being advertised right there, above the bed. This 'personality through brand commitment', and the rest of the ways that a culture that we do not own is being sold to us.

We live our lives on this terrain which, at best, we rent—all of these cultural icons whose cultural productions, first of all, are cultural in name alone, but secondly, we have *no rights to*! We are serfs on this soil; we're able to consume, we're able to send money off, but that's the extent of what we are able to do with it.

If we contrast that with—I mean, it's difficult even to imagine in some way. But if those elements of culture were either rooted within the community instead of rooted within the economy, or if those elements of culture, even if rooted in the economy, were at least *available* to the community, this would be very different. If they were available as something that the thirteen-year-old girl could remix, that she could strip out the vocal track of and record her own. Like, look at mash-ups, or these amateur music videos up on YouTube—these are, I think, just fascinating! All of this illegal art that kids are creating now; it's wonderful, and that's what culture *ought* to look like and it doesn't.

JIM MOWATT: That's right, and . . . I mean, you always have to go back to the question, "Why would someone put in this effort?"

because to create anything, to make a new work of art, requires effort, requires thought, requires input, requires some creative impulse and requires actually putting it together. And what we have now is recognition and respect from your peers, or maybe even further afield, that's what we have now through YouTube. You have all these comments where you'll either get slagged off or people will say "Yeah, you're great, do more!"

There are artists I've seen on YouTube that are stunning, amazing—people that have created art I would never have imagined in a million years. They've created it by putting things together to create sort of musical collages with picture-scapes built in. And, my view of the world is that we do a lot of what we do in order to connect to other people, and we want to get some feedback from other people. So most of our motivations are either to survive, or to get some kind of recognition from or communication with other humans. We're social creatures; it's what we do. And so, we can do that; we can be social creatures through the Internet and with YouTube, and I think that's the reason why we're seeing this sort of artistic impulse; why we're getting this explosion of art and the desire to create it and make the world a more vibrant and interesting place.

One of the problems though . . . You mentioned the thirteen-year-old girl—one of the problems that will sort of stunt the growth of this is that, just as a river will always flow downhill and electricity will always choose the shortest path, in the same way, if a great brand-name comes along and makes itself easy to identify with, makes it easy for the conservatism of youth to join it—because, you know, there is nothing more conservative than a fifteen- or sixteen-year-old that wants to fit in with the crowd—the brand names can come in and say "you're mine," and they'll say, "Oh, yes, that's easy, we'll be yours then."

SEAN MCGAUGHEY: I think I'm going to try to steer this wonderful conversation back to where we started, which is: we're all LibriVox volunteers.

We've talked about the Internet, we've talked about the philosophy of why we're doing this, of creating, of remixing, of so many wonderful things. All three of us are involved in a project, that . . . well, here are just some of the stats I've been reading that boggle my mind: at the moment there are four-hundred-and-eighty-or-so open projects to record audio books, and we record seventy-plus audio books a month. We currently have two hundred and thirteen completed non-English projects in twenty-four different languages, and contributors from at least six of seven continents. And we give all of these to the world; it's done entirely by volunteers, it's done entirely on a non-economic model, people donate everything from our servers to the time to listen to the time to record; it's all done for free, no money touches our accounts—we don't *have* any accounts.

It's just amazing; two thousand and eighty people have recorded something for us, four hundred and seventy-seven have recorded ten or more chapters for us, and we have released a total of sixteen hundred and sixty-eight works, with a full run-time of three hundred and twenty-seven days—almost a full year.[2] Dedicated people, all over the world, can come together using this technology and really enrich the public domain—do something for what I think is really a worthy cause, sort of as a gift to the world.

Comments? Thoughts?

JIM MOWATT: It's a bit of a complete statement there! It's not a question, you're not throwing something out there, that's a complete statement—that's what we do!

D.E. WITTKOWER: There's something related to this that I'd thought of, actually, when first ringing you up—and, Jim, your comments right before this were relevant too: we're doing all of this on a volunteer basis, but why are we all doing this? Well, presumably, because we care about the public domain and we care about these texts; because we want them to be available, and we want them to be accessible. But also, presumably, because we want to share our *joy* with these texts; because we want to share our enjoyment of them.

SEAN McGAUGHEY: Well, I want to thank my, it turned out to be two guest hosts. Jim Mowatt, thank you very much, for joining us from over 'across the pond' at a much more reasonable hour.

JIM MOWATT: Thank you, Sean, at half-past-twelve, over here in England!

---

[2] These numbers in these paragraphs have been updated to represent figures current as of August 8th, 2008.

SEAN McGAUGHEY: And Dylan Wittkower, thank you so much for joining us.

D.E. WITTKOWER: Thank you for having me on. It's been fun.

SEAN McGAUGHEY: Do you want to take us out, Jim?

JIM MOWATT: Yep. Enjoy the snow if you've got it, and enjoy recording! Let's have another *thirty* recordings of Jane Austen! I love every one of them, and she's probably our most favored author. There are so many, and I love the feeling when people come on and record another Jane Austen, and they love doing it, and I love that enthusiasm! Please keep it up, I love listening to it.[3]

---

[3] This transcript has been edited for clarity. Thanks to Sean McGaughey, for doing such a fine job putting together the podcast upon which this was based (LibriVox Community Podcast #66), and to Britt Patterson, for help producing this transcription.

17
Podcrastination

REGINA ARNOLD

"We are tools of our tools," intones Neil Postman in *Technopoly*, his 1993 lament over the advent of electronic and digital culture, adding lugubriously that new tools, or technologies, "alter those deeply embedded habits of thought which give to a culture its sense of what the world is like . . . of what is reasonable, of what is necessary, of what is real."[1]

As with everything that grumpy man ever wrote, there is a grain of truth Postman's anti-technology rant, and few new "tools" illustrate his words better than the iPod mobile digital device, which has enslaved millions with its needy cries for more memory, more iTunes, more uses, more sizes and color, more time spent alone with it. It has even tinkered with how the world looks and feels, worming its way into our most intimate moments. Nevertheless, next time you're seated on a bus or an airplane next to a mom with a crying baby—next time you *are* a mom with a crying baby— you'll find it pretty easy to argue that the iPod has altered reality for the better.

As with all new tools, there is a downside. We're all familiar with the sight of individuals people plugged into iPods; buds sprouting from their ears like wire vines off flesh trellises, locking each individual consciousness into its own private media landscape. For some, the sight is an annoying sign that the world is

---

[1] *Technopoly: The Surrender of Culture to Technology* (New York: Vintage, 1993).

becoming ever more depersonalized and inhumane. Others believe that a private consciousness is now a privilege bordering on a necessity.

Love it or hate it, there's no denying that, since its inception in 2001 and almost universal adoption by music fans, the MP3-playing *object d'art* has done more than merely enliven our lonely hours on planes, trains and automobiles: it has reshaped our relationship to both time and space. The reason is a phenomenon I call *'podcrastination:'* that is, the *voluntary suspension* of one's engagement with reality, a kind of super-enhanced version of the dream state that capitalism is so famously said to induce in us all. That is why, as tempting as it would be to view the army of cyborgs that the iPod has created as a Donna Haraway-inspired promise for a new and post-human future,[2] it may be that they—that we—are something else entirely.

It would be nice to think that iPods—and podcrastination—have changed our inner as well as our outer experience of the material world, but even a modicum of hard thought on the subject will force the thinker to acknowledge that, in the case of iPods, 'consciousness', however private, has been acquired only through the consciousness *industry*—that is, the notion that, according to head Frankfurt School shout-pot Theodor Adorno, the mass media is 'administered' to the public in the grossest possible form with the express purpose of keeping everyone quiet. Adorno would certainly argue that podcrastination is a kind of cyborgian opiate; that to plug one's mind directly into a media-driven device is to simply to deepen one's thrall to the Man. But Adorno is a known sourpuss, and there's another possibility as well.

Perhaps, as Simon Frith once suggested, the iPod allows us to live "not without capitalism, but within it."[3] If it does so, I'd like to suggest that it's not the device itself that is driving this, but its ability to deliver other recorded media wherever and whenever we want it. For although not widely written about to date, the podcast is really the aspect of the MP3 player that separates it from the walkman or the transistor radio before it. Those devices also offered an escape from the hell-like noise of daily life, but only the podcast also un-tethers us from the space-time continuum.

---

[2] Please see Chapter 11 in this volume for more on Donna Haraway.
[3] Simon Frith, *Sound Effects* (New York: Pantheon, 1981).

Tools Rush In

A podcast is something—audio or video—that appears automatically on your hard drive, just as radio and television appear automatically in their respective delivery devices. But unlike those media, which distribute only corporation-made content, podcasts can be privately-made recordings; the equivalent of mix-tapes made by young men for their crush objects, only more easily distributed.

Not only does the podcast allow consumers to create their own broadcasts and distribute them via the net, but it also allows listening to occur away from that listening-post known as your television or radio. At its simplest, a 'podcast' may be what your iPod calls an "on-the-go" set; that is, songs it has grouped together from your own play list, based either on a random shuffle, on the number of times you play them, or on your own grouping. At its most complex, a podcast is something downloaded from a third-party site or sites, via the Internet, which addresses your own interests in some particular way. Moreover, it's something which will renew itself—that is, update its own content—whenever you plug your MP3 player back into your computer.

A podcast can be an oral recording your child sends you from abroad or a set of soothing music a yoga teacher has put together for a ninety-minute class. It can be an hour-long special downloaded from a radio website, or a five-minute daily news commentary on celebrity gossip, or a two-hour discussion of World of Warcraft. It can be sent to an individual or to a list serve, or to an even larger group, such as the endless nameless pool of ears that makes up the world wide web. But briefly put, as these myriad descriptions indicate, a 'pod' cast is the opposite of a 'broad' cast.

As such, the technology that affords us the podcast conforms strangely to Hans Magnus Enzensberger's utopian vision for digital technology which that he presciently laid out in his "Constituents of a Theory of the Media."[4] Way back in 1970, Enzensberger presented a challenging theory of how the media could be made empowering and emancipatory, rather than monolithic and impersonal. He believed that then-new media devices—things like news satellites, color televisions, cassettes, video tape recorders and pho-

---

[4] Originally published in *New Left Review* 64 (1970).

tocopying machines—were potentially explosive forces, sort of like high-tech stealth bombs that could break apart the monopoly that gripped consumers of the media.

At this remove, when we take rather miraculous things like email and GPS systems for granted, it seems kind of amazing that Enzensberger was so wowed by so little, but the times were different then; more rigid, more hierarchical. He clearly thought the fact that a copy machine could be used by employees to photocopy their own butts was the dawn of a new age, and although we now know it wasn't, we wouldn't want to be back in the days when we couldn't, either.

Moreover, it's important to bear this innocence in mind when considering the iPod, for many of the things we find so amazing about it now may seem just as quaint, ten years hence. However, there's no telling. Besides, we're now standing at a point in time when many of the things he envisioned for a digitized media have already come true without noticeably altering much about the power of the media. That being the case, it's worth examining whether the iPod, and more particularly the podcast it enables, can indeed fulfill his predictions, and perhaps provide a platform for a more participatory culture.

Chain of Tools

The main explosive force that Enzensberger saw within new media technology was its mobilizing power. This, as he beautifully points out, means, literally, "to make men more mobile. As free as dancers, as aware as football players, as surprising as guerillas."[5]

It's easy to visualize how the pod cast *mobilizes* individually in exactly these three ways, since the iPod advertisement silhouette does, in fact, dance, feint, block, and, in the six years or so since it came into being, surprise us so much (hence, this volume in the *Philosophy and Popular Culture* series). And of course it mobilizes us by allowing us to take it, and its contents, with us wherever we go. But does it, with the help of the net, encourage the kind of mass-participation Enzensberger goes on to postulate is true politicization?

---

[5] Hans Magnus Enzensberger, "Constituents of a Theory of the Media," in *Media Studies: A Reader* (New York University Press), p. 69.

That's another question, and one that hinges on one's definition of 'iPod users'. Is it fair to call them a mass, or are they each an individual? The silhouette in the iPod commercial looks like some zombie-like creature in between the two, a troubling specter that argues for neither.

It also may throw a spoke spanner in our hopes for the medium, since, in his argument for a socialist media theory, Enzensberger distinguishes between masses and individuals by saying that only the latter can be politicized. "Anyone who thinks the masses are only the object of politics cannot mobilize them," he tells us. "He wants to push them around. A parcel is not mobile; it can only be pushed to and fro. Marches, columns, parades, immobilize people. Propaganda, which does not release self-reliance, but limits it, fits into the same pattern. It leads to depoliticization." The depoliticization of the twenty-first century is alas a *fait accompli*, and it seems unlikely that podcrastination will undo it.

That's one view of it. On another level, however, podcasting seems to conform almost miraculously to the list of emancipatory potentials that Enzensberger proposed for a utopian new media. He lists at least eight processes that he believes would free the media from its repressive functions:

- **Decentralized programming**
- **Each receiver a potential transmitter**
- **Mobilization of the masses**
- **Interaction of those involved**
- **Feedback**
- **A political learning process**
- **Collective production, and**
- **Social control by self-organization**[6]

All these once-hyperbolic ideals are fulfilled by the podcast, and what's more, podcasting as a means of self-expression provides the perfect platform wherein the specialist (in this case radio broad-

---

[6] "Constituents of a Theory," pp. 80–81, altered slightly for formatting and clarity.

casters) could "learn as much or more from the nonspecialist as the other way around." But each of these functions carries within it a potential danger; the same danger that has turned every media technology before it into a relatively repressive apparatus: the danger of co-option. If one considers each of Enzensberger's ideals individually, one can see both the pitfalls that Postman would have us beware of, and the podcast's possible uses. (Note that some of Enzenberger's eight strategies must be grouped together when considered in light of the podcast.)

Decentralized Programming

What Enzensberger envisioned here was a media system that didn't rely on one, or a few, large corporate entities controlling the content. In theory, DirecTV and cable television, with its many privately-owned channels, have already done to television-watching what Enzensberger hoped. But of course in practice it has merely fallen into what's called "the Long Tail effect:" that is, Chris Anderson's theory that there has been a cultural shift toward away from 'lowest common denominator' towards niche markets that effectively target and exploit ever-narrower fields of interest. Similarly, podcasting breaks down programming modules into smaller, more individual units, but there is the possibility that they are small enough—individual enough—to elude Long Tail marketing strategies.

How does this affect us today? Consider, perhaps, some new streamed radio stations that have appeared, both on my radio and in my computer. One is called KYOU. It can be heard online, and also on air on an AM band. KYOU is owned and operated by CBS, but its programming is 'created' by listeners—or so its home page says. It consists of privately made podcasts of other programs that have been chosen (no doubt) by the powers that be—they are, as Adorno says 'administrated'—but this still exudes an authenticity that is lacking on more rigid broadcast models, where programming is essentially carried out by a single person.

Other music models now exist that can lead to podcrastination. Pandora, LastFM, and SOMA radio are just a few sites where listeners can load up their MP3 players with music that's not chained to the terrestrial, corporately owned, radio station. (These are mainly streamed sites, but podcastability is built into their models.) More obscure podcasts can be found via podcast sites like pod-show.com, but clearly, two things need to occur before the podcast can reach its liberating potential: first, there will need to be some kind of revolutionary search engine for podcasts, wherein listeners are able to find what they want to listen to without already knowing where to find it and what it's called, and second, more people will need to become aware of the real opportunities offered by podcasts. At the moment, few people seem to take advantage of their MP3 player's ability to automatically stream material from the Internet. I believe that this will become a much more widespread practice as more and more new-model cars make MP3-playing devices a standard feature in car radios.

Each Receiver a Potential Transmitter, Interaction of Those Involved, and Feedback

A third thing is needed as well: a wealth of material not tied to commercial radio—possibly consumer-made material, as with YouTube—that citizens will have a desire to access and to share.

At the moment, the discovery and acquisition of podcasts tends to be tied to terrestrial radio; for example, a sports fan who tunes in to CBS radio on his morning commute may know that John Madden's show is available via podcast, for days that he stays home from work. Although the barrier to entry as a podcaster is very low—merely the cost of a microphone and a software program—it's not, like email, a case where the delivery system and the retrieval system are exactly alike. It's still the realm of the specialist, rather than the individual, and it probably always will be. But the number of individual podcasts worth listening to is still bound to grow exponentially once there's an audio search engine worth its salt. And even if it doesn't, there are already small alternative worlds where transmitting and receiving are somewhat interchangeable.

Consider, for example, the podcast bar, where podcasts are submitted by bar patrons for fifteen minutes of dance programming. Popular sets—which are determined, of course, by how many people are dancing—create popular pod-jays, whose ability to program can then translate into a form of (at the very least, club-wide) fame. Interaction, feedback, and individual submission are all part of this equation in a way that they aren't in the previous example.

In his thirty-year-old essay, Enzensberger (utopianly) envisions things like "a mass newspaper, written and distributed by its readers, a video network of politically active groups" (p. 78). These things of course have long since come to be—and with less effect than he perhaps hoped, because the people really had nothing to say. The same problem might be said to be endemic to podcasts. They can do everything Enzensberger wants them to do, but to what purpose? At the moment, many only demonstrate clearly that certain dyed-haired pierced guys are eminently on top of techno.

Mobilization of the Masses, a Political Learning Process, Social Control by Self-organization

This potentiality—mobilization, learning, and social control—is one that can be taken quite literally. iTunes already has a segment called iTunesU; YouTube is currently broadcasting nine UC-Berkeley courses, which are a natural for podcasting. If you're "taking" Anthropology 101 via the Internet, what better way to ensure that you remember to "go" to class than to have it syndicated into your computer via podcast? And if education is available for free—to be imbibed at whatever time one wishes (rather than in a large lecture hall at 9:00 a.m.) then the entire social order is about to be overthrown.

The concept alone gives new meaning to the term 'smart mob'—Howard Rheingold's concept of a group that has formed through some kind of computer mediated digital network. Rheingold's version is generally done through text messaging, but it's just as feasible that it could form via some kind of podcast, especially because podcasts are automatically downloadable.

The defining characteristic of a 'smart mob' is that it behaves intelligently, or at least predictably, as opposed to more-or-less randomly, as is the case with regular old mobs. A smart mob is a form of social co-ordination and is touted by some as a source of possible collective wisdom. Examples of smart mobs include groups of teenagers who stalk celebrities via text messages, political crowds that gather in specific places—most famously in EDSA Plaza in Manila, during the unrest preceding former Philippine Presedent Joseph Estrada's resignation—and as a way of warning protesters of where police are located in a given situation, as during Critical Masses in San Francisco, or the French riots of 2006.

Originally, the smart mob seemed to be a phenomenon of text messaging, but the podcast simply enlarges that potential—particularly as the iPhone and other multi-purpose devices take hold of the *Zeitgeist.* If a simple text message ('meet at EDSA') was responsible for a change in government, how much more effective could a widely circulated podcast be; one which, say, appears in your PDA or iPod via automatic download?

If we widen out the concept of the podcast to include video, and consider the possibility of a popular, audience-created show that is able to suddenly circulate video or audio, one can imagine the potential it would have to perhaps capture a flame of anger and employ it at a particular moment. What if, for instance, there were a recording of Dick Cheney saying something virulently racist, warlike, or conspiratory—*and it had reached iPods right after Hurricane Katrina?* What if Barack Obama's inspiring speech from the 2004 Democratic Convention has been beamed automatically into synched iPods on the eve of the 2004 election? What if we were all suddenly confronted with a privately-made video of John McCain in particularly ill-advised drag?

Tools Like Us

Sadly, we have seen the effect of some of these events as mediated by YouTube: videos of Abu Ghraib, the beheading of Daniel Pearl, and Senator George Allen calling an Indian-born reporter a "Macaca" *have* been widely circulated, without creating the kind of explosive effect envisioned here. What's at stake, then, is not the publicity that media technologies like the iPod and the podcast can afford us, but something more ephemeral: a mere potentiality.

In her acclaimed essay "Regarding the Torture of Others," the late Susan Sontag wrote about the photos from Abu Ghraib that "the meaning of these pictures is not just that these acts were performed, but that their perpetrators apparently had no sense that there was anything wrong in what the pictures show."[7] The key point being forgotten in any socialist theory of the media is that when the media becomes two-way, when feedback is allowed, when each receiver is a potential transmitter, and when social control is exacted by 'self-organization', the potential for abuse could outweigh any social good that might momentarily occur in the

---

[7] Susan Sontag, "Regarding the Torture of Others," *New York Times* (May 23rd, 2004) http://query.nytimes.com/gst/fullpage.html?res=9503E5D7153FF930A15756C0A9629C8B63 (accessed March 12th, 2008).

space between invention and betrayal. The podcast is as open to this occurrence as any other medium, and betrayal is already hard on our heels.

Not only that, but we probably won't even hear it when it sneaks up on us. Our headphones will be turned up too high. While I do believe that individuals are becoming ever more savvy to the toils of the conventional consciousness industry (particularly to the news), there is no evidence that they will ever use their knowledge for any enlightening purpose; indeed, there is evidence to the contrary. This is the sole reason that the iPod and podcasting may *not* in fact represent the social panacea that it could be.

Yes, it has emancipatory potential; and yes, this potential will be squandered—not even co-opted, just flushed down the toilet—like everything revolutionary before it. This is the price we pay for the upsides of capitalism: a seeming inability to recognize liberation when we see—or in this case—hear it.

When it comes to revolution, Enzensberger said, "the individual's role is clear: the author has to work as the agent of the masses. He can lose himself in them only when they themselves," *the masses*, "become the authors, the authors of history" (p. 91). In the most immediate sense—that is, when you're sitting under headphones on a bus or a plane, indulging yourself in a spot of blissed-out private time shifting—podcrastination does not speak to history or to the masses, but to the moment, to the individual, to the body, and very much to the private self.

If we are indeed living in a state of post-modernity—and that's a question for another day—then podcrastination is not going to free our minds. It's only going to chain us to our seats. Upon reflection, as beautiful as the rupture of space, time, and the media is to experience, the iPod is not going to further a cyborg manifesto. It's only going to create a cyborg lament.

18

Is the Podcast a Public Sphere Institution?

MARC LOMBARDO

The technological story of the 1990s—the kernel of truth that made the dot-com bubble possible—was that the way that we communicate was undergoing a gradual but fundamental shift as cell phones, e-mail, and the Web became increasingly available to a broader spectrum of the population. This trend continued in the 2000s with the development of mobile digital devices, such as the iPod, which changed the ways in which music, TV, movies, and other forms of content were consumed. As one particularly drastic example of this change, consider that a significant portion of the population now carries the better part of their entire music library with them at all times.

Even the most avid music collector should be at least temporarily satisfied with the 160GB iPod Classic, which holds approximately forty thousand four-minute songs. If filled to its capacity, this model could play continuously without repeating a song for nearly a third of a year (111 days)! While CDs are considerably smaller than long-play records, nevertheless, to carry nearly nine hundred of them with you everywhere you go (on public transportation, while walking, in the car, in the bathroom) would be somewhat inconvenient. In *Gulliver's Travels*, Jonathan Swift ironically hypothesized that language originated because words were much lighter and easier to carry around than even miniature models of all the things that one would want to signify. How is the way that we talk about music changing now that an entire music library can be fit into a pocket?

As a culture, we're still in the process of negotiating how these new technologies should be integrated into our private and public lives: for example, the widespread use of the cell phone has led to an ongoing conversation regarding what constitutes appropriate and inappropriate cell phone etiquette. If anything is clear, it is that the meaning of these technologies lies not simply in the ways in which they extend our existing communicative practices to broader areas, broader populations, and broader social domains. The more interesting question that we are all trying to figure out—personally and collectively—is how these changes in communications technology and media dissemination are transforming the ways we actually communicate and the media that we produce.

User Intervention, Corporate Co-option

The podcast has been one such transformation that arose from the consumer reinvention and redeployment of the possibilities of the iPod. While Apple was quick to take advantage of this emerging use of their product, primarily by releasing various "official" podcasts of TV and radio programs on iTunes, the podcast was integrated into the profit structure only *after* it had arisen as a non-sanctioned and unpredicted side effect of the iPod's intended existence as a music player.

This story is but the latest iteration of the constant attempt by the manufacturers of technology to catch up with the evolutionary mutation of their products that occurs when they are used and transformed as a part of cultural practice. Engineers formulate the next devices for mass production in response to the reinventions and modifications that ordinary people applied to their previous efforts, most of which the engineers themselves could have never imagined.

The evolution of the iPod is a striking illustration of this mutual interdependence between corporations and non-sanctioned technological appropriations. The iPod was only conceivable at all as a consumer product because of the development of peer-to-peer file trading. Moreover, each subsequent "generation" of iPod came to incorporate more features (such as, video playback and the displaying of pictures) that had previously been developed by an international community of enthusiasts.[1]

---

[1] The iPod Linux Project deserves special mention: http://ipodlinux.org/Main_Page.

Hip hop, which is today thoroughly integrated within the corporate culture industry and has even become *the* hegemonic musical form, affecting and infecting nearly all others, arose as a musical form from the previously unimaginable reinvention of the direct-drive turntable and the mixing board. In the same way, the podcast has become a means for the dissemination of mainstream media sources only as a result of its being invented and practiced by people with no discernible relationship to those "official" sources.

This is not to say that new cultural deployments of technology are ever simply pure or authentic creations that exist without a relationship to the dominant corporate, governmental, and ideological power structures of the time. Even in its initial phase, hip hop had the electronic devices of corporate manufacturing and distribution to work with; similarly, the podcast community was only possible as a result of the massive investment of resources in the Internet's infrastructure by public and (in the relatively late phase in which it had proven to be profitable) private sources. The corporations that manufacture and distribute these devices depend, like parasites, *for their very existence* upon the markets that are unwittingly created for them by the subcultures that redeploy their products in new and often more interesting ways.

In examining the podcast as a specific site in which these issues are at play, we should try to maintain a perspective which is neither optimistic (concerning, for example, the new possibilities for democratic action and participation that the podcast may have made possible) nor pessimistic (concerning, for example, the fact that these possibilities wholly depend upon government and corporate structures of power and control) but rather *critical*. Such a perspective recognizes that the strategies and techniques developed by subcultures are always going to be co-opted, just as it recognizes that there is no technological device that cannot be used for purposes other than those for which it was constructed.

The podcast exists in a complex strategic situation within particular economic, political, and ideological systems. On the one hand, it exists as an outgrowth of corporate power and as a means of disseminating mass-media content. On the other hand, it provides individuals with a valuable means of being informed of vital issues that they may not otherwise hear about, and it also provides a means to communicate one's thoughts, views, or analyses to an audience that would likely be otherwise unavailable. The possibility that the podcast represents—and this possibility will survive the podcast, just as it existed long before the podcast ever came to be—is the possibility of a space for public debate and information-sharing that can function as a check upon corporate and governmental power.

The Public Sphere

While he's by no means the first to talk about the necessity for such a space of critical debate, the German philosopher Jürgen Habermas has made a significant contribution to the analysis of this phenomenon, which he called the "public sphere" (*Öffentlichkeit*). Habermas's work on this subject built upon the contributions of the great American philosopher of democracy and education, John Dewey. In his landmark 1927 work, *The Public and its Problems*, Dewey called for the founding of new institutions and techniques for communication relevant to the public; institutions that common people could *participate* in that were not simply reducible to the modes of passive reception encouraged by the mass media.

The concern of Habermas's first major work, 1961's *The Structural Transformation of the Public Sphere*, was identifying an actual historical example of the kind of institution of participatory communication that Dewey had in mind. To do this, Habermas turned to examine the institutions of debate that proliferated during the dawn of the liberal era (the late seventeenth and early eighteenth centuries) in Europe, primarily: the press, the coffeehouses of England, and the *salons* in France.

While Habermas's example of the public sphere was largely drawn from the institutions of the past, the primary significance of this historical study was to provide a basis for the task of analyzing, critiquing, and transforming the communicative institutions of the present. As we move into the digital era, many of Habermas's observations concerning the traditional forms of mass media (radio, TV, movies, and newspapers) seem even more applicable to some of the forms of "new media" that have sprung up in recent years.

Habermas contrasts the journals and periodicals of the liberal era with the later forms of mass media dominant in the late nineteenth through the twentieth centuries. These later forms of media were dependent to an ever larger degree upon advertising for their revenues. The significance of this change in the financing of media was far more significant than it might first appear. By flooding the cultural landscape with a proliferation of advertisements that attempted to forge products into unique brand identities, it became increasingly difficult to separate the actual merits of a product from the claims which were made about it. In response to this lack of transparency, consumers themselves began to do the work of communicating the relative advantages and disadvantages of various products, in effect providing a free source of advertising, which was necessary to supplement the purposefully opaque messages of the manufacturers.

The Consumerist Public

This process has arguably come to its culmination in recent years with the widespread use of so-called "Web 2.0" applications such as blogs, MySpace, Facebook, Flickr, YouTube, RSS feeds, and (last but not least) podcasts. One of the most prominent usages for these applications, quite possibly *the* most prominent—though this would likely prove difficult to assess in exact terms—is precisely that of individual consumers communicating information regarding the merits or detriments of various market commodities (movies, music, video games, computers, clothes, food, makeup, and so on). In a formulation that was eerily prescient of this phenomenon over forty years before the fact, Habermas referred to this activity of pseudo-debate, in which the exchange of ideas is replaced by that of mere product details, as "the soft compulsion of constant consumption-training."[2]

Far from being surprising (as many commentators suggested at the time), viewed in this light, Rupert Murdoch's purchase of MySpace for $580 million in July of 2005 was simply the latest acquisition in NewsCorps's longstanding strategy of pursuing the horizontal integration of media sources. The point is not that the advertising of the older forms of mass media (almost exclusively devoted to the production of brand recognition) is "dead," as some advocates of viral marketing have argued. The single fact of the large-scale cultural infiltration achieved by the iPod, and more recently the iPhone ads in itself disconfirms this. The rise of (purportedly) free-form and anarchic promotion via participatory media represents the conscious integration by the advertising industry of

---

[2] Jürgen Habermas, *The Structural Transformation of the Public Sphere: An Inquiry into a Category of Bourgeois Society* (MIT Press, 1989), p. 192.

the supplement upon which advertising has depended all along—public opinion.[3]

When consumers perform this function of supplementing the advertising industry by circulating product information, they're not simply acting as unwitting corporate dupes, or even acting in a way that is not in their interests. The citizens of industrialized countries—and industrializing countries are catching up fast—live in an environment which is populated and consumed by advertisements at all hours of the day and night. As Habermas argues, the purpose of advertising is not to demonstrate the utility of a product relative to its price, but actually the quite contrary one of obscuring the accurate perception of this relationship (what a product actually does versus how much it costs). On this point, Habermas writes:

> The decreasing transparency of the market, usually regarded as the motive for expanded advertising, is in good part actually just the opposite, that is, its consequence. Competition via advertising that replaced competition via pricing is what above all created a confusing multiplicity of markets controlled by specific companies offering brand name products all the more difficult to compare with one another in terms of economic rationality. (*The Structural Transformation of the Public Sphere*, p. 189)

Amidst this climate of the proliferation of advertising and the lack of transparency regarding the actual utility of commodities which results, it is natural and indeed inevitable that consumers will seek to find ways and means of communicating information regarding which products are actually worth what they cost. Various discussion forums (in the present day, those which we

---

[3] *Editor's note:* This consumerist public dialog has actually itself been commodified. What do I mean by that? For one thing, you might have to sit through an ad in order to get to a podcast, in which you might be told about whether a product lives up to its advertisement. So corporations can finally make ad dollars from our free conversational supplements to their advertisements! Strangely, one venture, ExpoTV.com, has begun paying people to record their thoughts about what they like to consume, and what they think others should consume, and why. In what may be a minor form of resistance, most videos contain virtually no useful information, and consist of bored-looking people basically reading the back of the product's box. The ones concerning condoms and tampons and such are awkward and amusing, though, perhaps because these are products regarding which we do not normally have this kind of conversation.

have come to know as Web 2.0, including the podcast) may perform this function.

While consumerist discussion can be seen as a supplement to the advertising industry, we must also recognize that the continued existence of such forums (and even the continued existence of the advertising industry as a whole) requires that they maintain a minimal level of autonomy from both the firms who produce the products being discussed and from the methods of uncritical persuasion with which such products are marketed. This space of minimal autonomy between discussion and advertising, which the market itself requires, might serve as the founding possibility of a sphere of debate that, if progressively developed, may turn into a check upon the forces of the market as a whole.

As Habermas detailed it, the development of the public sphere in the eighteenth century as a space of critical debate about the government arose largely out of the necessity for individuals to discuss their own economic interests in a manner that could be distinguished from those of the government. There's no inherent reason why the discussion forums of our own day could not be transformed in order to serve a similarly critical function, just as there's no inherent reason why these forums cannot direct their criticism upon the most powerful institutions of our day: the corporations. This is true despite, or perhaps even precisely because of the fact that these forums arise on the basis of their necessity within the corporate-dominated culture industry.

Public and Private Media Consumption

The podcast is but one piece of evidence for this claim. It illustrates how other present and future institutions of discussion and debate can evolve into properly critical public sphere institutions. The most unique aspect of the podcast, in comparison to other Internet-supported discussion forums such as blogs, social-networking sites, and wikis, is the personal and private way in which the content is consumed.

Computer users are often alone in a physical sense, but they are rarely alone in an experiential sense—they are usually in immediate communicative contact with others thanks to e-mail, instant messenger services, chat rooms, and so on. The podcast, however, may be consumed away from the computer, often by means of the *personal* media device which gave it its name, and thereby in a manner which is not just physically but also experientially removed from others (apart from the content of the podcast itself).

In his critique of postmodern consumerist society, Habermas emphasized the fact that the manner in which media was consumed in the home underwent a radical shift with the rise of mass media technologies. In the liberal era, the primary form of media consumption was the act of reading, which is most often done alone. The twentieth century, however, saw the introduction of forms of media which were primarily consumed collectively—such as the record player, the radio, the TV, and the VCR.

The introduction of the *personal* computer into the home in the latter part of the century was arguably the first large-scale break in this trend, but with the increased availability of Internet access, it has become merely a means of replacing the physical social sphere of the home with the virtual one of the net.

For Habermas, the significance of this change from the primarily personal consumption of media towards its increasingly social consumption was that the individual was less and less able to develop his or her own unique critical, aesthetic, ideological, and political sensibilities. The public sphere of the liberal era was essentially built upon (and even required as its precondition) the existence of the previously unheard-of phenomenon of distinctively *private* individuals, who had their own individually founded opinions, beliefs, and values.

In contrast to this narrative, when the iPod was introduced in the early twenty-first century, it was viewed by many social commentators as being only the latest and most extreme example of a host of technological developments that contributed to the isolation and atomization of the individual in the act of media consumption. This story runs like this: the transistor radio made it possible to listen alone; the decline in the price of TVs made it possible for an increasing segment of the population to watch alone in their own rooms; the proliferation of cable channels allowed for a vastly increased amount of programming tailored to smaller demographic segments; the Walkman freed the personal music collection from the social-sphere; and after their initial introduction in the family room, video games were increasingly designed for private consumption.[4]

---

[4] Coinciding with these technological developments, Robert Putnam has argued (in *Bowling Alone*) that the social-sphere as a whole has shrunken in the last forty years.

Taken together, what these seemingly contrary stories tell us is that technologies that are at the outset deployed for social consumption will likely be re-imagined for the individual, just as initially "personal" technologies such as the computer and the iPod will come to be incorporated into an environment of social reception and interaction.[5] One can view this process with respect to the iPod via the recent introduction of the iPhone and the iPod Touch, which reintegrate the personal media device with the social environment via the introduction of Wi-Fi and phone service.

While the increased connectivity of these devices seems a logical next step, it may very well compromise the personal aspect of the iPod that attracted people in the first place and that served as the basis for the podcast's mode of reception. As Habermas emphasized, the shift from primarily textual forms of media to primarily audio- and image-based media (though, in recent years, textual forms such as the Web *pages* and *text* messaging have reasserted themselves) was, above all else, a shift in the social context in which media was consumed. As opposed to TV and movies, the podcast is primarily consumed alone. Perhaps this could also be said for the radio since the development of the transistor and its introduction into cars and hand-held devices.

But what radically sets the podcast apart from the vast majority of forms of mass media is that the aspect of personal control extends far beyond the context in which the media is consumed, and beyond even the relatively unprecedented level of decision-making regarding what media is to be consumed and how and when it is consumed. While still primarily a mode of individual reception, the podcast is also a format that enables the individual to participate in a much more substantive sense than the comparatively trivial opportunities made possible by the mass media (such as voting for reality TV contestants, radio call-in shows, or letters to the editor). If he or she so desires, the individual can actually create their own podcast rather than serving as a mere representative of public opinion in formats designed by and for corporate interests.

---

[5] Avital Ronell argues that the telephone is the single technological apparatus that can be taken as a paradigmatic example for both these seemingly contradictory aspects of communications technology. The telephone meant never having to be alone, just as it meant the constant presence of the possibility of being "singled out," by being called. Ronell, *The Telephone Book: Technology—Schizophrenia—Electric Speech* (University of Nebraska Press, 1989).

Resistance to Advertisement

The participatory possibilities of the podcast; the individuality that it promotes in the processes of both production and reception; and the challenge that it poses for the wholesale integration of advertising—all these contribute to making it a form of media which is distinct from those technologies which are conventionally referred to collectively as "mass media" (radio, TV, movies, newspapers, magazines). This distinction can be made clearer by recalling Habermas's observation that the social function of the press changed drastically when advertising replaced subscription as the main form of revenue.

In the liberal era, when periodicals were financed by subscription (and many ran at a loss) they provided a space for debate that was openly and deeply critical of government power. The nineteenth century increasingly saw the use of advertising revenues as a means of increasing the circulation of periodicals beyond the small but dedicated audience of enthusiast-subscribers. At this time, and in direct contrast to the critical function that these institutions played previously, periodicals increasingly became a means for corporate and governmental interests to manage public opinion. This interrelationship between advertising and the streamlining of public debate became the paradigm for the mass media institutions of the twentieth century. The podcast is relatively distinct from this paradigm due to its resistance to advertising, its support by a small but dedicated group of enthusiasts, and the openness and accessibility to participate and air one's own views in a forum that—while it depends upon corporate technology and infrastructure—is not simply reducible to corporate ownership and control.

It's not for a lack of effort, but the advertising industry has yet to find a truly compelling and captivating means of communicating the interests of their advertisers via the podcast. Some podcasts do include advertisements, but unlike on radio, these can be readily fast-forwarded or simply deleted from the file entirely. This is but one more manifestation of the increasing manipulability of media content that has come with digital-era media technologies such as DVRs, satellite radios, and peer-to-peer file trading. Given these difficulties that the podcast format poses to the integration of the conventional forms of mass media advertising, content-producers are increasingly experimenting with other methods of revenue generation. These include the integration of merchandising, the obtaining of demographic and preference information from those who request programming, and, perhaps most interestingly, the charging of subscription fees (through iTunes for example).

Just as was the case in the history of print media, the subscriber model emphasizes the role of the consumer as an agent of rational choice in a way that cannot be said of advertising-driven formats, which appear "free" to the consumer only thanks to advertising. Whenever consumers of media are a source of revenue, the producers of content are accountable to the consumer in a much more direct manner.[6] Even in the case of podcasts which are merely extensions of content produced primarily for other forms of media, such as *The Daily Show* or *The Colbert Report* podcasts, one of the things that consumers are paying for, in addition to the freedom to watch the shows whenever and wherever they want, is the removal of ads from the content. This indicates a minimal level of resistance to the advertising paradigm even in one of the podcast's most corporate-controlled aspects. Over time, if this is able to develop into a significant form of revenue for the producers of these programs, they may find that some of the fear they have of their advertisers will have to be redirected towards their subscribers.

The Minority and the Marginal

What makes the podcast most interesting as a communicative practice is not the way that it has been adopted and adapted by mass media institutions, but rather the proliferation of unique, often individually produced, content that could not have come into existence any other way. This directly relates to another frustration that advertisers have with the podcast as a format: the relatively small audience that any given program commands, and the relatively small audience of the format as a whole. According to research conducted by the market research firm Arbitron in 2007, while approximately one third of the adult population in the United States owns some form of portable media device, only a slightly higher percentage of their sample (37%) knew what a podcast was, and only 13% had ever heard a podcast.[7]

---

[6] This is why the most critically-acclaimed TV shows are now being produced by subscriber-funded channels (such as HBO or Showtime).

[7] Arbitron Inc. and Edison Media Research, *The Infinite Dial: Radio's Digital Platforms* (New York: 2007). Available at: http://www.arbitron.com/downloads/digital_radio_study_2007.pdf

Unfortunately, there's no data available concerning how many of these persons are regular listeners, but this would certainly be a significantly smaller number. Combine this with the fact that this audience is split between over 150,000+ podcasts and it's not hard to see why the format isn't a favorite of advertisers.

The number of podcasts available at any one time is nearly impossible to estimate given all of the different sources by which they may be distributed. These include (but are by no means limited to) various podcast directories on the web, peer-to-peer file trading services, and the iTunes Store (which indexes many podcasts which are available free of charge in addition to the ones that require subscription fees). As of September 24th, 2007, Feedburner.com lists the number of total podcasts that it supports at 142,534. Another difficulty with calculating the number of podcasts is the fact that there isn't a clear, generally agreed upon definition of what a podcast is. As of October 8th, 2007, Wikipedia defines it as follows: "A podcast is a digital media file, or a series of such files, that is distributed over the Internet using syndication feeds for playback on portable media players and personal computers." This definition poses many problems; for example, should conventional TV shows distributed by such means be included? If so, then just about anything could potentially be a podcast, and so as a description of content the term would be next to meaningless. I would suggest that when the term is used as a description of content that is not originally produced in order to be podcasted, it should be reserved for programming which has some relevance to current affairs. So, we would refer to a podcast of *The Daily Show*, but not an episode of ABC's *Lost*, even though the latter is also distributed by similar means. This seems to agree with the term's general use.

While nearly all of the most popular podcasts (as listed in the iTunes Store, for example) feature content produced for other media, this still leaves a vast array of programming whose audience likely consists of only a handful of people. However, this intense diversification of programming and the relatively small audience which it implies for any given podcast is quite possibly what has allowed the format to serve as a venue for topics and perspectives that would not be welcome in the mainstream media.

This ability of the podcast to offer alternative views that would not be welcome in other media institutions can be readily seen by examining a small sampling of the podcasts with political themes. Mainstream media outlets confine the range of political debate for a number of reasons that do not apply to the podcast. For example, the media gatekeepers may avoid a particular viewpoint which they assume is representative of the interests of only a small segment of the population—such as that of the podcast *Right Side of the Rainbow*, which is described as "political news and commentary from a right-of-center, gun-owning, gay Texan." Other viewpoints could prove undesirable to broadcasters due to concerns that they would be likely to offend a large segment of the population or arouse the attention of the FCC—this would certainly be true of the podcast *National Socialist Radio*. However, there's another, more pernicious, and more fundamental reason that prevents mainstream media outlets from airing alternative viewpoints: a given viewpoint may actively threaten the interests of the advertisers or the interests of the media institutions themselves. It doesn't take a great deal of imagination to see why it might be difficult to get a television show produced on the same theme as the podcast *Turn Off Your TV.*

Given its ability to contain seemingly any possible perspective, its at-least-minimal resistance to advertising-driven mass media, and the potential for nearly anyone with the requisite technology and know-how to participate, the podcast has many of the elements of the public sphere institutions of the liberal era that Habermas praised. The institutions of the past which fostered similar opportunities for debate and discussion—the coffeehouses, salons, and the press—were constituted by individuals who came together out of the desire to share their own opinions and to give thorough consideration to the opinions of others, whomever they may be.

As Habermas emphasizes, the significance of these institutions had more to do with the *process* of open debate that they fostered than it did with any specific area of content that was being discussed. Because these institutions conducted discussion in a manner that was potentially open to anyone—in which all participants were viewed as being equally capable of seeking the truth, and no particular authority was taken as having a monopoly upon truth—their potential to perform a unique critical function upon the operation of power was in some way always present. However, this implicit potential of any given public sphere institution to limit the influence of the structures of power upon the citizenry, and thereby to influence society as a whole, can only be realized when the diverse institutions which constitute the public sphere can be linked together in order to form a larger, more cohesive entity.

Unity in Diversity

While the institutions and individuals of the public sphere are always multiple and diverse, the public sphere itself must strive for singularity and universality. The podcast has shown itself to be an excellent format for encouraging the cultivation of a great many discussions on a wide array of subjects from numerous perspectives. This is significant: the existence of a diversity of viewpoints and expressions is an essential precondition for expanding the influence of public debate in society. However, no matter how much they proliferate, as long as these discussions remain fragmented, mutually distinct, and concerned only with addressing small subsets of the population they will not amount to a public sphere worthy of the name.

This is the dilemma that the podcast faces. The broader relevance of the viewpoints expressed by various podcasts depends upon the recognition of their mutual interdependence as institutions of public importance. This would require a broader conversation between various individual podcasts (and other forms of participatory media) concerning the ways in which particular issues affect the public as a whole, across demographics, political affiliation, religious persuasion, personal temperament, and aesthetic taste. The point is not to pursue anything like homogeneity in either information or viewpoint (this is after all an unfortunate characteristic of mass media) but rather to communicate the fact that the problems, concerns, and interests of a given subset of the population are always somehow of broader public relevance—and they become even more so when they are recognized as such. If the podcast can limit its fragmentary and isolative aspects and continue to resist its integration into the corporate media structure, it may provide a valuable resource for the creation of a socially-transformative public sphere.

19

The Rhodesian Stranger

SOCRATES, PHAEDRUS, and STRANGER

SOCRATES: Enough appears to have been said by us of a true and false art of speaking.

PHAEDRUS: Certainly.

SOCRATES: But there's something yet to be said of propriety and impropriety of writing.

PHAEDRUS: Yes.

SOCRATES: I have heard a story from the ancients, whether true or not they only know; although if we had found the truth ourselves, do you think that we should care much about the opinions of men?

PHAEDRUS: Your question needs no answer; but I wish you'd tell me what you say you've heard.

SOCRATES: At the Egyptian city of Naucratis, there was a famous old god, whose name was Thoth. The bird which is called the Ibis is sacred to him, and he was the inventor of many arts, such as arithmetic and calculation and geometry and astronomy, but his great discovery was the use of letters. Now, in those days, the god Thamus was the king of the whole country of Egypt. Thoth came to him and showed him his inventions, desiring that the other Egyptians might be allowed to have the benefit of them. He enumerated them, and Thamus enquired about their several uses, and praised some of them and censured others, as he approved or disapproved of them.

When they came to letters, "This," said Thoth, "will make the Egyptians wiser and give them better memories." Thamus replied: "O most ingenious Thoth, the parent or inventor of an art is not always the best judge of the utility of his own inventions. And in this instance, you who are the father of letters, from a paternal love of your own children, have been led to attribute to them a quality that they cannot have. This discovery of yours will create forgetfulness in the learners' souls, because they will not use their memories; they will trust to the external written characters and not remember of themselves. Letters are an aid not to memory, but to reminiscence, and you give your disciples not truth, but only the semblance of truth; they will be hearers of many things and will have learned nothing."

I cannot help feeling, Phaedrus, that writing is unfortunately like painting; for the creations of the painter have the attitude of life, and yet if you ask them a question they preserve a solemn silence. And the same may be said of written speeches. You would imagine that they had intelligence, but if you want to know anything and put a question to one of them, the speaker always gives one unvarying answer. And when they have been once written down they are sent around among those who may or may not understand them, and know not to whom they should reply. And, if they are misunderstood or misused, they have no parent to protect them; and they cannot protect or defend themselves.

PHAEDRUS: That is most true.

STRANGER: Oh, excuse me. I couldn't help overhearing your conversation.

SOCRATES: Why, Phaedrus, look at how strangely dressed he is!

PHAEDRUS: Perhaps he is from Rhodes?

STRANGER: Er. Yes, that's right; I'm Rhodish. Um. Rhodesian. Are you Socrates?

SOCRATES: I am, and this is my friend Phaedrus.

STRANGER: Just now, were you saying that the written word is like a painting?

SOCRATES: Writing is but thought placed into water, through pen and ink. Only speech and argument can place words and thoughts into the souls of men.

STRANGER: But don't I turn the ink into words and thoughts when I read them?

SOCRATES: When you, as you say, turn the ink into words, does the ink disappear, or does it remain?

STRANGER: Well, of course it remains there on the page—but that's not . . .

SOCRATES: And is it changed when you hear this speech in your head?

STRANGER: No, Socrates. But . . .

SOCRATES: And when something, like speech, is made, do you think there must be something from which it is made?

STRANGER: Yes. Yes, Socrates.

SOCRATES: Then you must make the words on your own, from your own soul. But if you make the words, why then do you pretend to use this 'ink' to think, when only the soul can think?

STRANGER: I, uh, use it to think about things that the writer thought about, and which I wouldn't have otherwise been thinking about.

SOCRATES: So, the ink tells you what to think? Is thinking then just repeating the words that someone else once found meaningful?

STRANGER: No, Socrates, I suppose not. It reminds me of something Arthur Schopenhauer once said—

PHAEDRUS: What a strange name! It doesn't even sound Greek!

STRANGER: Um, he's also Rhodesish. Er, from Rhodes. Anyhow, he said that thoughts put down on paper are nothing more than footprints in the sand—we see the path that was taken, but we know not what was seen along the way.

SOCRATES: He sounds like a wise man. Perhaps I may one day go to Rhodes and speak with him.

STRANGER: Wait—I read those words of his, which he wrote because they were meaningful to him, and I remembered them because I also thought they were important, and repeated them to you, and you seem to think that they have value. Didn't those words, then, teach us something?

SOCRATES: Isn't it true that grain is enjoyed by and makes a horse excellent, although a dog does not like it, and a dog fed only on grain is made sickly?

STRANGER: [*sigh*] Yes, Socrates.

SOCRATES: And when you wish to steer a ship, you consult the stars to find your direction, but when you are building a ship, you consult not the stars, but a diagram?

STRANGER: Yes, Socrates.

SOCRATES: In the same way, is it not the case that some words are enjoyed by and make excellent some people, while other people do not care about and are not helped by those same words? And that some words serve as true guides to some people, while other people may be led astray by those same words?

STRANGER: Yes, I suppose that is right, Socrates.

SOCRATES: So then these words of this wise man of Rhodes, as they are spoken between us, may be guiding, but if they are written, they may end up in the hands of those who will not understand them, or are not helped by them?

STRANGER: Yeah, okay. Fine.

PHAEDRUS: Boy, you sure walked right into that one!

STRANGER: Shut up, Phaedrus. Okay, but *we* found them to be wise, didn't we? If I write something down, and send it out into the world, those who are interested in the same kinds of issues as I, or those who think about things the way I do—they will find value in those words, even though everyone else won't care. Right?

SOCRATES: When you chose to come here to Athens, did you consider your task completed when you had obtained a ticket upon a ship?

STRANGER: Crap. I have no idea where you're going with this, but—

SOCRATES: When you bought the ticket, was it the ticket you desired, or the journey?

STRANGER: It was the journey. You'd have to be a total idiot to just want the ticket.

SOCRATES: You should not speak so harshly—after all, it's you who think that to send out your words to someone else is the same thing as speaking with them, which makes no more sense than mistaking the ticket for the journey!

STRANGER: I'm totally lost here. Don't you roll your eyes at me, Phaedrus!

PHAEDRUS: Sorry.

SOCRATES: You admitted before, did you not, that it is the soul which thinks, and that ink can be a guide to repeating the words of another, but does not create thought?

STRANGER: Yes, Socrates.

SOCRATES: And that some words are useful for some people, but not for others?

STRANGER: Yeah.

SOCRATES: But to be useful is to be useful for some purpose, and to think is to seek what is true and good, not merely to seize upon a single thought and repeat it for its own sake. Words are then more like a ticket for a journey than they are like a destination, aren't they?

STRANGER: Well, yes, but if some people understand my words correctly, and can use them to continue their journey towards truth, then haven't I helped them? Phaedrus!

PHAEDRUS: Sorry.

SOCRATES: When you wish to travel somewhere with a friend, do you travel together or separately?

STRANGER: Together, Socrates, of course.

SOCRATES: And when you wish to guide a friend to a certain location, perhaps some place of great beauty, do you walk alongside your friend, or do you charge ahead?

STRANGER: . . . Look, do you think you could cut to the chase a bit?

SOCRATES: If you wish to speak to someone, it seems like you must have something to say to them. If you speak to them as a friend, rather than by giving orders or making accusations, it seems that you wish to bring them towards the true and the good. But if you are a true friend, you will not wish to simply put up a sign-post, but instead to come along on the journey. This is not only because a journey is better when taken together, but because directions given ahead of time cannot take careful note of where the terrain is treacherous, or address the many things which will come up along the way, such as whether another path may be shorter or less dangerous, or even whether another destination, discovered along the way, might be preferable. Further, you will walk alongside one another, and when you must walk ahead in order to guide your friend, you will turn around frequently to be sure that your friend has not gone astray or fallen behind.

When you simply write something, it is like an order or a sign-post. It may be of some use to those who wish to travel there, but it is not a guide. A book simply runs ahead of you, heedless. You may choose to follow it or put it down, but you cannot ask it ques-tions, and it will not help you; nor will it take you on any path other than its own narrow way.

When you speak with a friend about the true and the good, you are able to be a guide. You are able to stop and reconsider the claims you are making, to explain to him what you meant by something, to relate it to his concerns, and to follow his lead when he sees a clearer path. This is why thought is better spo-ken than written, and why dialog better serves our journey in thinking.

STRANGER: Yes, Socrates, I understand. I see why what I said before was mistaken, and I think I understand why you said that a written speech is like a painting, and why dialog is important if we want to strive towards knowledge. But there's still something else that I would like to hear your thoughts on.

SOCRATES: Oh, I do not have any knowledge to impart. I am only trying to help you speak with clarity so that I might gain from your knowledge!

STRANGER: Whatever. Let me tell you an ancient myth that I once heard. It is an ancient myth . . . uh . . . from the East. That's why you haven't heard of it before.

There were once a people who were so enamored of writing that they wrote down everything important to them. Anything that anyone thought of that he felt was important, he would write

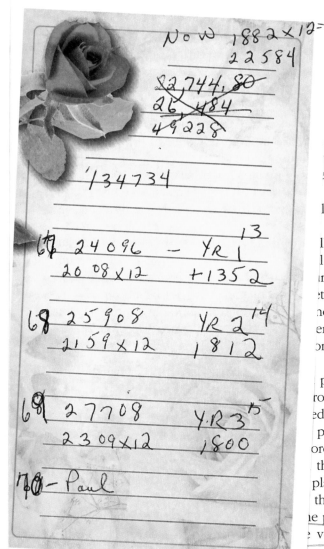

ple would discuss

eing that the gift of
as a community, to
—was being used
eir gods took back
abused. From that
d their mouths to
word, only a small,
ll of these peas.

of their ways, and
lly were. Everything
l way, and was said
niversal broadcasts,
ther, and smaller or
ncerns were ignored
ere no longer based
om people working

pleas of the people
rom the people, who
d that the seeds pro-
planted, and would
ording to what kinds
the speech that had
planted in the fertile
their city, they grew
e pea-pods produced
e voice of the person

The people began going to the ~~~~ ularly. They would go
and cast their own pea-pods widely, so that all who were interested
in hearing their words could find the resulting plants easily. They
would also look about for plants that were similar to their own, so
that they could hear the speech of those who shared their concerns
and interests. Using harvesting devices called pod-catchers, they
were able to automatically get just the pods from the particular
pod-casters they were interested in hearing from. They were even
able to carry these around with them as individual-pods, or i-pods,
so that they could hear the speech of their fellow citizens whenever they wished.

Once they were accustomed to this practice, these pod-casters began to hold dialog with one another—to reply to each other, to work through ideas with one another, and to co-ordinate action together. Although they might never meet or come to know those whose pods they consumed, they were able to consider their words and then compose a reply which they would then cast out into the field.

Although separated from one another, they could still, through the medium of the field, form communities of common interests and concerns, and to help one another forward, as friends, even as they were apart.

SOCRATES: Well, that is an interesting myth, and you were right to think it might be unfamiliar to me. It is a very strange story. I wonder, though, whether this kind of disconnected communication can really be called a dialog; whether these people, communicating separately and perhaps coming to exchange speeches with each other, can be said to approach each other as friends who are working together towards the true and the good?

Don't you think that these people, accustomed as they had become to speaking only about useless things, would produce and consume the pods cast that were of the least real interest or importance? And that these people, accustomed as they had become to the universal written word—disconnected from their own lives, concerns, journeys, and projects—would produce and consume pods which were also disconnected from their own lives, and from their truest concerns? And, even if they were able to have a real dialog, based in their real interests, do you think that this would be enough to produce communities of common concern strong enough to bring about collective and collaborative thought or action?

STRANGER: Yes, Socrates, those are all very good questions, and I am not sure how realistic the story is. But it is a beautiful myth, isn't it?

SOCRATES: Yes, it is. And surely beauty is as faithful a guide towards the good as is truth.[1]

---

[1] Special thanks to co-authors Plato and Ben Jowett, and a big shout-out to H.G. Wells for technical assistance.

ID3 Tags:
About the Artists

REGINA ARNOLD—sometimes known as Gina—is a doctoral candidate in the program of Modern Thought and Literature at Stanford University and a lecturer at the University of San Francisco, where she teaches courses on media audiences. Her dissertation, "Rock Crowds and Power," is an attempt to make sense of her former predilection for mosh pits. As a former rock journalist for *Rolling Stone* and *Spin*, she wishes very much that the iPod had been invented before she quit the business.

JON AUSTIN is an Associate Professor and Deputy Dean of the Faculty of Education at the University of Southern Queensland, Australia. His areas of interest include cultural studies, whiteness, autoethnography, and the grossly underrated place Neil Young is accorded in the music canon. His new black iPod contains the best distillation of music, both White and Other. He can be contacted at austin@usq.edu.au.

CRAIG A. CONDELLA is Assistant Professor of Philosophy at Salve Regina University in Newport, Rhode Island. In addition to Heidegger and the philosophy of technology, his academic interests include environmental ethics and the history and philosophy of science. Though he admits to using his iPod while exercising in the gym, he would not even be able to turn it on were it not for the help of his wife. If the iPod functions intuitively, his intuition must be outdated.

MATTHEW DEWEY is a graduate student of Communication at Boise State University, studying media reform and participatory discourses. He usually has a video project that needs editing and can't wait for the day when iPods and the woven 'Wearable Instrument Shirt' fuse into walking musical skin.

237

Delia Dumitrica is a doctoral student in Communication Studies at the University of Calgary. She is usually obsessed with nationalism and how it affects our understanding and use of new media. She's interested in all cool gadgets and online applications, and is now doing some research in *Second Life*. She downloads tons of academic and news podcasts on her chic iPod Touch and then wonders when she'll find the time to listen to them.

Andrew Wells Garnar is a Lecturer of Philosophy in Clemson University's Department of Philosophy and Religion where he teaches classes on ethics and science. His writing is chock-full of subtle musical references that are far too obscure for the unaided human eye to detect. You should try getting that guy with the beard who works at that record store to explain them . . . you know, the one who won't make eye contact and sneers at your purchase? And yes, Andrew has been known to give up punk for Lent.

Andrew Hickey is a lecturer in Cultural Studies and Social Theory at the University of Southern Queensland, Australia. He is particularly interested in the way technology mediates our contemporary existences, but actively refuses to own a mobile phone. He is however warming to the idea of iPod ownership after now being refused borrowing privileges to his friends' iPods.

Ruud Kaulingfreks is a reader in Philosophy and Organizations at the University of Humanistics in Utrecht, the Netherlands and at the School of Management at the University of Leicester, UK. Besides interests in organization critique he loves popular culture and electronic gadgets. He often uses his iPod in order to avoid unpleasant conversations.

Librivox Volunteers:

As a child, **Mark L. Cohen** was told: "You can do whatever you want with your life . . . once you finish medical school." He is Professor of Pathology at Case Western Reserve University. With his virtual colleague, Robert Scott, he records and produces free audiobooks at www.freeaudiobooks1.com.

Sean McGaughey has a bachelor's degree in philosophy, which has served him well for many years as a teacher. However, as a primary school teacher, he rarely gets the opportunity to discuss Aristotelian philosophy with his six- to ten-year old students. Sean is also a podcaster and musician who is deeply interested in the free culture movement. You can find him at http://seanmcgaughey.net.

JIM MOWATT is of middling age and voracious curiosity. An avid student of history, he produces the podcast, *Historyzine*. He adores being part of the sheer energy and productivity on the net that has become the Open Culture movement, and is involved in several projects that connect the past to the present, and maybe on to the future.

MARC LOMBARDO is Faculty Associate in the Departments of Communication Studies and Social and Behavioral Sciences at Arizona State University. His interests include: American pragmatism, novelist James Baldwin, and political philosophy. He recently managed to reanimate his four-year-old iPod by throwing it on the ground.

SCOTT F. PARKER has done and will again do philosophy in the academy. Meanwhile, he studies on his own, and contributes to books like *Lost and Philosophy*, and *Football and Philosophy*. He does not own an iPhone.

JOSEPH PITT is Professor of Philosophy at Virginia Tech where he teaches history and philosophy of science and technology. He is currently Editor-in-Chief of *Techné: Research in Philosophy and Technology*. Joe's own research focuses on the impact of technological innovation on science. He and wife live on a farm in Newport, Virginia where they raise Irish Wolfhounds and combined training horses. They do not own an iPod.

FRANCIS RAVEN is a graduate student in philosophy at Temple University. His books include *Shifting the Question More Complicated* (Otoliths, 2007), *Taste: Gastronomic Poems* (Blazevox, 2005) and the novel, *Inverted Curvatures* (Spuyten Duyvil, 2005).

ALF REHN is a Party Shuffle of a Professorship of Innovation and Entrepreneurship (Royal Institute of Technology, Stockholm, Sweden), a Chair of Management and Organization (Åbo Akademi University, Finland), the Ethel Merman Disco Album, www.alfrehn.com, a generous helping of caffeine, and the complete works of the divine Patsy Cline. He can be browsed through Cover Flow, but might browse back.

PETER SCHAEFFER is Assistant Professor of Communication Arts at Marymount Manhattan College, where he teaches classes in media and communication theory. His research explores the relationship between social theory and communication technology. He is currently enjoying the smells of a New York City summer.

SOCRATES is a jerk who enjoys harassing people in public. When he's not hanging with Phaedrus—who is just a friend—he wanders shirtless through the streets of Athens, insults poets, and corrupts the youth.

DAN STURGIS is an instructor at the University of Colorado at Boulder, where he teaches classes in environmental philosophy. He wrote his chapter during breaks in the surf, in backcountry ski huts, and in a bar with a mechanical bull, while pumping his fist to the Drive-by-Truckers. When he's not posturing as some badass mountain man, this skinny suburbanite is probably reading *The Economist* or making his wife pancakes while listening to NPR.

DONALD L. TURNER teaches Philosophy at Nashville State Community College. His writing deals mostly with ethics and philosophy of religion, blending attention to absurdity with a persistent mirth that confounds his hardheaded analytic colleague. He jockeys for iPod space and iPod time with his wife and three-year-old son, and when he listens to Black Sabbath at high volume he feels omnipotent.

SAMANTHA WARREN is a Senior Lecturer in Human Resource Management at University of Surrey, researching organizational aesthetics and fun at work using visual methods. Philosophically speaking, she continues to be fascinated by the magic and sorcery that is modern technology – her latest i-project is making video podcasts for use in teaching, although she much prefers using her iPod to listen to free dance mixes downloaded from talented DJs so she can dance to them in her kitchen.

DYLAN E. WITTKOWER is a Lecturer in Philosophy at Coastal Carolina University and studies the ways that technology either encourages or prevents the formation of collaborative creative communities. In other words, he is basically like your standard "Web 2.0" tech geek, except with a whole lot more fretting, fussing, and Marxist rhetoric. He has recorded numerous philosophy texts, which may be downloaded at librivox.org.

Keyword Search